W9-AKM-105

Mindful
Inquiry
in Social
Research

"The truth, however nobly it may loom before the scientific intellect, is ontologically something secondary. Its eternity is but the wake of the ship of time, a furrow which matter must plough upon the face of essence. Truth must have a subject matter, it must be the truth about something; and it is the character of this moving object, lending truth and definition to the truth itself, that is substantial and fundamental in the universe."

George Santayana, *Realms of Being*

"Wisdom not steeped in method is bondage.
Wisdom steeped in method is freedom.
Method not steeped in wisdom is bondage.
Method steeped in wisdom is freedom."

Tsongkapa, *The Principal Teachings of Buddhism*

Mindful
Inquiry
in Social
Research

Valerie Malhotra Bentz
Jeremy J. Shapiro

SAGE Publications
International Educational and Professional Publisher
Thousand   Oaks   London   New Delhi

For information:

SAGE Publications, Inc.
2455 Teller Road
Thousand Oaks, California 91320
E-mail: order@sagepub.com

SAGE Publications Ltd.
6 Bonhill Street
London EC2A 4PU
United Kingdom

SAGE Publications India Pvt. Ltd.
M-32 Market
Greater Kailash I
New Delhi 110 048 India

Printed in the United States of America

Library of Congress Cataloging-in-Publication Data

Bentz, Valerie Malhotra, 1942–
    Mindful inquiry in social research / by Valerie Malhotra Bentz
    and Jeremy J. Shapiro.
        p.   cm.
    Includes bibliographical references and index.
    ISBN 0-7619-0408-5 (cloth: acid-free paper)
    ISBN 0-7619-0409-3 (pbk.: acid-free paper)
    1. Social sciences—Methodology. 2. Social sciences—Philosophy.
I. Shapiro, Jeremy J. II. Title.
H61 .B4713 1997
300'.7'2—ddc21   98-19720

98 99 00 01 02 03 04   7 6 5 4 3 2 1

Acquiring Editor:	Marquita Flemming
Production Editor:	Sherrise M. Purdum
Editorial Assistant:	Karen Wiley
Designer/Typesetter:	Ravi Balasuriya/Rebecca Evans
Cover Designer:	Candice Harman

To our parents,
Norma Bentz Sajeck and George Sajeck
and Judah J. Shapiro and Florence I. Shapiro,
who raised us both to become
reflective scholars, musicians, and critical thinkers;
and to our siblings,
Daniel Shapiro and Lorelei Cederstrom,
who are always alongside us in our lifeworlds.

Contents

■ CHAPTER TEN
Comparative–Historical Inquiry and Theoretical Inquiry   **134**

■ CHAPTER ELEVEN
Critical Social Science and Critical Social Theory   **146**

■ **CHAPTER TWELVE**
Conclusion and Magic Formulae   **160**

Preface

There are a number of introductions available to research in the social and human sciences. In fact, there are more than 150 introductions to research listed in *Books in Print*. A number of them are very good at what they intend to do. But we believe that the beginning researcher has fundamental needs that they do not address. We have written this book to try to meet needs that we have encountered in recent years among students with whom we have worked, needs that were not being met by other introductory books, including books that we like and advised them to read. We do not assume that our book is the only introduction to research that you will read. In fact, we hope that it is not, because we are deliberately not duplicating standard material that is covered elsewhere. We believe that you need to consider multiple perspectives—that is a main point of our book. But we imagine that you will find that this book contains information, ideas, and a perspective on research that is not to be found in other books and courses and that will help you reframe that other material and use it more effectively for your own purposes.

We have found that for students—and for us—the challenges in undertaking research are not mainly about the details of research methods. Rather, they are about making choices about which research approach to take; trying to figure out how to integrate your research with your underlying sense of who you are and what you want out of life; being aware of your intellectual and social context and how your research relates to it; deciding what your "knowledge values" are; trying to figure out if your research is significant; learning to be an intellectual peer of other scholars; finding your own niche in the world of scholarship and research; situating yourself in the cross-cutting discourses that exist in the academic world; finding the right way of conceptualizing the topic in which you are interested; making sure that the topic and approach are "right" personally and existentially; relating to the social worlds that you inhabit and in which you do your research; and managing personally the conflicts, ambiguities, fears, and confusions that the research can bring to the surface. This short book—and it is short intentionally—obviously does not provide the solutions to all of these problems, but we try to take them into account and help people deal with them constructively.

What is distinctive about our approach is that we pay attention to the intellectual and cultural postmodern, chaotic situation in which human and social science research takes place today, to the social and historical changes that are the background context of intellectual work today, and to the multicultural, interdisciplinary, multiparadigmatic trends in the social and human sciences. Most textbooks either do not address this situation at all or do so peripherally, at best. This is especially true of textbooks and courses that are operating within a framework passed down from a previous intellectual generation. In consequence, we believe, students are not prepared adequately either to make sense of the scholarly work that they encounter or to fit their own work into current intellectual discourse. We believe that, in such a situation, you—the researcher—have to place yourself at the center of the research process because of the need to make choices in a chaotic environment; and you need to become a bit of an applied philosopher to be able to make these choices. You also need to be aware both of the social and cultural context of research today and of the multiple research modes, or cultures of inquiry, that are available to you in the human and social sciences. In contemplating your research, have you thought, for example, of building your own theory? Analyzing your own consciousness? Changing your own social environment? These are among the many options available to you (although your immediate environment may not be receptive to all of them).

Instead of presenting research as a neutral tool kit to be used in any kind of intellectual or philosophical or value framework, we present and recommend our own philosophical framework, which we call *mindful inquiry*, as a way to think about inquiry and research. Our framework is not value-neutral: It is a synthesis of critical social science, hermeneutics, phenomenology, and Buddhism. Do not worry if these terms are unfamiliar to you. We explain them in the text and in a glossary at the end of the book. We believe that mindful inquiry will help connect, in a meaningful way, you as a researcher, your inner self, your research interests, the world in which you live, your philosophical assumptions and commitments, and your moral and political values.

Our conception of the book has shaped our bibliography. We have provided bibliographical information for all the works to which we refer in the text. We have limited recommended readings to a short list of introductions to the major topics that we cover. We believe that the interested reader will be best served by using those works in combination with our references and with bibliographic searches guided by her own particular interests.

We wish to thank, first of all, the faculty of the Human and Organization Development (HOD) Program of the Fielding Institute, particularly those involved in the development and writing of the program's *Study Guide for Research and Inquiry,* from which we have borrowed considerably in the present work: Anna DiStefano, Will McWhinney, Rich Appelbaum, Judy Stevens-Long, and Frank Friedlander (Jeremy Shapiro was also involved in this project). Other faculty have contributed to ongoing discussions about research through their participation on the HOD Research and Inquiry Committee and in other faculty contexts. These include Jody Veroff, Elizabeth Douvan, Peter Park, Bob Silverman, Sara Cobb, Matt Hamabata, Willy DeMarcell Smith, Keith Melville, Dottie Eastman, and Morris Berman. We are also grateful to Linda Ford and Paul Bundick for permission to use their descriptions of their experiences of research, to Elyse Kutz for reading the manuscript and suggesting editorial changes, and to Daniel Shapiro for graphics consultation and for making the helix used in the diagrams. We wish to especially thank editor and colleague Tamera Bryant of Five Oak Editorial, who "midwifed" the book from her Ohio office as Jeremy, its East Coast mother, completed labor and Valerie, its West Coast father, paced the floor. We are indebted to our editors, Marquita Flemming and Sherrise Purdum, of Sage Publications, for nurturing this manuscript through a long process of conceptualization, production, and revisions.

From Valerie: I wish to thank those who sustained my lifeworld as I worked toward and completed this project: my daughter, Pamela Malhotra; my dear friends and colleagues Jeanette Day, Frieda Karr, Ellen Pratt, Amanda Samaha, Frank Jankowitz, and Jonathan Freedman; my friend and yoga teacher, Abhaya (Susan MacDonald); my kundalini yoga teachers, Dr. Bede Kuntz and Amrit Joy of the Center for Inner Peace; my dear niece, Greta Cederstrom; and my teachers and colleagues at the Body Therapy Institute of Santa Barbara. Others with whom I have worked and whose work supported and inspired me are cited in the text. The love and friendship of my kittens, Spitfire and Lovejones, were invaluable in alleviating the stress of the process of bringing the book to completion. I thank the Great Spirit for bringing Steven Figler into my life just as this book was born.

From Jeremy: This book grew out of a decade of thinking and working with friends—graduates of and students at the Fielding Institute—whose doctoral work shaped my understanding of inquiry and research, and I would like to thank especially Jan Elliott and Kelly Rae Reineke, as well as Gail Suttelle, Barbara Rusness, Andrea Zintz, Theresa Russell, Viola Harrison, Jenny Wade, Anita Jensen, Mike Terpstra, Pat Salgado, and Karin Bunnell. Coteaching critical theory with Kelly Rae Reineke has also contributed to my reconceptualizing it. During this period I also benefited from the thought, conversation, and friendship of Bert Somers, Virginia Mullin, Trent Schroyer, Barbara Einzig, Hannah

Davis Taieb, David Guss, Linda Ford, Terry Winant, Judy Adler, David Bellin, Mike McCullough, Billy Stoneman, Kathleen Rubin, Marty Rubin, and Charlotte Riley. I am particularly grateful to the friends, collaborators, and family who sustain my intellectual and personal life on a daily basis: Shierry Nicholsen, Shelley Hughes, Pamela Walsh, Florence I. Shapiro, and Daniel Shapiro. And I want to acknowledge Hallock Hoffman and the late Renate Tesch for the gift of their special friendship and mentorship.

A note about masculine and feminine pronouns:
We have chosen to alternate at random between masculine and feminine pronouns because we feel that slicing or mutilating everyone's pronoun gender identification makes it difficult for each of us, as gendered beings, to identify with the text.

Research

The New Context and a New Approach

"It was the best of times; it was the worst of times." These words by Charles Dickens truly describe your situation today if you are starting out as a social science or human science researcher. We are "in over our heads," as Robert Kegan's book (1994) suggests, not only as people facing life in postmodern society but as researchers. The postmodern period follows the supposed triumph of science and rationality, calls them into question, and produces an array of diverse and divergent conceptions of knowledge. Over the past quarter century, and increasingly in the past decade, the human and social sciences have been undergoing the proliferation and diversification of the following:

- epistemological paradigms, or models of valid knowledge; research methods, or how knowledge is produced;
- intellectual disciplines, or how knowledge is organized;
- modes of interdisciplinary collaboration, or how knowledge is shared and linked;
- media of scholarly communication, or how knowledge is transmitted, accessed, and integrated;
- the volume of scientific information available, or how much knowledge is stored and retrievable; and
- cultural voices and social perspectives claiming to be represented within the public arenas and discourses of knowledge.

This situation can be disorienting and confusing. Previously, researchers were exposed to a restricted set of techniques that were the research methods of their discipline, and graduate students had to learn just this set or the set of the particular school of thought that their departments or professors occupied within their discipline. Students today, however, are made aware not only of a larger set of techniques but of an array of research methods so different from one another that they do not even fit into previous definitions of the field, of research, or of scholarship. Consider the following:

- A historian no longer works only with the traditional approaches of historians but may be using anthropological methods as well.
- A piece of sociological research may not look like what would have been found in a sociology journal 20 years ago; instead it may look like literary criticism. By the same token, literary scholars are using the methods of demography, sociology, anthropology, and philosophy to understand literature.
- A philosopher may argue that philosophy is dead.
- A political scientist may be doing research using conversational analysis or may be analyzing videotapes.
- A psychologist may be studying emotions in on-line environments using e-mail as data.
- Intellectual discussions are occurring via mailing lists on the Internet.
- Anthropologists are writing studies in which their own emotions about being in foreign cultures are as important as the behavior of the people in those cultures.
- People of various ethnic and gender groups are proposing models of knowledge that reflect the situation of their group, and they are contesting scientific and research traditions that reflect the worldview, biases, and emotions of White European and American men.
- Philosophers and theorists are debating whether it is possible for knowledge to be objective, whether there is such a thing as rational agreement, whether selves exist, and whether any phrase, text, or document has an unambiguous meaning.
- Where social scientists used to talk as though there were such things as sexuality, identity, and personhood, they now look at them as "constructs."
- Popular culture is studied with the same discipline and scholarly apparatus that used to be reserved for the classics.
- Information in the world's libraries and databases is doubling every 5 years.

There is an undercurrent that exists beneath these phenomena, a crisis about what knowledge is, what makes it valid, and whether and how it can be objective if it is shaped by historical, social, and cultural contexts. This has been called the "epistemological crisis of the West" (Harding, 1996). For a society that defines itself as based on knowledge, an epistemological crisis—that is, a crisis about the legitimacy and validity of knowledge—is a serious matter.

On one hand, because becoming a researcher is about becoming a producer of legitimate and valid knowledge, doing so in an epistemological crisis is a serious personal matter. Perhaps it is a bit like learning to drive a car in a wrecking yard, learning good health practices in the midst of a plague, or learning to build a house in an area devastated by a flood. The situation can disorient, scare, frustrate, or depress you if you are entering the world of social science and human science research at any level. That is why we say that this is "the worst of times."

On the other hand, these new aspects of knowledge creation are exciting. They provide you with an amazing array of possibilities for creative research work: new fields of study, new things about which to inquire, new methods of inquiry, new ways of combining knowledge of different fields, new ways to incorporate your self and your social background into your research, new technologies to play with, new social relationships with peers. Existing knowledge is being critiqued and revised in light of these innovations, and uncharted territory expands on all sides, offering you exciting new vistas, whether you are a beginning or an established researcher. This is why we say that this is also "the best of times."

In addition to the new research questions and challenges arising from the expansion of the modes of knowledge, new intellectual issues have been arising both from the progress of scientific disciplines and from the social, cultural, and technological changes of the present period. The human and social sciences are being asked to face an array of momentous and unprecedented social and human problems. Some examples include how to

- manage the transition to a new phase of social organization—a global economy, which some see as the harbinger of an era of prosperity, peace, and freedom and others see as the sure cause of global poverty, social injustice, exploitation, and environmental devastation;
- manage the transition to an information society, one in which information technology is part of the social infrastructure and in which information products, commodities, and services are reshaping organizations, daily life, relationships, and experience;
- respond to and manage a global environmental crisis and also incorporate ecological and environmental awareness into our ways of thinking about and dealing with human affairs;
- organize political life after a century in which political issues were shaped by the now concluded Cold War;
- develop methods of resolving conflicts in a nonviolent manner;
- determine what kinds of cultures and education to develop around family and sexuality now that conventional conceptions of family and sexuality are no longer taken for granted;
- bridge differences among people of widely divergent cultures;
- develop new philosophical conceptions of the meaning of life, identity, love, community, work, justice, democracy, leisure, and freedom when the traditional conceptions have been called into question.

So far, the work of the human and social sciences has been largely determined by the social, psychological, economic, political, and cultural problems posed by the surrounding society. There is every reason to expect that this new set of social issues will generate new and challenging sets of research questions.

As work in advanced industrial society has become more knowledge based, social and human science research has moved farther out of the exclusive domain of academia into the world of work and business. Corporations have hired anthropologists to study how human beings interact with computers, sociologists to study and help manage organizational change, and psychologists to help design products and media. These changes in the production, diffusion, and consumption of knowledge are not just "an academic matter." They are a matter of everyday life.

We believe that this new situation is a uniquely confusing and disorienting one that we all face as researchers. Our aim in this book is to help you navigate the situation of postmodern chaos.

We believe that you need to figure out your relation to the postmodern situation in order to develop a coherent, grounded approach toward your own research. And we believe that the only way to do so is through centering your research in yourself through what we call *mindful inquiry*. Because we agree with those interpreters of the current situation who see it as being beyond coping, we believe that what is needed is not just more information that will help you cope but a different, mindful approach.

The rest of this chapter briefly summarizes our own approach to responding to the current situation faced by social researchers. After each section, we present one or more activities that we recommend you engage in as part of developing your own response.

▬ Putting the Person at the Center

Research is always carried out by an individual with a life and a *lifeworld* (explained later in the chapter), a personality, a social context, and various personal and practical challenges and conflicts, all of which affect the research, from the choice of a research question or topic, through the method used, to the reporting of the project's outcome. Most research textbooks and courses do not bring the living reality of you, the researcher, into the discussion of research. We believe that the person is always at the center of the process of inquiry—that you will always be at the center of your own research, which in turn will always be part of you. We believe this to be true not only in a psychological sense—for example, in the way that being insecure about your intellectual ability can create ambivalence about your work or that your personality style can shape your choice of a research method—but in a philosophical sense—for example, in seeing research not as disembodied, programmed activity but rather as part of the way in which you engage with the world. Phenomenologists consider life projects and plans to be of fundamental importance. Research endeavors are central plans and projects. In this book, we try to address the nature of research and its challenges as personal or existential. For a wonderful illustration of the way research interacts with our identities and life plans and projects, see Wagner's example of the life of Alfred Schutz, a prominent phenomenologically oriented social theorist (Wagner, 1983a).

In our own work with students, we always try to locate an individual's research interests and projects within her being-in-the-world or personally configured universe. We recognize that scientific research is only one of our "ways of knowing" (Belenky, Field, Clinchy, Goldberger, & Tarule, 1986) and needs to be connected with the other ways. We have also seen how one's research can contribute to the transformation of one's self or identity. We have experienced this ourselves and seen it in our students. We are always noticing how values shape conceptual frameworks, and we believe that research needs to be thought of in connection with all of the ways that it is part of individuals' lives and lifeworlds.

In particular, our whole conception of mindful inquiry is based on the idea that your research is—or should be—intimately linked with your awareness of yourself and your world. We strongly believe that your awareness of and reflection on your world and the intellectual awareness and reflection that are woven into your research affect—or should affect—one another. Good research should contribute to your development as a mindful person, and your development as an aware and reflective individual should be embodied in your research.

One advantage in taking a philosophical approach to research is that it enables you to confront the vital question—why do research in the first place?—which so few research guides have asked, let alone answered. We believe that clarifying why you want to do research, even if your reason is a requirement of a degree program or an employer, will be of immense value to you in your research, as well as a tool of self-knowledge. We hope that when you have finished this book, you will have more clarity about why *you* do research.

Because research has become institutionalized and industrialized, it is possible to engage in it like a cog in the wheel of the modern industrial apparatus, without reflection as to its purpose or one's own purpose in engaging in it. Indeed, because much actual research is carried out to solve problems, the problems are often given prior to the research and exist outside of the researcher.

There are presently strong debates over the nature of knowledge and the types of knowledge that are appropriate to providing useful "scientific" understanding. Choosing a research method necessarily requires one to make conscious choices about the assumptions underlying the inquiry. One must, in other words, take responsibility for one's approach and its consequences. One's choice of research approach, therefore, ought to be made consciously.

Activities

Go to a quiet place and let go of all thoughts and feelings, making your mind a blank. After you have cleared your thoughts, think of your life and a possible research project you are thinking of carrying out. Do not consider any possible limitations and constraints. Does this idea relate to your current research projects or ones you have thought you would actually do? If not, why not? Think of ways in which your fundamental interests and your actual research could become more congruent.

■ Mindful Inquiry: Our Philosophy

Most guides to research present themselves as "without philosophy," or they present their philosophical biases such that they are common knowledge or can be taken for granted. We, to the contrary, come to the research process "with philosophy," and we want briefly to say something about it here, so that you know our biases and framework. In a nutshell, our philosophy of research, which we call *mindful inquiry,* is a synthesis of four intellectual traditions: phenomenology, hermeneutics, critical social science, and Buddhism. Some or all of these may be unfamiliar to you; they are explained in Chapter 3 as well as later in the book. For right now, *phenomenology* is the analysis of consciousness and experience; *hermeneutics* is the analysis of texts in their contexts; *critical social science* is the analysis of domination and oppression with a view to changing it; and *Buddhism* is a spiritual practice that allows one to free oneself from suffering and illusion in several ways, one of which is becoming more aware.

Mindful inquiry includes a number of ideas from those four traditions:

1. Awareness of self and reality and their interaction is a positive value in itself and should be present in research processes.
2. Tolerating and integrating multiple perspectives is a value.
3. It is important to bracket our assumptions and look at the often unaware, deep layers of consciousness and unconsciousness that underlie them.
4. Human existence, as well as research, is an ongoing process of interpreting both one's self and others, including other cultures and subcultures.
5. All research involves both accepting bias—the bias of one's own situation and context—and trying to transcend it.
6. We are always immersed in and shaped by historical, social, economic, political, and cultural structures and constraints, and those structures and constraints usually have domination and oppression, and therefore suffering, built into them.
7. Knowing involves caring for the world and the human life that one studies.
8. The elimination or diminution of suffering is an important goal of or value accompanying inquiry and often involves critical judgment about how much suffering is required by existing arrangements.

9. Inquiry often involves the critique of existing values, social and personal illusions, and harmful practices and institutions.
10. Inquiry should contribute to the development of awareness and self-reflection in the inquirer and may contribute to the development of spirituality.
11. Inquiry usually requires giving up ego or transcending self, even though it is grounded in self and requires intensified self-awareness.
12. Inquiry may contribute to social action and be part of social action.
13. The development of awareness is not a purely intellectual or cognitive process but part of a person's total way of living her life.

We do not expect you to accept these ideas on faith. We simply want you to know the particular perspective that shapes this book. Later we will explain how we see mindful inquiry as an encompassing framework within which research can be carried out using a variety of approaches and methods.

Activities

Review each one of the assumptions about mindful inquiry. On reading each one, take a deep breath and ask whether you accept it fully, do not accept it, or do not know if you do but wish to look into it for the future. We ask that you be open to the cases we make and to the assumptions we hold as you read this book.

■ Researchers

Every introduction to research makes some assumptions about its readers. Although there are some notable exceptions (see, for example, Robson, 1993, which includes practitioner–researchers among its intended audience), most writers of guides to research assume that their readers are either young graduate students who intend to become full-time scholars in an academic setting or undergraduates for whom research training will serve as preparation for graduate school. The intended audience can also be students in particular applied fields who are learning special research techniques employed in those fields and will need to read such works as *Introduction to Market Research, Introduction to Research in Speech, Introduction to Criminal Justice Research,* and so on.

We hope that prospective full-time scholars will find our book useful, and we assume them to be among our audience. But we make some additional assumptions, based on both our experience and our knowledge of changes in work and education. First, we believe that, as knowledge work expands, the ability to conduct, evaluate, and plan research is increasingly coming to be considered a general skill, or set of skills, that people will need in order to work in knowledge-based occupations (Reich, 1991). Many people in graduate school do not, in any case, become full-time scholars in academic environments but instead pursue occupations in the private sector, public sector, or nonprofit sector in which their research skills and activities are part of a wider range of skills and activities.

Second, we have been working for years with adult students who have decided, either independently or with encouragement from their places of work, to become researchers and add scholarship to their work and lives as professionals and practitioners. Because adult students are a growing fraction of the student population, the underlying assumption that the developing researcher is a young person can no longer be sustained. That is why we have tried in our book to keep in mind the needs and perspectives of adult practitioners or professionals who are adding research thinking and skills to their existing skill set and ways of knowing.

Third, we have seen, especially with these adult students, that learning research and conducting research is not just an added item to check off on a list of requirements but rather something undertaken deliberately to enhance and enrich life. Although we believe and hope that our philosophy of mindful inquiry will be helpful as well as exciting for all of our readers, we think that adults entering the path of research as part of expanding their life options will find it particularly valuable. In addition, we have tried to make the book as suitable for independent study as for use in classroom contexts.

Activities

Think of various social roles you have played in your life. For each one, imagine yourself to be a researcher who has received a large grant to learn more about these social roles. What questions most interest you about each one? (In this exercise, it is important that you think of real concerns, questions, or problems in your actual experience, regardless of whether you know it to be an accepted use of actual research.) As C. Wright Mills pointed out in *The Sociological Imagination* (1959), the key contribution of sociology to the world is to show how personal troubles connect with social issues. Sometimes, the things that we think unimportant or perhaps uniquely troubling only to us are actually troublesome to others as well. For example, Clark Moustakas, in his path-breaking phenomenological study of loneliness (1961), described his loneliness from being out of touch with himself and not having enough time to be alone and to cultivate his uniqueness. His study showed loneliness to be an important feature in the landscape of everyone's life.

■ Multiplicity of Approaches, Cultures of Inquiry

One consequence of the new intellectual situation of the human and social sciences is their increasingly interdisciplinary character. That is, the methods of inquiry used in different scientific disciplines borrow frequently from one another—history from anthropology and sociology, anthropology and sociology from linguistics and literary criticism, psychology from computer science, economics from history, and so on. Indeed, the social sciences and humanities frequently merge, as art historians and literary critics borrow sociological and economic categories and concepts, and sociologists and political scientists learn from philosophy. Even the boundaries between the natural and social sciences are less clear than they used to be, as sociologists and management scientists draw on biology and ecology. Furthermore, according to a tradition in the social sciences going back to the late nineteenth century, knowledge that tries to explain phenomena has different intentions and rules than knowledge that tries to understand them in the sense of knowing their subjective meaning. Some philosophers have added to this list of knowledge intentions (Apel, 1984) the idea of knowledge that tries to emancipate people or help them gain more freedom, justice, or happiness (Fay, 1987). In any case, it is clear that inquiry is pursued according to varying conceptions and models of what knowledge is, how it is created, and what it looks like.

What we have done to help you make your way amid this variety—and here we owe a great debt to our colleagues in the Human and Organization Development Program at the Fielding Institute who have collaborated in developing this conception—is to provide introductions to what we are calling "cultures of inquiry." These "cultures," which are far broader than research methods, are general approaches to creating knowledge in the human and social sciences, each with its own model of what counts as knowledge, what it is for, and how it is produced. Our array of cultures of inquiry is quite a bit more extensive than what is to be found in most introductions to research. For example, we consider phenomenology, critical social science, hermeneutics, action research, and theoretical research as cultures of inquiry, although many research textbooks do not even mention them. We also discuss ethnography, quantitative and behavioral science, historical research, as well as evaluation research. We are convinced that this will broaden your range of choices and your ways of conceptualizing your interests when planning and carrying out your own research.

This book is designed to introduce you to the principal approaches to scholarly inquiry that characterize the community of human and social science at large and the world of "reflective practitioners" in particular. A generation ago it was widely assumed that, depending on what school of thought you belonged to, there was either one valid approach to all knowledge gathering—the highly quantitative methods customarily associated with the natural sciences—or two: the natural–science and the interpretive–qualitative–humanistic approaches.

Today, we recognize that the study of people and their institutions may rightfully entail a variety of approaches. Some are quantitative, and some are qualitative. Some call for the researcher to be detached and impersonal, others call for direct engagement and involvement. Some require strongly developed skills in data manipulation and statistical analysis, others require "people" skills. A good research project will match the research approach to the problem to be studied, and it will ensure that the researcher is comfortable and competent in his or her role.

After reading this book, we expect that you will be better able to intelligently sort through the variety of existing research approaches, choosing those both personally compatible and adequate to the needs of your research. This book will introduce you to these approaches and give you a sense of the kind of knowledge that they produce, their strengths and limitations, and their applicability to your particular concerns. Given that each of these approaches comprises dozens of actual research techniques, this book is not intended to provide you with a sufficiently deep understanding of the methods you will eventually use to conduct research intelligently and defensibly in your field. For this, you will need to go into greater depth about the general approach to inquiry that you adopt— what we call *a culture of inquiry,* such as phenomenology, action research, or critical social science—and you will need to master the specific set of methods and techniques used in that approach. This can be done through a combination of organized research training in courses or training sessions; a research practicum, internship, or apprenticeship; independent study; observation of researchers at work; and acquaintance with exemplars of research-classic or outstanding research studies.

We strongly believe that researchers should be familiar with the language, culture, intent, and purposes of inquiry and research in their disciplines in a way that reflects the goals of integrating personal, professional, and intellectual competence and development. Hence, you should develop understanding of fundamental issues about the different ways in which we know, what constitutes reliable knowledge, and how one makes learnings credible and incorporates them into the culture of inquiry. You should also reflect personally on the psychological, intellectual, and social meanings of your research interests and your personal ways of engaging with ideas, data, methodologies, and decisions. And because inquiry and research in the human and social sciences occur within a number of divergent cultures of inquiry and research traditions, you should work at comparing and critically evaluating several cultures of inquiry and the research traditions in which they are embodied in your area of intellectual interest or professional work.

Finally, before engaging in a major research project, whether a thesis or dissertation research or research as part of your work, you should develop specialized competence in the methods that are appropriate to its question, including current trends and methodological controversies. As we said, this volume is an introduction to the general cultures of inquiry and not to the specific and detailed research techniques of which they consist.

Activities

Think of two very different kinds of skills you have learned in your life-time—for example, riding a bicycle and cooking. How did the "culture of learning" about each skill differ? What elements in each learning process were the same?

■ Becoming a Researcher as Socialization into a Community

Thinking about research and science has changed over the past generation in major ways. The most important change has been the shift to thinking of disciplined inquiry and scientific research, whether in the natural sciences, the social and human sciences, or the humanities, as social processes. Previously, research was often thought of and described as the activity of a solitary individual—the scientist, researcher, or scholar—facing reality or the world or nature and applying a body of universally valid scientific methods to it. To the extent that other people entered into research, as an afterthought it was called "the audience," that is, the people who would read the results of those solitary activities. This is still the view of research that shapes almost all introductions and guides to research. They focus primarily on learning certain methods or techniques through which this lone individual will produce a piece of knowledge or research.

In the view that has evolved over the past quarter century, however, science and research are understood as embedded in concrete communities and social groups, as processes that occur as part of dialogues, conversations, or discourses among members of communities of scientists or researchers. The individuals who are members of these communities are motivated in as various and complex ways as other human beings: by ambition, competition, desire for material success and recognition, generosity, religious and political beliefs, nonrational impulses, neurosis, and self-transcendence. Scientific communities, in turn, are governed by (often nonrational) social norms, rules, rituals, myths, ideologies, and "totems" (Hess, 1995) as are other kinds of communities. Individual scientists as well as scientific communities live in multiple, complex relationships with the society that surrounds them, which also affects how they live, think, feel, and behave. Furthermore, these communities of researchers are not static. They are continually evolving in time, changing their rules for producing knowledge, their "hot topics," their heroes and stars, their achievements and scandals.

Just as joining a fraternity, social club, firm, or religious order is a process of socialization in which people develop new ways of acting and new identities—that is, new ways not only of behaving, thinking, and feeling toward the rest of the world but new ways of thinking about, behaving toward, and feeling about themselves—so becoming a scientist or researcher means becoming a member of a scientific community or community of investigators, which therefore also means taking on new values, behaviors, and identities. In scientific communities, many of the values and social rules have to do with the creation of knowledge, with what counts as knowledge, how one goes about creating legitimate knowledge, how one establishes claims that something is or is not knowledge. But there are also values and rules that have to do with such things as the "ownership" of knowledge, propriety in distributing knowledge, and originality in knowledge, which are cultural and social values rather than purely knowledge-based values. (See James Boyle, 1996, for an excellent and illuminating discussion of some of these issues surrounding "intellectual property.") For example, if I write a paper copying verbatim from someone else's paper, it is as "knowledgeable" as the first person's paper. Yet almost everyone who has been in school knows that this is plagiarism and is one of the most morally reprehensible acts in the world of knowledge. Just as in joining any other community, one joins the community of researchers in history and at its current point in time. If one migrates to a new city or country, it is not enough to know about that place in general. One wants to understand what is going on there right now, which usually means knowing something about what went on before.

What we want to emphasize is that becoming a researcher consists largely of becoming socialized into a community of researchers, and much of the learning involved is social learning. This means learning not about research methods in the abstract but the research methods that are currently in use and the controversies surrounding them. It means learning the language and social conventions of the community. It means learning where the action is. Textbooks and introductions teach these things only to a limited extent. That is a primary reason why our book is not a textbook in research methods. Rather, we want to encourage you to develop intentionally and mindfully both your individuality as a researcher and your membership in one or more research communities.

Despite differences among scientific and research communities, all scientists, whatever their worldview, tend to agree on one thing: Following rational procedures of argument, criticism, and evaluation is the one best way to get at that ever-elusive "truth." Despite the influence of money, politics, spiritual beliefs, imagination, and sheer adventure on the practice of science, it is still the case that only what will stand up to rational argument will count as scientifically valid knowledge—that is, rational argument combined with some information about the world.

Activities

1. Interview an active social researcher. Ask him what other persons, groups, and societies he thinks about and communicates with about work. Ask about what it means to be a part of this group of colleagues.
2. Log into a discussion group or join a Listserv on the Internet about a research topic. Who are the primary participants? What theorists, researchers, and others do they frequently refer to?

3. Are there terms in the discussions you do not understand? Ask questions in classes and in on-line forums and report on any responses you receive.

4. Scan the past several years of a scholarly journal in which you are interested. Look for themes in the areas of questions, vocabulary, frequently cited authors, articles, or books.

■ Mode of Serious Play

We write in the mode of serious play. The play we write is a comedy, not a tragedy. We are willing to expose our blind spots, as well as the weaknesses and limitations in our orientations—not as a ritual or confession that would force us back into the tragic mode, which, after all, came from religious rites. That mode of thinking and writing places us too close to the skewer, to be deep-fried by our critics. Our mode is that of comedy, which encourages others to laugh with us at our limitations (Duncan, 1964).

Approaches to social knowledge will not always be laughing matters, however, as the results of research can hurt those who are affected by the interpretations and truth claims that such research asserts. Research on race is one such example. The concepts and categories researchers employ may skew and distort the results that, in turn, may taint the forms of practice that result. For example, the concept of leadership has been picked up from everyday use and built into a stream of research. However, just because it exists, attention has been drawn away from questions of power and manipulation. This illustrates the importance of clarifying concepts before proceeding with an investigation.

Once again, we say that this is the worst of times as well as the best of times. It is the best of times because it offers opportunities for social researchers to more freely select their questions and research approaches. Although many social science programs are still dominated by traditional scientific ways of knowing, they are increasingly including courses in alternative approaches. Recent social science and humanities journals and books reflect this new diversity of research approaches and knowledge perspectives. It is the worst of times because of the breadth and depth of knowledge and understanding that one needs to acquire in order to make appropriate, justified, rational decisions about frameworks and principles. In addition, one needs detailed empirical knowledge to investigate any aspect of human and social reality. However, the "worst" is also a "best" because working from the epistemological level offers openings, insights, and opportunities that are closed to the orthodox. This is especially important, we feel, for a student who comes with lots of work and life experiences. Epistemological openings may reveal opportunities in practice. For example, Jewel Ray Chaudhuri, after learning of hermeneutics as an approach to inquiry, used it to redeem a training situation in which a measurement instrument did not have its intended result (Chaudhuri, 1996). She was conducting a training session with executives in a Fortune 500 company using a well-known measurement instrument. However, the results did not provoke the anticipated discussion from the group. Whereas before she would have written this off as a session that did not work out well, having learning of hermeneutic epistemology she now asked participants to critically interpret the instrument itself and discuss their varying interpretations. This turned out to be one of the better training situations she conducted.

▬ Conclusion

In this chapter we have introduced our concept of mindful inquiry as an approach to social sciences research. We have stated why we believe each researcher should place herself at the center of the process. Focusing attention on the demographic changes in who researchers are, we realized that more scholar–practitioners are learning to become researchers in applied settings. We have briefly introduced the concept of cultures of inquiry and how you, as a researcher, will become part of a community of scholars with shared research cultures and subcultures.

In Chapter 2, we will explore the current historical and intellectual situation through which you must navigate as you conduct your research. If you wish, you may skip this chapter now and go on to Chapter 3, where we explain mindful inquiry in more detail. We hope that if you do this you will come back to Chapter 2 later, because it is important for you in understanding the postmodern situation, positivism, and why we developed our concept of mindful inquiry.

From Positivism
to Postmodernity

*The Mindful Inquirer
as a Philosopher*

We believe that being a researcher means far more than mastering research methods and techniques. As we have said, it means entering into the community of researchers, its conversations and its debates. Moreover, to be a full-fledged member of that community means entering into its traditions and its historical situation. In the social and human sciences in particular, that means entering into the historical situation of the community of researchers, facing the issues that it faces, and understanding something of how they have emerged.

■ Research Methods as Historical Products

It is almost inevitable, in such a historical turning point, for old intellectual frameworks, problems, and paradigms to be replaced by new ones, for old intellectual traditions and political and social perspectives and policies to give way to new approaches. It is just as inevitable that these changes will be reflected in how knowledge is produced—in research. Yet many textbooks present their introduction to research seemingly oblivious to these historical changes, as though their repertoire of research methods could just run on its own steam, independently of history. Research methods are often presented as a collection of tools that are just lying around, outside of space and time, to be used when needed. In reality, research methods and traditions come and go, and new tools replace old ones. When we were in graduate school a generation ago, many of the tools currently being used in the human and social sciences either did not exist or were quite unfashionable. Indeed, these methods are not "pure" methods at all, because they depended on theories and schools of thought that shape how social and human scientists conceive of social and human affairs.

Although we do not purport to be able to identify unambiguously the coming research approaches of the emerging historical phase, we do look at the tools of research as ever-changing historical products that meet the historically changing research needs and knowledge models of researchers—researchers who are always redefining themselves historically. And we do believe that our own approach of mindful inquiry is particularly suited to this context, because it includes explicitly defining your research in terms of your understanding of your own historical context. Thus, we take a critical, historical, and nonpositivistic approach to research methods themselves.

Activities

Ask yourself these questions: How is the historical situation in which you are contemplating doing social research different from the setting for research 10 years ago? How is it different from the setting for research you have recently read? Who are the founders of the discipline or area of interest in which you are working or interested? What was going on at their time, and how did it affect their work and ideas?

■ Living at a Historical Turning Point

Inquiry and research always take place within a historical and social context, not merely in an intellectual context, such as the postmodern situation in the human and social sciences, but in the wider context of social, political, economic, cultural, technological, and environmental trends of which that intellectual situation is a part. We are living through a major sociohistorical turning point now. In fact, if we include the ecological crisis, it is a sociohistorical–natural turning point, which includes at least five major aspects.

1. A truly global market economy is emerging—one in which all of our fates are shaped more than ever before by economic forces around the world. International trade, investment, and economic competition have had some significance for centuries, increasingly so since the second half of the nineteenth century. But in recent decades, the globalization of the economy has taken a qualitative leap, propelled by the growth in size and scope of multinational or transnational corporations, the emergence of the computer and network infrastructure that makes instantaneous financial transactions and business manage-

ment possible, efficiencies in transportation and shipping, and trade and commercial treaties and arrangements that facilitate global trade. These developments have led to truly global markets for capital, labor, and commodities. Firms from the United States can employ cheap labor in South America and Asia; Chinese citizens can eat McDonald's hamburgers in Beijing; Moroccan villagers watch American, French, Indian, and Egyptian videotapes on their VCRs; transactions move around world financial markets 24 hours a day. Furthermore, the spread of the commercial and commodity culture of advanced industrial nations to the rest of the world has created a global symbolic system in which people all over the world, despite cultural differences, share images, symbols, and media transmitted to the entire planet by global media (Iyer, 1988). This creates common or overlapping need structures throughout our planet.

2. The push toward an information society is accelerating. A second industrial revolution, in which information technology—through the integration of computers, networks, and multimedia—is restructuring many aspects of our public and private lives, is even, in some views, creating a new type of human being (Bolter, 1984) and a new type of reality (Heim, 1993; Levy, 1987). Human and social life have always been shaped by technologies, and the current "informatization" of the world, to use a French term, is one of the most extensive and rapid technological shifts in human history. People work in new ways, interact with others in new ways, conduct their daily lives in new ways, and relate to space and the environment in new ways, for all of these sectors of life are mediated by computer, network, and multimedia technologies. Some human beings are working in distributed groups for virtual organizations in cyberspace, producing, distributing, and consuming information commodities (Mowshowitz, 1992, 1994). Indeed, an entirely new branch of the legal system is being developed to organize information commodities in a way that will maximize private property in information (Boyle, 1996).

3. Humanity is coming up against environmental and natural limits to human activities, which also means rethinking the ancient split between "nature" and "culture" (Catton & Dunlap, 1980; Latour, 1993).

It is only within the past quarter century that there has been widespread recognition in advanced industrial societies that human beings exist and live not in a vacuum but in continuous interaction with a natural environment that is affected by them and that affects them. All human production and consumption has environmental impacts and costs. The gigantic growth of the global human population in this half century, combined with the tremendous output into the environment of the products, by-products, offshoots, efflux, and externalities of industrial production, has given rise to serious environmental problems for which no substantially effective policies have yet been devised.

4. The end of the Cold War is redefining the issues of capitalism, socialism, democracy, and authoritarianism that have shaped the politics and social move-

ments of the past century. Until very recently, the political and social life of the twentieth century was based on the interplay of four main conflicts: that between capitalism and socialism; between liberal democracy and fascism; between imperialism and national liberation; and between the Communist political, military, and economic system under the control of the Soviet Union and the Western capitalist coalition led by the United States. The disintegration of the Soviet Union just a few years ago has changed the world's economic, military, political, and ideological shape, with consequences that can hardly be foreseen. Nevertheless it is clear that a change of this magnitude in the world's political, military, and ideological frame is bound to affect, in a serious way, many aspects of life.

5. Previously suppressed or marginalized groups, as a result of their enfranchisement, are taking an active role in political and social power and public cultural and intellectual dialogues. Developing nations previously dominated by imperialism; members of dominated ethnic minorities in many lands; women deprived of their voice and power by patriarchal social systems; gays and lesbians hiding their sexual orientation for fear of violence, humiliation, or discrimination—members of all of these groups have entered the long process of reclaiming their rights, power, and identity and wresting from the ruling groups the right to control and to define. This process is also changing the meaning, context, and experience of the traditional voices that dominated these dialogues in the past, primarily the voices of "dead, White, European (and American) males," as well as living ones.

These factors are changing who we are as human beings, how we see ourselves and define ourselves, and the problems we face both individually and collectively. The human and social sciences, as they have been handed down to us, are largely a human and social attempt to respond to the set of problems distinctive to modern society. These arose in the nineteenth century as the industrial revolution, capitalism, urbanization, population growth, and bureaucratization met new ways of thinking derived from the scientific revolution and the Enlightenment. Eric Hobsbawm has pointed out that, in the period from 1789 to 1848, many words came into existence that are now part of our everyday vocabulary: *industry, industrialist, factory, middle-class, working class, capitalism, socialism, aristocracy, railway, liberal, conservative, nationality, scientist, engineer, economic crisis, utilitarian, statistics, sociology, journalism, ideology, strike,* and *pauperism* (Hobsbawm, 1962). As Hobsbawm noted, "To imagine the world without these words (i.e., without the things and concepts for which they provide names) is to measure the profundity of the revolution which broke out between 1789 and 1848 and forms the greatest transformation in human history since the remote times when men invented agriculture and metallurgy, writing, the city and the state" (1962, p. 17). This transformation was at the origins of the human and social sciences.

We imagine that it would be possible to make a list of words and terms from the present that would suggest another major transformation and, correspondingly, the need for new efforts, achievements, and creativity by the human and social sciences: *globalization, cyberspace, virtual organization, ecosystem, CNN* (instantaneous, ubiquitous moving pictures of current events), *McDonald's* (instantaneous, ubiquitous hamburgers), *greenhouse effect, robot* and *knowbot, electronic funds transfer, downsizing* and *outsourcing, gay liberation, decolonization, moonwalk, sisterhood is powerful, deep ecology,* and *World Wide Web.*

The five trends that we have mentioned are bringing about new realities; it is only to be expected that they will bring about new human and social problems. They are also principal causes of the postmodern intellectual situation.

At some point, any researcher must be able, with regard to proposed or completed research, to answer the questions "So what?" and "What is the significance of your research?" One consideration, although not the only one, in evaluating answers to these questions is whether the research helps us understand these trends, their consequences, and their implications. It seems that an introduction to research that does not pay specific attention to the new historical situation in which we live and work is bound to seem somewhat "out of it." Because we see ourselves—and you—as "in it," we pay attention to it, which does not mean trying to be "with it."

Activities

List material, political, social, personal, and environmental streams in your immediate environment. How do these affect your desire to do research? How do these affect your ability to do research? What kind of research will be the most likely for you to do? How do the people in your social environment—fellow students, coworkers, family—see their relationship to these larger historical trends and forces?

▬ The Postmodern Situation and the Crisis in the Foundations of Knowledge

Postmodernism is a concept that some thinkers have used to grasp our living in a new historical situation. It has become not only a major intellectual trend but also a fad and an object of consumption. At the time of writing, there is a song on some airwaves titled "Postmodern Sleaze," and the word *postmodern* has started to appear in advertisements. You may have noticed that many books and articles in every field either use the term *postmodern* or are about *modernity* and *the modern,* often from the perspective of our being in a postmodern period.

There are books out not only on the *postmodern organization* but even on *postmodern marketing* and *postmodern consumer research!*

Whenever a word is applied to everything, it runs the danger of becoming meaningless. What does *postmodern* really mean? In essence, it means three different but related things that, taken together, constitute *postmodernity:* the postmodern historical situation, postmodern culture, and postmodern theory.

1. The idea of a postmodern historical period is that a new historical epoch has arrived, one that is distinguished in several important ways from the modern period of history. A number of social theorists believe that the five trends we described previously, along with some others—such as the transition from mass production to customized, just-in-time production; the conversion of most aspects of goods, services, and cultures into commodities; the tremendous time–space compression of contemporary experience and consciousness; the role of the media in everyday consciousness; and the prevalence of mass migrations— set the present off in significant ways from the preceding period of modern history and project us into a "condition of postmodernity" (Appadurai, 1996; Harvey, 1989; Lyon, 1994).

What is the difference between calling these trends a new historical situation and calling them postmodernity? The point of the postmodernity label is to assert that the present period (i.e., within approximately the past two decades) represents a qualitative break with the entire modern period of at least the past century or two, depending on what people mean by *the modern period* or *modernity*. A number of historical watersheds are used by historians to distinguish the modern from the premodern period:

- the nominalist philosophy of the end of the Middle Ages in the fourteenth century, which severed human knowledge from correspondence with an objective divine and cosmic order and saw order as originating in the human mind's abstractions from particulars of experience (Dupré, 1993; Haag, 1985);
- the Renaissance of the fifteenth century, with its humanism and resuscitation of the heritage of Classical Antiquity (Hale, 1994);
- the Reformation of the sixteenth century, which broke with the hierarchy and spiritual monopoly of the Catholic Church and transferred religious authority to the individual (Dickens, 1966);
- the scientific revolution of the seventeenth century, which produced both a new mathematical and experimental method for understanding nature and a new cosmology derived from that method (Gillispie, 1960);
- the Enlightenment and the American and French revolutions of the eighteenth century, which placed human reason and the critique of irrational authority in a central role in culture and political institutions (Hazard, 1963; Hobsbawm, 1962);
- the emergence of capitalism from the sixteenth through the nineteenth centuries, which spread commercial exchange, production based on the organization of

free labor and the accumulation of capital, and a culture of financial calculation to most sectors of social life (Dobb, 1947);

- the development of the modern state apparatus from the seventeenth through the nineteenth centuries, which subjected increasing areas of life to formally rational administration and procedure (Weber, 1961);

- the Industrial Revolution of the nineteenth century, which linked capitalism with technological revolutions in the production of goods and the generation of power (Landes, 1969).

In reality we can regard modernity as an overlap of all of these. A common feature of most conceptions of modernity is what the sociologist Max Weber called "rationalization"—that is, the expansion to more and more sectors of behavior, thought, and social life of "formally" or "technically" rational conduct, which is based on efficiency, calculation, predictability, procedures or algorithms, and the adaptation of means to ends (Habermas, 1984; Weber, 1968a; Weber, 1992). Especially since the late eighteenth and early nineteenth centuries, this rationalization of social life has been associated with the economic and social priority given to the intertwined growth of economic production, technological mastery, scientific knowledge, and bureaucratic administration of public and private institutions.

In the modern period as a whole, this rationalization has been accompanied, although in an ambivalent way, by the growth of rationalistic and secular belief systems—that is, the belief that there is a rationally structured world and that human beings are rational and autonomous individuals or "subjects," capable of objective knowledge of this world, rational action, control of their natural and social environment, and self-knowledge. "Modern" culture has believed and emphasized the centrality of the human being, the human self, the human subject, over and against the centrality of either God or nature. One version of this theory is what the philosopher Immanuel Kant called the *Copernican revolution* in philosophy. According to Kant, our knowledge is relative to the knower, who may not be central to the physical universe but is central to the world "as known." Another version of the centrality of the human subject is Friedrich Nietzsche's statement, "If God existed, I could not be God. Therefore there is no God." Modern thinkers see human beings, rather than God, as the source of meaning. In James Mensch's words, "This positioning of the subject or self as normative has worked for hundreds of years. In fact, in a broad sense, modernity is this appeal to subjectivity" (1996, p. 21).

This emphasis on the centrality of the human subject points to another important part of modern culture: the philosophical idea that it is both necessary and possible to find an absolute, secure, rational basis for knowledge. This was rooted in the rational human subject's ability to reflect on itself and identify in its own human mind the basis for objective and certain knowledge. This philosophical notion runs from René Descartes's "I think therefore I am" through

Kant's "Copernican revolution" to Edmund Husserl's twentieth-century attempt to ground knowledge in the transcendental dimension that can be attained through "phenomenological" (see Chapter 7) reflection on the nature and structure of consciousness. And part of the modern belief system is a particular philosophy of history—the notion that human beings and civilization are on a course of progress to a better, freer, more knowledge-based, peaceful society based on science and the recognition and valuing of human rights. Different philosophers and theorists of the past two centuries have formulated this idea differently, seeing the path of modernity as leading, for example, from a military to an industrial society (Herbert Spencer), from feudalism to capitalism to socialism (Karl Marx), from community to society (Ferdinand Tönnies), from traditional to rational–legal authority (Max Weber), from religious to secular society (many thinkers), and so on. But all modern thinkers, from the eighteenth century to the present, define the history of modern society as progressive, even if they are ambivalent about this progress.

Postmodernity is considered to be a break with characteristic modern social and cultural forms, structures, and processes. For example, whereas within a segment of modern consciousness there was the belief that culture would become more secular with the advance of science and technology, we now see that the spread of modern science, technology, and commerce in fact can be accompanied by the intensification of religious belief, participation, and consciousness (Barber, 1995; Bloom, 1992). Because in the twentieth century science and technology have been used to build concentration camps, develop nuclear weapons, wreak destruction on the environment, and create "information media" that end up making people less informed (McKibben, 1992), doubts have been raised about the reality and inevitability of progress, to the point where some thinkers have criticized "enlightenment" as a new myth (Horkheimer & Adorno, 1975). Whereas modern thinkers saw technological progress as helping moderate the human struggle for existence and reduce human labor while increasing leisure, anthropologists have shown that precisely the reverse is true—that technological progress, associated with the infinite expansion of human needs, has intensified the struggle for existence, reduced leisure, and increased labor (Sahlins, 1972; Schor, 1992). The emergence and expansion of information technology is taken by some to constitute a break with the technological and social basis of modernity (Lyon, 1994; Lyotard, 1984), and others see the break as being the end of modern mass production or Fordism (Harvey, 1989). The historical context has become both more multicultural and more universal or transcultural than it was before. Because of the globalization of technology and the availability of communication among cultures via electronic means and jet air travel, a global culture is evolving. At the same time, we are aware of more cultures with more diverse points of view both within our own countries and outside. We are becoming aware that there are differences that are not a result of ignorance of each other but a result of knowledge of each other (Pearce & Littlejohn, 1997).

Whether postmodernity is a genuinely new historical period or merely a phase of modernity that just intensifies certain of its characteristics is a controversial question (Calhoun, 1995) whose answer is not essential for our purposes. For us it is enough to note that the present is a time of major social and historical shifts and that these shifts form the basis, as we shall see, of major changes in the climate and content of the human and social sciences.

2. The idea of postmodern culture is that certain characteristics of contemporary culture, especially in the arts, constitute a distinctive style that is different from the "modern" art of most of the twentieth century. Here *postmodern* is distinguished not so much from *modernity* as from modernism, the radical artistic movements of the early twentieth century. Starting in the first decade of the twentieth century, the arts ruptured with traditional artistic languages and forms to create the distinctive styles of modernist visual art (e.g., Pablo Picasso, Georges Braque, Wassily Kandinsky, Piet Mondrian), music (e.g., Arnold Schoenberg, Igor Stravinsky), architecture (e.g., Walter Gropius, Ludwig Mies van der Rohe), and literature (e.g., Franz Kafka, James Joyce, T. S. Eliot, Ezra Pound; Butler, 1994). As avant-garde art, modernism distinguished itself from the "common sense" of artistic tradition and the surrounding culture and from the "common sense" of the commercial products of mass culture and popular culture produced in increasing volume by the "culture industry" (Adorno, 1991a). Many of the modernist artists considered themselves to be both on the bandwagon of modernity and in revolt against it. That is, they saw themselves as part of the logical extension of urbanism, science, technology, and secularism. But they also protested the overrationalistic, bourgeois, traditional, repressive culture and the alienation, suffering, meaninglessness, and hypocrisy that they experienced and saw as accompanying modernity (Butler, 1994). In Nietzsche's words, "Too long, the earth has been a madhouse!" (Nietzsche, 1887/1967, p. 93). Regardless of this ambivalence, modernity in the arts was widely interpreted, by some modern artists and critics, in terms of the modern philosophy of history as progress. Modern art was supposed to be "progressive," recognizing a distinctive modern situation (Spender, 1963).

Postmodern culture erases the distinctions between *modern* and *classical* or *traditional* culture on the one hand and between *avant-garde* or *high* culture and mass culture on the other by drawing on all of them and mixing them together (Docherty, 1993; Jencks, 1989). For a number of people who use the concept of postmodern culture, it also includes the notions of the surrounding influence of media and advertising and of culture as representing or expressing anything, critique of the idea of artistic progress, and objection to the idea of artists being in the vanguard of some superior, more authentic or expressive stage of civilization. Thus postmodernism in the arts severs the artists from the modernist philosophy of history.

One could divide the recent history of culture into three phases: (a) classical–traditional, when art and culture were thought to represent an objective external reality, as in the art of the Renaissance, the novels of the nineteenth century, the music of Johann Sebastian Bach; (b) modernist, when art and culture were thought to represent or express deep layers of consciousness, the unconsciousness, or the realm of spirit and symbol, as in the art of Picasso and Kandinsky, the short stories of Kafka, and the music of Schoenberg and Stravinsky; and (c) postmodern, in which artistic and cultural creators deny both that there is an objective reality to represent and a self to express. It may be worth pointing out that postmodernism only originated after modern, or modernist, art moved from being avant-garde art (i.e., the art of a small group of outsiders who rejected the social and artistic "establishment") to becoming the official art of the late-twentieth century. That is an important reason behind postmodernism's challenge to modernist culture.

In any case, modernity consists not only of certain objective social trends (e.g., industrialization and urbanization) but in the consciousness that different social groups have of what it means to live in and with those trends. Developments in the arts have been important turning points in the self-interpretation of the modern world. When historians see the Renaissance as the beginning of the modern world, it is not only because of economic and social changes but because of the view of the world opened up by Renaissance painting and architecture. In a similar way, the rise of modernism in the arts just before World War I is taken as the transition to a new historical period. Postmodern culture is an important ingredient in the postmodern situation because it represents a break with the consciousness of modernism in the arts.

3. Postmodern theory is a particular body of thought and theory, especially in philosophy, the humanities, and the social sciences, that constitutes a break with the main tradition of modern philosophy and social theory since the seventeenth century. As we noted, modern thought has maintained, in different forms, that human beings are rational subjects capable of clear, accurate, and objective knowledge of a knowable and rationally structured natural and social reality. Although postmodern theory includes a wide variety of intellectual positions and ideas (Best & Kellner, 1991; Docherty, 1993), some of its prominent features are

- the idea of the "death of man," which asserts that the "rational autonomous subject" is just a fiction or construct of a particular period of cultural history and that there may not be any such thing as a subject or even a self;
- the idea of the "death of history," which asserts that the notion of history as progress is just a fiction or "metanarrative" and that there is no overarching meaning or direction to history;
- the idea of the "death of metaphysics" or "the end of foundationalism," which asserts that it is impossible to provide an absolute foundation for knowledge,

and that knowledge itself does not "represent" reality but merely "constructs" it in different ways (Benhabib, Butler, Cornell, & Fraser, 1995);

- the idea that the meanings of signs, symbols, and texts are not unequivocal but rather are temporary and unstable moments in an ongoing process of interpretation—a process that depends as much on the interpreter and the context of interpretation as on anything that the texts and symbols stand for;
- the idea that facts, meanings, and theories are constructs that reflect the temporary power of social classes, ethnic groups, and genders in an ongoing power struggle about defining reality and knowledge, and that such facts, meanings, and theories need to be not so much explained, interpreted, or critiqued as *deconstructed*—that is, to have their cultural, historical, and power bases exposed.

Whatever one thinks of these postmodern theses, they represent a challenge to the human and social sciences to examine their philosophical assumptions, their theories, and their understanding of how they fit into their social and historical context. Here are some of the current challenges and confusions:

1. There is confusion and conflict over what constitutes valid knowledge and over what valid knowledge looks like. We can no longer just assume that we can ride on the coattails of our intellectual predecessors and teachers and adopt their definitions. In the face of the extreme relativist challenge of postmodern theory, we need to construct our intellectual edifice from scratch.
2. There is conflict about the value and purpose of knowledge (knowledge for what? knowledge for whom?).
3. There is disagreement about whether knowledge is discovered or socially constructed and subject to deconstruction.
4. There is disagreement about whether knowledge should be deconstructed—that is, taken apart in a way that reveals its limitations, assumptions, biases, and historical conditions.
5. There is disagreement over whether truth and objectivity are possible, and if so, what limits there are to them.

We believe that the postmodern situation is fundamental with regard to the context of present work in the human and social sciences. This does not at all mean that we are postmodernists in the sense of the postmodern theorists. To the contrary, we are highly critical of some of the "official" doctrines of postmodernism (Bentz & Kenny, 1997). In some ways, we are old-fashionedly modern and even unfashionably premodern. But we do think that there is a postmodern situation and that you cannot become a social or human science researcher without being aware of it.

Activities

The most important and useful thing that you can do as a researcher with regard to postmodernism is to figure out how you stand with regard to it. Do you believe that there is a postmodern situation, that the current period of history is a new historical phase that bears on the nature of knowledge and research in the way that the theorists of postmodernity maintain? If so, how do you see yourself, your family, your social network, your environment, your future prospects as affected by this situation? How would you define any differences you believe exist between the modern and the postmodern? Are there cultural works (scholarly books, novels, songs, movies, television shows, websites, etc.) that you would describe as postmodern, and if so, why? Are there people you know who seem more or less aware of being in a postmodern situation? If so, how do they demonstrate this awareness?

The place to start in thinking about these questions is to read some of the characterizations of the postmodern age and of postmodern thought and see if they make sense to you. The next is to look at cultural phenomena to see if they reflect a postmodern consciousness. The final step, especially as a researcher, is to look at people who are doing intellectual work explicitly in a postmodern vein and see whether this seems like a fruitful or stimulating line of work to you.

■ The Mysterious Death and Afterlife of Positivism

To understand the philosophical and methodological aspects of the postmodern situation in the social sciences, it is important to understand something of positivism. Until the past quarter century, much of the philosophy of science and the theory of knowledge were highly influenced by the current of thought known as positivism. Much recent philosophical thought has been a reaction against positivism and cannot be understood without it. Some philosophers of science try to base human and social science research on an explicitly postpositivist theory of knowledge (Polkinghorne, 1983). Yet current research training and research textbooks in the social sciences are often still based on positivist ideas. Indeed most of us, before we ever knew that there were such things as epistemology and the philosophy of science, were indoctrinated into positivism in high school, when we were told that there was such a thing as "the scientific method" based on observation, hypothesis, and verification, and when we were given the general idea that the march of science and technology is the key to human progress.

During the heyday of the Cold War, when Communism was the reigning enemy of the "free world," a public opinion survey found that many Americans had never heard of Communism. Far more numerous, we are sure, are those from all walks of life who have never heard of positivism. Nevertheless, positivism—the adoption of a rather limited notion of the scientific method as not only a prescription for conducting research and producing scientific knowledge but a comprehensive worldview, social ideology, and definition of the meaning of life—is an important force in the history of modern culture and, in particular, in the history of intellectual life and research. This is because positivism has been not only a philosophy of science but a major version of the modern philosophy of history. It has linked certain ideas about the nature of science and knowledge with a notion of modernity as scientific progress.

So what is positivism? The term *positivism* is sometimes used ambiguously or incorrectly in a way that contributes to confusion about epistemology and about the conduct of research. As Anthony Giddens wrote, "The word 'positivist,' like the word 'bourgeois,' has become more of a derogatory epithet than a useful descriptive concept, and consequently has been largely stripped of whatever agreed meaning it may once have had" (1974, p. ix). This is especially true because, as Giddens noted, "After Comte, no philosophers or social thinkers willingly called themselves 'positivists'" (1974, p. 2). Thus it is easy to concoct a positivist straw person, a construct of the writer's worldview rather than a description of something identifiable in the world.

Positivism originated in the nineteenth century in the thought of Auguste Comte (Comte, 1974; see also Marcuse, 1954; Simon, 1963) and received its most extreme formulation in the logical positivism and logical empiricism of the 1920s and 1930s (Ayer, 1952; Ayer, 1957; Russell, 1956). Because positivism is a complex, composite phenomenon, because it is also a controversial and partisan set of ideas, and because it is not just a theory of knowledge but a cultural and political orientation, it is not something that can be covered by a simple, dictionary definition. Not all people who have called themselves positivists hold all of their ideas in common. Not everyone who has ideas that have been considered positivistic calls herself a positivist. More important, there are thinkers who hold, either explicitly or by implication, ideas and intellectual positions that are positivistic in significant ways, although they themselves are explicitly critical of or opposed to positivism.

Positivism has characteristics of both clearly defined doctrines and of large, amorphous worldviews. In Appendix C, we have provided a more detailed summary of positivist ideas as well as of their critics. Here we would like to emphasize certain key positivist theses and beliefs.

1. The modern "positive," empirical, factual sciences are the only legitimate form of knowledge, replacing religion, metaphysics, and philosophical speculation as valid knowledge. Science is its own justification and requires no philosophical justification or validation. Philosophy can provide no genuine knowledge, but can merely clarify scientific method and help determine whether something is scientific or not. In Comte's idea, human thought and knowledge naturally develop from religion to metaphysics to "positive" science.

2. There is, or should be, a unitary form for science, with the implication that there is a single, canonical model, that particular disciplines are more or less scientific and more or less "mature" to the extent that they conform to this model, and that ultimately they will all converge in a "unified science." Usually a natural

science is taken as the exemplar, with the implication that it could serve as a model for the human and social sciences.

3. The world and knowledge are structured *atomistically*. That is, reality consists of a collection of disconnected facts, and experience consists of a bunch of disconnected perceptions or observations.

4. Ethics, values, and politics have no rational basis, on the grounds that they are not scientific. Rationality can exist only in the realm of science and not in the ethical or practical realm, which is seen as the expression of irrational or nonrational emotion, will, instinct, or arbitrary decision making.

5. Human and social progress are interpreted in terms of scientific progress. Here positivism has not only tended to regard the advancement of science as the key motor of human and social progress, it has defined human and social progress in terms of scientific progress, on the grounds that there are no rational nonscientific criteria of progress. And, because it tends to think of science in terms of prediction and control, it tends to think of human and social improvement or change in terms of "social engineering." As Gillispie has said of Comte, "he converted sociology from the science to the engineering of humanity. . . . He would know in order to predict, and predict in order to control, and such was the program of positivism" (Gillispie, 1960, p. 496). The social message of positivism has tended to be that the social order in which we live is fundamentally alright as it is, requiring for improvement simply the piecemeal extension of scientific method to problem areas. Although Comte thought of positivism as part of the "religion of humanity"—of which sociologists were to be the priests—it was a scientific, technocratic, managerial religion.

We would like to emphasize some problems with positivism that underlie the current epistemological situation in the human and social sciences.

1. As a particular doctrine about the nature of science and the scientific method, positivism has been criticized as false as a theory of science and of scientific development, even in the natural sciences.

2. There is a substantial tradition arguing that the unrestrained application of a single, natural–scientific method to every domain is inappropriate, especially for the human and social sciences.

3. In seeing the world as a bunch of disconnected facts, positivism thinks about both facts and knowers or inquirers as having no context or history. The recent philosophy and sociology of science emphasize the extent to which knowing is always embedded in history and in cultural and social context. From this point of view, any approach to knowledge, whether it is natural–scientific or objectivistic or subjectivistic, can be positivistic if it does not look at the broader history and context in which knowledge is generated.

4. There is a long philosophical tradition, from ancient philosophy to the present, that argues that it is possible or necessary to be rational in the realm of ethics, values, and politics—that it is as possible to give a rational justification of or motivation for a moral action as it is to give a rational explanation of a physical event (Benhabib & Dallmayr, 1990).

5. Positivism is also a general doctrine about the relation of knowledge to ethics, politics, and society. In its stress on the power of facts and on the limitation of knowledge to facts, its rejection of the potential rationality of norms and values, its denial of the possibility of a critical perspective on the whole of society, and its making a fetish of science and technology, it functions as an ideology (Habermas, 1970a) that is uncritical, antihumanistic, and politically conservative, propping up the status quo and contributing to the development of a "one-dimensional society" (Marcuse, 1966b). In this view, positivism helps prevent radical or progressive social change by rejecting as irrational any norms or goals that go beyond the facts and transcend the status quo.

Radical critics of positivism point out that during the early modern period and the rise of modern science, philosophers, scientists, and political thinkers linked the advancement of science and knowledge to the general education of the population and to the growth of individual, political, and social autonomy and freedom. They believed that the advancement of science would or should lead to the elimination of archaic, barbaric, or repressive institutions. After the French Revolution, positivism attempted to liquidate the connection between the advancement of knowledge and the growth of freedom by defining scientific progress as the primary issue. Comte himself saw the purpose of the advancement of science as serving humanity and reorganizing society. But the primacy positivism gave to science, as well as its idealistic, religious, and vague conception of such a social reorganization, ended up in the worship of science regardless of its political, social, or human consequences. Even though the positivists wanted benign human consequences to occur, they were concerned that these consequences occur in an "orderly" way. Hence the positivist motto, "order and progress."

If positivism is so controversial and has so few adherents, why do we believe that it is important to know something about it? First, because, as Richard W. Miller pointed out, though he has "never met a self-proclaimed positivist . . . in a broad sense of the term, positivism remains the dominant philosophy of science" (Miller, 1987, p. 3). We have already pointed out that much of the postmodern situation in the social sciences is still a reaction against and debate with positivism. Therefore, because you are in this situation, it is important to understand the theory and the reactions to it.

Second, the term is sometimes simply used incorrectly. For example, it is sometimes used to refer to the use of quantitative methods in the social sciences. The association between positivism as a way of knowing and its preference for no-mothetic (law establishing), quantitative research methods has created confusion about the meaning of the term *positivism* as well as about positivism as an intellectual current. Positivism is not a particular way of doing research. There is no such thing as a positivist research method per se. Any research method or culture of inquiry, not only quantitative and behavioral science inquiry but phenomenology, ethnography, action research, and so on, can be carried out in either a positivistic or nonpositivistic way. Rather, positivism is a philosophical position about knowledge and research and their social context and consequences, one that also takes on ideological functions. Whether a particular piece of research or scholarship is positivistic or not is something that must be decided in each individual case based on the structure and operative assumptions the researchers employed and not on their self-described philosophical affiliation or the particular research method they employed.

Third, over and above its particular views about the nature of science, positivism, explicitly or implicitly, is at the core of the modern worldview of scientific, technological, bureaucratic, commercial civilization. The advancement of science and the adoption of scientifically and technologically rational procedures are basic components not only of that civilization but also of its self-justification and self-legitimation, part of the achievements on which the citizens of that civilization pride themselves and on the basis of which the civilization is "sold." Thus positivism has cultural, symbolic, political, and social significance as well as epistemological meaning. That is why the critique of and crises of advanced industrial civilization—of modernity—of the past 30 years have been intertwined with the critique of positivism. Positivism is part of "the system," part of the phase of modernity that started in the nineteenth century.

That is why we do not accept the idea of a new, "postpositivist" theory of knowledge that has superseded positivism. That idea implies that there was a time when everyone was a positivist but now, through either increased wisdom or a paradigm shift, everyone sees the light and recognizes the limitations and defects of positivism. This would imply that the positivist age has given way to a "postpositivist" age. In fact, positivism was always just one stream of thought and has been criticized since its beginnings. Conversely, even though few philosophers and social scientists currently accept the philosophy of science of the logical positivists of the 1930s, positivism as a general worldview is still alive and well, not only within the philosophy of scientific method but within prevailing orientations to knowledge and its relation to society. One could almost say that the idea of postpositivism is itself a positivistic idea, because it just adds a phase—postpositivism—to Comte's phases of the development of knowledge, of which the last is always the truest. Postpositivism can become, like positivism did, an excuse for not reflecting on the grounds of one's beliefs and practices about knowledge and about one's social and historical context.

We mentioned previously that Jürgen Habermas has argued that, at root, positivism is simply the denial of reflection, that is, of the need to reflect explicitly on the philosophical and social conditions of knowledge (1971). From this point of view, any "official" philosophy of science, whether positivistic or post-positivistic, is inherently positivistic, because of the implication that there is a basis for knowledge that does not need to be questioned. We believe that the method of mindful inquiry that we propose will help you stay in a reflective mode, be conscious of the basis of your knowledge claims, and make explicit choices about the philosophical, value, disciplinary, theoretical, and socio-political framework within which you work. Regardless of your research method, this will make your work less likely to be positivistic in the ideological sense. If you choose positivism as an explicit reflective choice, as some recommend (Turner, 1992), then you will have avoided some of the problems that have troubled positivism's critics.

The single most important consequence of the recent critique of positivism is this: By removing a taken-for-granted account and justification of science, it forces the researcher to become her own philosopher. To be an inquirer in the human and social sciences, you now have to become something of an epistemologist, a theorist of knowledge. Because you cannot simply fall back on positivism as your ultimate foundation, you have to create your own. Even if, along with contemporary philosophers who are "antifoundationalist," you do not accept that there is or can be a foundation to knowledge, then you have to show why.

Activities

List four assumptions of positivism. To what extent do you accept or reject them? Why?

■ The Researcher as Applied Philosopher

We are old-fashioned in believing that the scientist or working researcher is always a kind of philosopher, at least an applied philosopher. We are even pre-modern in the sense that before the nineteenth century the sciences did not exist as separate disciplines and were considered part of philosophy. We believe that it is impossible to fully understand the nature of research or to make the best choices about it without some attention to its philosophical context, its assumptions, its a priori constructions of reality, its knowledge values. No matter how technical and mechanical research may be, at least at some points in the process, it always is also a form of philosophical inquiry. That is, it always involves philosophical assumptions about the nature of knowledge and of the world and about what the point of knowledge and research are in the first place. Consciously or unconsciously, research is always contributing to the advancement of some philosophical "project"—and to a personal and social one as well.

In most research textbooks and courses, research tools (and research itself) are presented as "value-neutral"—that is, as having no ethical, moral, or political content or significance. This, in turn, is part of research being presented *without philosophy* or as requiring no philosophy. The way this works is that the author will say that research is about creating *science* or *knowledge* about *the world* or *reality* or *society* or *human behavior.* But what is *science?* What is *knowledge?* What is *reality?* These are precisely philosophical questions, and any statement about them is a philosophical one. In fact, you already have to have some idea about them in order to engage in research. Does knowledge mean being able to predict? Does it include intuitive knowledge that I have about something? Does it have to be generalizable? And what is this *reality?* Does it have an *essence?* Is it a collection of facts? Is the reality that I know the same as yours? These are all philosophical questions that you have to have some tentative answers to before you conduct disciplined inquiry, because they shape how you do research and what you may find.

We believe that some attention to philosophical issues is as important as learning to use a specific research method, and we pay some attention to them. Perhaps you do not normally think of yourself as a philosopher, but we believe that, to the extent that you are engaged in research, you are a philosopher and need to think of yourself as such.

The researcher today must be aware of the epistemological grounds on which his inquiry rests. Epistemology is the branch of philosophy that investigates the basis of knowledge claims, or the grounding of knowledge. What model of knowledge is being adopted here? What grounds are there for accepting this model? What makes it valid? Are there alternative models? What is my personal definition of knowledge, and on what do I base it? In our view, having to answer these questions—even having to ask them—is a sign that today's researcher must become what her predecessor was half a millennium ago: a philosopher. All of the modern sciences are offshoots of philosophy. Physics and biology emerged from natural philosophy just as political science and sociology did from social philosophy. This specialization has produced wonders of scientific and cognitive achievement. But, without eliminating the need for specialization, the present situation also requires us to return in some ways to the philosophical origins of science—if not to spin new systems of metaphysics, at least to be able to take responsibility for our actions, decisions, and beliefs about knowledge and science.

A generation ago, research methods were often learned as mechanical procedures. Just the way a carpenter learns that a hammer is for pounding nails into wood or an auto mechanic learns that a torque wrench is for applying just the right amount of pressure to make the parts of an engine fit together, social science and human science researchers learned survey techniques, interview methods, and tests of statistical significance as algorithms that, when used properly, produced knowledge. To say this is not to deny that algorithms and mechanical rules can contribute to the generation of knowledge. But the broad variety of methods available for social and human science research today are not merely "chips off the old block" of science. They reflect fundamentally different ideas of what knowledge is, what it looks like, how it is obtained, how it is validated, and what it is for. A student encountering, for example, phenomenological research, hermeneutic interpretation, feminist analysis, or postmodernist film criticism may find herself in an alien intellectual world, literally unable to make sense of it either in the detail or in the underlying cognitive intent. It may not look anything like what she has been educated to recognize as knowledge. Her situation can resemble that of a person who has grown up eating in burger chains and coffee shops and wanders into a neighborhood of people who eat foods prepared according to the traditions of other cultures and continents. She may find herself not merely unfamiliar with the tastes and textures of new foods but asking herself, "Is this food?" Someone picking up a scholarly journal or book from an alien epistemological paradigm may find herself asking, "Is this knowledge?" Or even, "Do these sentences even mean anything?" As with cultural differences about food or anything else, the differences may have been created according to very different conceptions or meanings. It is, therefore, not just a question of finding the right tool for the task but of coming to realize that some people formulate the tasks so differently that tools appropriate for one are inappropriate for another.

Although diverse approaches to knowledge and research can be overlapped, blended, or integrated, because of the underlying divergence of their assumptions and orientations they cannot simply be stuck together willy-nilly. Two tablespoons of statistical analysis, a teaspoon of phenomenology, a quarter cup of feminism, and a liberal sprinkling of action research do not add up to a delectable dish. The researcher needs to have thought in enough depth about the meaning of different pieces of knowledge or analysis to know if they really address the same question, are from the same corner of the cognitive universe, or have legitimate points of overlap or "interface." This requires understanding both the research method and how it is typically used as well as the philosophical assumptions on which it is based.

The need for epistemological grounding—for understanding and being able to justify what makes something count as knowledge in a situation of methodological and epistemological pluralism—requires more from the student than a deeper exploration of the epistemological assumptions and paradigms underlying contemporary methods of inquiry. It also requires a kind of reflective personal commitment to the ones with which she or he chooses to work. In a certain sense, researchers before the postmodern period were like people in sociologists' conceptions of a traditional society. Working within a commonly accepted value system, they did not have to make choices about the value system itself but only about individual situations. In comparison, today's scholars have to choose the underlying cognitive framework in which they work. Although this choice is also an existential one, it is not *merely* an existential one. That is, it is not only an act of will or ethical decision but one into which a number of scientific and philosophical reasons and arguments enter. It is a situation that demands the integration of personal and intellectual self-awareness and self-reflection.

For this reason, we believe that the contemporary situation in inquiry and research is one that is conducive to an integration of personal and philosophical self-reflection and also requires it. The intellectual situation of the present seems to cry out for both personal and philosophical awareness and self-reflection. In our work with students, we have observed over and over again the way in which the process of carrying out a research project seems to promote psychological and even spiritual development and transformation. We have seen repeatedly the way in which engaging in research as a philosopher—that is, as a person who takes responsibility not only for producing knowledge but for knowing why it is knowledge and defining what knowledge is and integrating it into one's self— leads to deepening one's experience of the meaning, value, and richness of life.

Under the reign of a unitary model of scientific knowledge such as positiv- ism, it was possible, even inevitable, for research training to be focused on tech- niques and methods of research. The researcher could be an epistemological ignoramus, because the nature and definition of knowledge could be taken for granted, and the only thing to be learned was how to produce it. The end of this reign forces the researcher back to epistemology—the study of how we know— and even to ontology—the study of what there is that knowledge is about. Be- cause without some reflection on what the "it" of knowledge is, training in how to produce "it" does not make much sense.

These are not armchair questions. It is quite possible for a researcher to complete a study and be confronted not merely with methodological chal- lenges—"your sample wasn't random," "your population was too small," "your questionnaire isn't valid"—but with epistemological ones—"your assumptions are sexist," "that's a positivistic approach to history," "your interpretation of that text is hermeneutically naive because you didn't take into account either its context or your own," "you didn't pay attention to the socially constructed nature of your variables," "you didn't ask how these features of the culture are pro- duced," "your data analysis is ahistorical," and so on. In other words, after a long period of being able to get by as a kind of engineer, the researcher in the human and social sciences must be a practicing epistemologist.

We are not claiming that the social scientist needs to be a trained philosopher and follow the ins and outs of technical philosophical discussions of epistemol- ogy. We are claiming that being aware of the fundamental issues and making conscious epistemological choices is essential to today's social scientist. In our view, methodology is parasitic on epistemology and ontology, and we believe that an individual who uses a particular research method without being able to articulate its epistemological and ontological assumptions and preconditions is not a fully human, fully responsible researcher.

Activities

Make a list of some of the likely consequences of the type of research you are planning to carry out. Do those outcomes justify the effort? What are the assumptions about knowledge that your methods and techniques assume? How do you personally distinguish between scientific or scholarly knowledge and other kinds of knowledge? What are your criteria?

▬ Conclusion

We have discussed how all research takes place in a historical situation, which allows some aspects of a situation to come to light but which conceals others. Currently, the social researcher is at a historical turning point at which positivism and its modernist assumptions are challenged. At the same time, ardent critics of positivism find themselves ironically falling into positivistic modes of thinking and analysis.

Postmodern theory asserts that all knowledge is socially constructed and that we do not, in fact, exist as human subjects. Rather we are modules in information flows. Mindful inquiry takes issue with this virulent form of postmodernism. By putting the person at the center of the research process we are choosing to hold on to the view of ourselves and of you as rational, creative, ethical persons. As such, you must be an applied philosopher. The mindful inquirer is an applied philosopher, not an information-processing machine.

You may be asking yourself how we are proposing, in the rest of this short introductory book, to meet all of the goals we have set for ourselves and to cover all the topics we have introduced. In truth, to meet our own goals fully would require a book many times the length of this one—one that, precisely because of its length, might scare off more readers than it would attract. Our aim for this project is different. We will not try to meet each of our goals thoroughly. Rather, we will attempt to provide enough grounding and to initiate some thought processes with regard to all of the goals so that readers will feel empowered to continue these thought processes on their own and know where and how to do that through suggestions and pointers that we provide.

In recent years, we have been teaching inquiry and research by giving short workshops that students attend, participate in intensively, and then leave, following up on them through independent study. To a certain extent, we conceive our book in analogy with these workshops. There is never enough time in a workshop to cover all the topics in depth or to meet everyone's needs completely. Nevertheless, people leave them with new perspectives that enable them to make great leaps forward in their own intellectual development. We will be quite satisfied if you experience something similar in reading this book.

From these first two introductory chapters, you are now in a good position to decide whether reading the rest of the book will be worth your while.

Mindful Inquiry
as the Basis for
Scholarly Practice

Persons engage in social research primarily to answer questions or solve problems. These may be problems at home, at work, or in the community, or things that seem to be problems or questions in themselves. The vast majority of students of the social and human sciences will not become professors or pure researchers. They are interested in knowledge they can put into practice. Scholar–practitioners increasingly must also be able to navigate the vast network of available information, selecting what is essential and most helpful to maintain and enhance their lifeworlds. In addition, scholar–practitioners must be "knowledge brokers," able to help their colleagues and students evaluate, select, and build viable and practical theories from the assault of massive amounts of information. The best way to do this is to become a mindful inquirer and to teach others to do likewise.

There are two reasons why mindful inquiry is a good basis for scholar–practitioners operating in the context of the age of information. The first is that it helps the scholar–practitioner sustain her or his own personal identity amid the onslaught of the information age (Shenk, 1997). It is easy to become engulfed and overwhelmed by the mass of available information and by Internet and e-mail access to more persons, more words, and more facts than one can absorb. This phenomenon has become so prevalent that some theorists have warned of the demise of the identity, or self, as a hallmark of entering the postmodern age. Persons' selves will split into multiple identities or exist merely as ever-changing nodes or agents in information networks (Weinstein, 1995).

Contrary to some radical postmodernists, such as Deleuze and Guattari (1983), who advocate dissolution of personal identity (e.g., schizophrenia), most persons do not wish to be so deconstructed. Indeed, schizophrenia and fractured identities are experienced by those who are so afflicted as painful and extremely difficult ways of being (Glass, 1993).

The second reason for scholar–practitioners to approach their research as mindful inquiry is in order to use available information in a productive way. Knowledge of social sciences inquiry methods and theories for interpreting results and data will help practitioners evaluate the quality of the information being conveyed and make intelligent selections of quality material. Mindful inquiry will allow them to stave off the flow so that they are in control of it, rather than vice versa.

■ Mindful Inquiry as Critical Hermeneutic Buddhist Phenomenology

Four Knowledge Traditions

We want to make it clear what epistemological choices we have made and where we stand. There are three Western research traditions, each of which is essential to mindful inquiry on the meta (or more general) level and each of which has specific contributions to make in the areas of theory building, methodology, and research techniques. Mindful inquiry has elements of hermeneutics, phenomenology, and critical social science, which we will explain briefly in this chapter. Later in this book, we discuss these approaches in some detail as cultures of inquiry—that is, as three specific traditions among a number of others, such as quantitative and behavioral science, ethnography, and action research, within which research is currently carried out in the human and social sciences. Here, however, we are looking at them in a different way, namely as part of a larger framework or metaperspective, which we recommend for all inquiry and research, including quantitative and behavioral science, ethnography, and so on. In other words, we consider them as part of the philosophical foundation of research, not merely as research methods. They define and clarify those general issues that we believe are essential for all research, such as your philosophical orientation, the relationship between yourself and your research, and how you see yourself in relation to your historical and cultural context. In turn, this is a philosophical and value position on our part. Mindful inquiry is not a research method that you have to adopt to engage in research. It is a choice, one that we believe will lead to significant research, promote a personally meaningful and rewarding experience for you as a researcher, and contribute to the surrounding society and world. But it is a choice nonetheless.

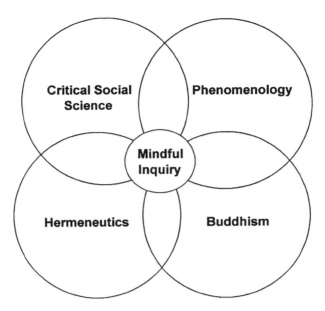

Figure 3.1. The Sources of Mindful Inquiry

There is a fourth, non-Western knowledge tradition that we consider part of mindful inquiry, and this is Buddhism. For more than two millennia, Buddhist doctrine has been intimately concerned with the elimination of suffering and with the role of desire and consciousness–unconsciousness in creating suffering. Buddhism is also concerned with overcoming illusions, especially those that create false separations between ourselves and other human beings and between ourselves and the rest of nature. In particular, Buddhism asserts that extricating ourselves and others from suffering involves direct engagement, pursuing a rightful life in which mindfulness and awareness play a key role. For only through awareness can we reduce the effect of our desires and illusions on our perception of the world and our action in the world. The Noble Eightfold Path of Buddhism consists, in the Buddha's words, of "right view, right thought, right speech, right action, right livelihood, right effort, right mindfulness, right concentration" (Buddha, 1974).

In a recent best-selling book, Jon Kabat-Zinn has commented on mindful inquiry. He is not talking about social sciences research but about looking at everyday life as an inquiry into self and other mysteries. Nevertheless, his words are relevant to the approach of mindfulness:

> The spirit of inquiry is fundamental to living mindfully. Inquiry is not just a way to solve problems. It is a way to make sure you are staying in touch with

the basic mystery of life itself and of our presence here. . . . Inquiry doesn't mean looking for answers, especially quick answers which come out of superficial thinking. It means asking without expecting answers, just pondering the questions, carrying the wondering with you, letting it percolate, bubble, cook, ripen, come in and out of awareness, just as everything else comes in and out of awareness. Inquiry is not so much thinking about answers, although the questioning will produce a lot of thoughts that look like answers. It really involves just listening to the thinking that your questioning evokes, as if you were sitting by the side of the stream of your own thoughts, listening to the water flow over and around the rocks, listening, listening, and watching an occasional leaf or twig as it is carried along. (1994)

The connection with the Buddhist concept of mindfulness is echoed in the life of the Buddhist monk. Thought is the most vital ingredient in the monk's life, and in spite of the many activities in which monks participate—teaching, farming, building, ceremonials, political life—the most vital ingredient of that life is thought (Bechert & Gombrich, 1984, p. 116). Even the most mundane daily activities are carried out in an attitude of mindfulness (Nhat Hanh, 1974).

Besides the concept of mindfulness, mindful inquiry shares with Buddhism tolerance for varying ideas and frames of reference. This tolerance extends to having the ability to hold several beliefs in different areas of knowledge. Many Buddhists, for example, are also Christians (Bechert & Gombrich, 1984, p. 10). The mindful inquirer may practice both ethnography and quantitative and behavioral science, even though these cultures of inquiry come from different assumptions.

In summary, mindful inquiry incorporates some fundamental notions of Buddhist philosophy. In this way, it overcomes some of the criticisms against Western social sciences, for example, that they are fused with Western bias. Mindful inquiry shares the following principles with Buddhism:

1. the importance of mindful thought itself;
2. tolerance and the ability to inhabit multiple perspectives;
3. the intention to alleviate suffering;
4. the notion of the clearing, or openness, underlying awareness.

Critical theory (short for *critical theory of society*) is a tradition of theory and research that focuses on the alleviation of suffering through the critique of sources of oppression. It was founded by a group of social scientists, including Max Horkheimer, Theodor Adorno, Herbert Marcuse, and Leo Lowenthal, in Frankfurt am Main in Germany. These Frankfurt-school theorists wanted to explain such events as the rise of fascism and to understand how and why modern society, with its emphasis on rationality and knowledge and on increasing the scope of individual freedom, could bring about extreme barbarism, authoritarianism, irrationality, and the manipulation and brutalization of consciousness. Influenced by the theories of Karl Marx, Max Weber, and Sigmund Freud and the philosophies of Kant, Hegel, and Nietzsche, they wanted to develop a general theory of society that was also a critique of that society from the perspective of trying to realize human potential that was suppressed or denied by society. Part of this critique addresses the conception of knowledge that is completely detached from the world and that exists only to observe and explain it. Critical theory attempts to create a contemporary version of Marx's idea that "philosophers have only *interpreted* the world in various ways; the point is, to *change* it" (Marx, 1844/1969, p. 402). The Frankfurt theorists, most of whom were Jewish, fled Nazi Germany and immigrated to the United States where they had an important impact on social science research. The sociologist and philosopher Habermas is an important contemporary theorist who works in this tradition.

Hermeneutics means, initially, the interpretation of texts and in general the theory of interpretation and understanding. It comes from the tradition of Biblical interpretation, which was later picked up by historians and social scientists who wanted to apply those methods to different kinds of texts, especially historical and literary texts, but lately including films, conversations, and even fashion (Barthes, 1990; Brown, 1987, 1992).

In the twentieth century, hermeneutics has been extended, under the influence of Martin Heidegger, into a general approach to our understanding of our existence and of Being in general. In the work of Hans-Georg Gadamer, it involves our understanding of all human culture and history and our own situation in culture and history. For everything human, including both our own and other selves and cultures, is expressed in language and symbols that must be interpreted to be understood. Therefore, we are beings whose knowledge—even our own self-knowledge—is always bound to processes of understanding and interpretation. Our ability to do this is formed and limited by the systems of culture, meaning, language, symbols, and interpretations that we inhabit and that form our context. Even our own self is something that we continually construct through our own interpretation and reinterpretation of our self, the languages and symbols in which our consciousness expresses itself, and the culture and world around us (Frank, 1988).

Hermeneutics emphasizes that all of our understanding and interpretation are bound to, and shaped by, our existing in a particular historical and cultural context, because we use the concepts, language, symbols, and meaning of our time to interpret everything. Therefore, hermeneutics involves us in perpetual asking, of anything meaningful that we study as well as of ourselves, "Where are you coming from?"

Phenomenology is a school of philosophy that focuses on the description of consciousness and of objects and the world as perceived by consciousness. Formulated by the German philosopher Edmund Husserl in the tradition of the philosophy of Descartes and Kant, phenomenology attempts to take seriously the fact that we are conscious beings and that everything we know is something that we know only in and through consciousness. Phenomenologists reframe our knowledge of the world by focusing on the complex and elaborate structures through which this world and our knowledge of it are constructed in our consciousness. Alfred Schutz extended this approach to the study of our social world and its foundations in our consciousness. Harold Garfinkel developed a school of sociology and anthropology called *ethnomethodology,* which extended and modified the phenomenological approach to other kinds of social research.

A primary focus of phenomenology has been to help us get ourselves out of everything that we take for granted about the world and about ourselves through a process that Husserl called "bracketing" (1962). All research procedures and other cultures of inquiry are performed within brackets from the perspective of the mindful inquirer. Bracketing sets aside aspects of a situation in order to focus full attention on other aspects of it. It is especially important and useful for noticing what things we take for granted and for trying to step outside of them in order to see things in a new way.

For example, right now you probably are reading this book in what you think of as "the real world." And you "know" that you are not dreaming. You know that you are doing so today, rather than yesterday, although if you started the book yesterday, you have some memory of having done so. In everyday life, we take the waking, everyday world of the present as more "real" than the dream world or the world of the past. But a phenomenologist would have us bracket that everyday definition of reality and notice that, as facts of consciousness, my consciousness of being in the everyday real world and my consciousness of dreaming and my consciousness of the past are all equally real as phenomena of consciousness. Studying their similarity and difference as phenomena of consciousness may help us understand things about reality, dreams, time, and consciousness that are invisible to us when we adopt what phenomenologists call the *natural attitude* or *natural standpoint*—that is, the definitions of reality and knowledge that we adopt unthinkingly in everyday social life.

Bracketing is different from simply executing a method or technique. If one works from within an assumed epistemological frame, one can carry out a technique perfectly, but this does not make for mindful inquiry because it is done with epistemological blindfolds. That is, phenomenology makes us stop taking for granted the things that we normally take for granted, and that is part of mindfulness. A useful way to think of this is contemplating coming to understand another culture. Many people, much of the time, take the concepts and categories of their culture as "real" and the concepts and categories of other cultures as weird or alien things that do not capture "reality" in the same way that one's own culture does. Phenomenology can help us see our own culture in just as bracketed a way as we often see other cultures.

Although phenomenology, critical social science, hermeneutics, and Buddhism overlap in their ways of working, each brings a distinctive contribution to the practice of mindful inquiry. One way of looking at this is that *phenome-nology* brings clarity and attention to the consciousness of the researcher, to the importance of relating research endeavors to deep structures of culture and persons, and to the actual lived experience of those involved in the problematic. It also assists in clarifying the subject or object of study by providing a way of shaking down concepts to prevent reification, or unreflective use of empty categories.

Hermeneutics makes texts and contexts, and the interpretation of texts and contexts, central to awareness, and it thematizes the process of the flow of interaction between interpreter and text or event. *Critical social science* focuses attention on the political, economic, social, and psychological barriers to seeking truth in a power-saturated environment that can distort understanding. It focuses attention on the ethical aims of inquiry and places its heart firmly on the goal of emancipation.

Buddhism focuses on the ways in which our personal way of being, thinking, perceiving, and feeling can create distorted understanding and on the need for the personal, existential choice of mindfulness as a way of life. Mindful inquiry requires careful attention to all four meta-aspects of any research process, regardless of the possible use of research techniques from other streams of activity within the social sciences.

■ The Spiral of Mindful Inquiry

Mindful inquiry springs from the lifeworld of the researcher. A *lifeworld* is a concept from the philosophical perspective of phenomenology. It means the entire ongoing social world as actually experienced by living human beings—in other words, the world of everyday life (Schutz & Luckmann, 1973; Wagner, 1983b). It is based on lived, embodied relationships located in time, place, space, history, and the natural environment. All social research is about aspects of lifeworlds and, therefore, is responsible for the condition of the lifeworlds it affects.

Within the lifeworld, you may view the entire research process as a journey between yourself and texts—that is, something to be interpreted. Hermeneutic thinkers use the notion of a "hermeneutic circle" to describe the interpretive process. In this circle, we move cyclically in interpretation between the whole and the part of a text, and between ourselves and the text. We visualize the journey of the research process as a spiral to emphasize the sense of expansion and forward motion that comes from circling in time and touching various points, each time from a new point in time and in one's own self-development.

This journey may begin with an interest in a theory or in testing a theory or with a practical problem from the lifeworld. Or it may begin with a question suggested by an impressive researcher in the literature. Whatever the beginning point, the process involves centering you as a mindful inquirer and interpreter and reaches from this starting point to the other points. If you begin with a

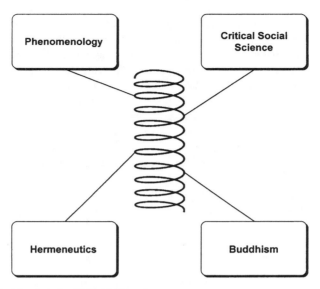

Figure 3.2. The Spiral of Mindful Inquiry

problem or concern related to your work experience, such as in Michael Prior's case in his study of the negative impact of downsizing (1997), you would go from that experience to personal reflections or interpretations of its meaning to you and, perhaps, even of its impact on your body. You could then move around the spiral to streams of research related to the topic, to methodological literature, and to theoretical literature.

In mindful inquiry, each step of the process is mediated by an empty space on the spiral, indicating that you are moving though lived time and you are living through the meaning of this new aspect of becoming a mindful inquirer. These meditative openings in the spiral indicate that the mindful inquirer makes space and time for this reflection before and after each move forward in the endeavor. Because of this, all of the components of our view of research are equally essential. It would be correct to call our approach critical hermeneutic Buddhist phenomenology, or phenomenological hermeneutic Buddhist critical social science, or any other permutation of these four traditions.

As a mindful inquirer, when you immerse yourself in the project, you also steep yourself deeply in the techniques of the chosen research methods and in existing research and theories about your question or interest. With each turn of the spiral, you create a deeper and richer understanding both of the phenomenon, problem, or question and of yourself as a reflective, mindful inquirer.

Remember, in mindful inquiry, you may choose to halt a particular journey to enter another pathway. You may change the direction of the path of the spiral.

There are some essential, unavoidable turns or stopping points on the pathway of critical hermeneutic phenomenology for mindful inquiry. There will be periodic returns to reflect on the critical aspects of the situation you are studying, as well as on your own situation as an inquirer. There are many ways each turn in the spiral may be taken, depending on which theorist you are following. The order of the spiral may be changed. You may do step G first, then D, and then come back to A, for example. You may alternate between two steps until both are completed at about the same time. You may skip some of them, but ultimately, the more you are conscious of each of them, the more your mode of inquiry is mindful, alive, aware, and reflective. All of the turns are part of the art of the spiral of mindful inquiry.

In each of the sixteen turns in mindful inquiry, we will describe our turns as we became engaged in the inquiry of writing this book for you.

Critical Turns (A Through D)

A. Examine the historical, political, economic, and cultural circumstances in which you are working.

We framed mindful inquiry in relation to the history of the social sciences and how they respond to the economies and cultures of the time. We assessed the current need for social scientists, well trained in theory and research, to work successfully and ethically. Within the culture of our home institution, we made it clear that we were working on the book, based on our academic program's study guide for inquiry and research (of which Jeremy was a coauthor and editor), and invited participation from colleagues. We also were facing difficulties in setting aside time from the ongoing demands of our jobs as academic professors and administrators to work on this book. On one hand, these were personal problems. But we are aware that our colleagues in universities all around the country are facing overload and work pressure in their jobs. We know that there is evidence that the workweek is getting longer and work life more demanding everywhere (Schor, 1992).

More important, both of us have a long history of seeing our intellectual endeavors as linked both to our personal lives and to political and social activism with regard to basic social issues of our time. So we have been aware, both intellectually and in our lifeworlds, of the changes being wrought by globalization of the economy, information technology, multiculturalism, and postmodernism. From working at an institution that is particularly oriented toward adult students and that uses computer networks for academic work and for the maintenance of social relationships, some of these social changes enter into our daily lives. In our teaching of research, we have experienced the limitations of some of the standard approaches, and of students' wishes to integrate inquiry into the rest of their lives. So, for us, our inquiry is a response not only to our immediate

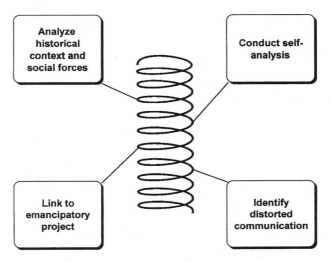

Figure 3.3. Critical Turns

circumstances but to the larger social and historical context as it is manifested in those circumstances.

B. As a mindful inquirer, you look into your own psychology, psyche, childhood emotional experiences, and so on, and how they may be distorting your perceptions and actions.

We were sensitive to how our own aging bodies and our current life circumstances mitigated against completing this book. During the time of its writing, Jeremy moved twice and had two surgeries, Valerie had an eye infection and was in an automobile accident. Both of us meditate regularly and consult with our own teachers, gurus, and therapists regarding the state of our emotions and psyches as part of our individual quests for both self-knowledge and relief from stress and distress. Jeremy has been a teacher of peer counseling, and Valerie practiced psychotherapy for 20 years and is currently a practicing massage therapist dealing with intellectual, emotional, and bodily connections. Over the years, both of us have been in psychotherapy of various kinds and received deep body release work. Both have helped us not only personally but also intellectually and professionally.

The body dimension is important to us not just as some personal matter of fact but intellectually. Some important modern philosophers have emphasized that, ultimately, all of our knowledge is held bodily, because it is through our bodies that we are rooted in the world. The French phenomenologist Maurice Merleau-Ponty made this central to his philosophy (1964, 1981; see also Landgrebe, 1968). The American existential phenomenologist Hubert Dreyfus has made this notion central to his critique of artificial intelligence. Ultimately, the reason computers cannot think is not that they do not have minds but that they do not have bodies; therefore, they do not have the world that is given to us through our body (1992). In his wonderful book *The Tacit Dimension* Michael Polanyi points out that our explicit and articulate knowledge of the world presupposes a prior, tacit, bodily connection to the world. "Our body is the ultimate instrument of all our external knowledge, whether intellectual or practical" (1966, p. 15).

Both of us are faculty in a situation in which we live in geographic distance from each other, other faculty, and most students. The value system of our institute stresses service to students and to the community, but we are often overextended to the point where we do not attend well to ourselves or each other. We live at the edge of limited resources that we are constantly besieged to stretch. Yet we attempt to do good in the world and sometimes believe that we are. We do not understand all of the implications of this. Still, we write sincerely, in good faith, with the hope that we are contributing something that will help you, the researcher, ground and center yourself, because we find this the best way to do our own work. At the same time, we realize that our belief in mindfulness is a product of forces in our own lives that have made us attached to the notion of personal awareness and the integration of intellectual, personal, professional, and social–political life, and that not everyone else shares this view or is likely to do so.

C. Be sensitive to the way in which the communicative process of inquiry may be distorting the realization of emancipatory "truth," following Habermas (1970c, 1984).

Here, one will look at the kinds of communicative processes occurring in terms of the norms of "competent communication," which include "understandability," "truthfulness," "truth," and "rightness."

Habermas concluded that power differentials between participants would distort the outcomes in the search for truth. The pursuit of the truth implies a situation in which anyone can participate as an equal in conversation about the ideas being discussed, including raising objections and putting forward different or opposing ideas. If power is operating in the situation, individuals will not feel that they can say what they really think. This is a continuing problem between researchers and research participants, as is discussed by Bentz (1989). Indeed, we prefer and use the term *participant* rather than *subject* because we believe persons should be fully informed, willing participants in research, up to and including being coauthors.

The relationship between us as authors of this inquiry is deep and egalitarian. In the immediate sense, we did not have participants but were working with texts. But in another sense, we did and do have participants, because our ideas have been developed in ongoing interaction with our students, and we are putting them out to you. In our place of work, tremendous emphasis is placed on equality between students and faculty in an effort to minimize power differentials that would adversely affect learning. We know that we do have power as faculty members; therefore, we may not have been exposed to or had to fully absorb all relevant criticisms of our approach. We hope that our students have told us what they genuinely think of the limitations of our ideas, but we cannot be sure that they have.

Partly as a result of both of us moving geographically and partly as a result of personal issues between us, we lost contact with each other for a while. We made an explicit attempt to reconnect on a personal and professional level to assess whether we could still work on the book together, by regular long-distance telephone calls. *Understandability,* in Habermas's sense, means we communicated from similar norms and frames of reference. These telephone conversations were necessary in order for us to rebuild our collaborative and personal relationship so we would again understand each other to the extent that we know and fully trust where each of us is coming from. We both know that the other is coming from a state of "truthfulness." Our constant searching of the literature and our discussions with knowledgeable colleagues is a truth or reality check for our book.

Habermas's analysis of communication and dialogue raises another important issue—that of blocks to communication that the individual may not even be aware of because she has internalized them so that they have become part of her sense of self. For example, in almost every social setting, people have internalized rules about what can and cannot be said and done in that setting, and for most people, these operate instinctively. People do not take off their clothes in a supermarket, although they do so in their bedrooms. They do not express negative feelings about a person with whom they are dealing, although they may express them as soon as that person has left the room. In a scholarly or academic book, authors instinctively feel that there are certain personal things that they do not express—perhaps some of their feelings about religion, politics, sexuality, employers, their colleagues, the publisher, and so on. Yet observing these prohibitions can serve as a block not only to communication but to knowledge. Inversely, advances in knowledge sometimes come from violating prohibitions. For example, Freud used some of his own dreams and their personal context in his masterpiece *The Interpretation of Dreams* (1965). We decided to speak a bit personally in this book because the notion of mindful inquiry involves personal engagement and personal awareness, and we felt that it would be dishonest to advocate personal engagement in a completely impersonal manner. But this made us face the questions, "Can we say what we really think?" "To what extent can we 'tell it like it is'?" Our ideas of mindful inquiry came, in part, from our trying to say what we really think.

D. Link your inquiry to the project of reducing suffering or increasing freedom, justice, or happiness in the world, either locally or globally or both.

In conducting mindful inquiry, we can be openly human to one another instead of joining the logic of the "system," as Habermas calls it (1988), that is of the expansion of market, technological, bureaucratic, and military rationality into every province of life, a logic that expands the scope of acquisitiveness, manipulation, fear, oppression, inequality, and treating people as objects, and one that continually demands new sacrifices. We see our work as expanding the scope of the "communicative rationality" of the lifeworld (Habermas, 1988, 1990, 1996) in which people shape their world and lives according to values and understandings that evolve from discourse in which they are personally engaged and in which they treat one another as equals. It is essential to that communicative process that people can engage in inquiry in a way that is consonant with themselves and their values. This includes not subordinating themselves unthinkingly to ways of conducting research that are merely part of systems logic.

Phenomenological Turns (E Through I)

E. Pay attention to the nature of the phenomena being investigated by writing a deep phenomenological description of one's own experience of it.

A deep phenomenological description of an experience of mindful inquiry is to be found in an article I (Valerie) wrote. In a sense, it is a description of my experience of teaching phenomenology (Bentz, 1995). This article describes my teaching a student ("Paul") with a diagnosed "writing disability." Paul could only write from his heart. He expressed his experiences in story form. The stories were fictionalized expressions of the concepts under scrutiny in the seminar. I had to examine my own experiences of being in a situation of contradiction. There was a contradiction between my explicit purpose—trying to open up graduate students, who had learned to be objective, to direct descriptions. Paul went beyond this to writing emotionally accurate descriptions in the style of fiction, but he could not frame this in academic writing.

Actually, neither one of us has yet written deep descriptions of the experience of research. It is encouraging and enlightening, however, to read other people's descriptions of what it was like for them to carry out research, such as those in Golden's *The Research Experience* (1976).

F. Use "imaginative variations" to elucidate hidden aspects of the phenomenon. (How would it change if certain elements of it changed?)

The act of writing this book would have been radically different if either of us had written it alone. If I (Valerie) had written it outside of partnership with Jeremy, I would have functioned more as a creator of a collage, bringing in various faculty to write different sections. By thinking of this with Jeremy, it became deeper for us, and possibly, unacceptable to other colleagues who may have been involved. If I (Jeremy) had written it outside of partnership with Valerie, it would not have the same idea content, because the most important ideas came from our conversation and collaboration, and Valerie is the person

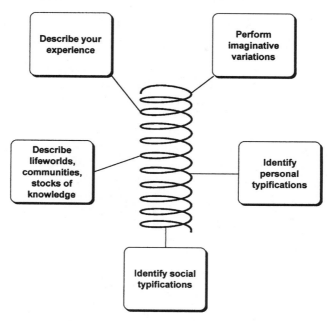

Figure 3.4. Phenomenological Turns

who actually formulated the idea of mindful inquiry, which seemed right to me as soon as I heard it.

What if we, coming from Lutheran and Jewish traditions, had framed it from those cultural traditions? What would Lutheran–Protestant inquiry look like? It would be critical of accepted tradition but would not broadly appeal to a sense of open consciousness, space, or the idea of grounding one's self, including body and breath, in oneness. Rather, it would base itself on a crusade for truth resting in sacrifice, motivated by a desire for salvation, and perhaps a desire to love. There is a connection between such worthy forms of Christianity and modern social science. There is also a connection between critical theory and social science and the Jewish experience. Much of critical theory arose as critique of the dangers of fascism in Europe, the foundational works brought together in the critical theory of Marx and Freud, both of Jewish heritage. If this work had been written primarily in the Jewish tradition, it probably would have been more politically messianic. As in many works of the Marxian and critical theory tradition, mindfulness would probably have been conceived more as "critical consciousness" in a cognitive way and less in a Buddhist and existential way. Christian, Jewish, and Buddhist heritage are all brought together in mindful inquiry. Hermeneutics was developed largely by Protestant theologians. Luther nailed his 95 theses on the door of the chapel at Wittenberg. He wrote these as a Catholic monk, based on his belief in hermeneutics. All persons, he believed, not just priests, were to read and interpret the sacred texts.

The depth of consciousness of the Buddha who does not condemn but comprehends, who does not punish but offers compassion, can include the Christian, Jewish, Muslim, and other heritages. All are part of the one, of Being. A powerful argument for a version of Buddhism (Maitreyanism) that encompasses all other religious heritages in a religion adequate to the emerging global, multicultural civilization can be found in Charles Morris's *Paths of Life* (1973).

G. Ask yourself these questions: "What modes of consciousness do I bring to bear in the situation?" and "What typifications am I using?"

We empathize with your plight as a reader trying to become a researcher. Anyone who buys and reads this book is someone we feel affinity toward, because it means you are going to conduct some research about important human questions.

Every aspect of research and all of the concepts in this book are typifications—socially constructed abstractions and simplifications of the complexity of experience that enable us to handle it in a regular, organized, and socially shared way. These typifications are not invented by us but by the discourse communities who use them. Becoming a mindful researcher means critically knowing the array of typifications.

We write this book from multiple modes of consciousness. Jeremy has had dreams about it that influenced his writing. He brings his compulsiveness to the project as well. He must straighten out the groundwork of it before he can move forward. He had to get the bibliography worked out flawlessly before he could let his imagination work on finishing the writing of the book. At the same time, he has a tendency to want to include everything and make it perfect, which can prolong the work. Valerie brings a flowing sense of creativity to it, as well as a begrudging "let's-get-the-job-done" frame of mind. She falls in and out of focus, reflecting alternately on the text, romantic fantasies, and her new kittens.

H. Get descriptions of the experience of those involved. Determine the typifications they use to function in their situations.

Our scrupulous use of references and our carefully chosen quotes express the typifications used in different scholarly communities. Each culture of inquiry or community of discourse builds and uses its own body of typifications—that is, conventions and abstractions about what is the case, interpretive schemes that organize the complexity and particularity of lived experience. This was challenging to us because we are trying to incorporate multiple views and take them all seriously and give them all credit. So we had to function as translators among different philosophical positions.

I. Describe the relevant lifeworlds and the intersubjective communities in which the situations occur. Look at the stocks of knowledge, the effects of predecessors, the interlocking web of typifications. (We paid attention to these worlds in our introductory chapter.)

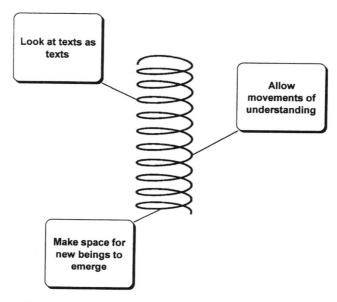

Figure 3.5. Hermeneutic Turns

Hermeneutic Turns (J Through L)

J. Look at the elements of your texts as texts. Elucidate the levels of preexisting interpretations of the situations and their relevance.

We have built the levels of interpretation into the text itself by discussing communities of discourse within the scholarly world and by putting ideas into their historical and social context. Footnotes and references, the foundation to which Jeremy devoted special attention, gives additional levels. Our editor helped us look at the text as one with potential readers beyond those we initially had in mind—graduate social sciences students—and include undergraduate inquirers and professional inquirers.

K. Allow the movements of understanding to happen on their own time.

The insights we had as we wrote the book occurred only in their own time. We had to be able to communicate with each other about the topics. Our relationship went through a time of estrangement, not of heart but of fact. Jeremy reached out to Valerie to span the gap so that we could write this text together. The external circumstances in the academic, political, and social worlds changed in the meantime, making the need for the text more clear to us.

L. Through presence and intention, allow for a release of new meaning to occur. Make a space, a clearing, for new "beings" to emerge.

Paul Ricoeur refers to this as looking for the world beyond the text. We found such a world, a "new being" to use Heidegger's phrase, and called it *mindful inquiry*. We were not explicitly aware of the concept of mindful inquiry and of the synthesis of the four traditions when we began work on this project. Rather, it emerged as part of a genuine inquiry, rather like Kurt Wolff's conception of "surrender and catch" (1995). That is, we surrendered to the process of communicating about how we think about and teach about the creation of knowledge in the human and social sciences, and we "caught" mindful inquiry. Heidegger's ontological hermeneutics speaks of allowing the totally new or unexpected to emerge through openness or "releasement" (1993, p. 184).

Buddhist Turns (M Through P)

M. Become aware of your personal addictions or addictive needs with regard to your inquiry.

Buddhism tells us that our desires and addictions are the source of our illusions and our suffering. Usually, when we engage in inquiry, such addictive needs attach themselves to our orientation to the research. Becoming aware of them can increase our awareness and decrease the extent to which we are unconsciously driven by them. Meditation is an important path to this sort of awareness. Note that this has a certain parallelism to the phenomenological injunction to bracket your own empirical ego and adopt a stance of transcendental reflection.

What ego needs are you trying to gratify through this inquiry? Where do they come from? Is there something that you need to prove? Some cherished belief that you need to validate? How would you feel if your research turned out differently than you imagine? How would you feel if no one ever read the results of your research? How would you feel if it did not save the world or even make an observable difference in it?

N. Become aware of how you define and construct the "other" of your research as other.

Buddhism tells us that our everyday sense of separateness from other beings is illusory and comes from attachment to the illusions of ego. In the way we experience the other (think here of the other that you are studying, whether it is other people, other cultures, other historical times, other ideas), we may be projecting illusions, fantasies, needs, or emotions. Said (1978) critiqued the way "Orientalists" (discussed later in this book) developed a conception of Asians and their cultures that was really a projection of their own psyches. Sexist interpretations constructed women as the "other" out of the researchers' own emotional and power needs. The more ego you have in your inquiry, the more likely that your other is really a projection of your ego.

O. Through the practice of compassion and right conduct, pay attention to the suffering of sentient beings in the world, and ask yourself what kind of inquiry and action would diminish that suffering.

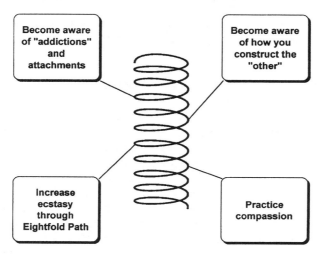

Figure 3.6. Buddhist Turns

Buddhism tells us that as we increase our own awareness of mindfulness, we become as concerned with the suffering of others as we were with our own suffering, and that helping free other beings from suffering, or just reducing their suffering to some extent, will contribute to our own enlightenment and spiritual perfection and thereby reduce our suffering. Note that this is related to critical social science's orientation to emancipatory knowledge, knowledge that will reduce suffering and increase happiness, freedom, and justice.

P. By following the Eightfold Path of Buddhism, focused on rightness of thought and action, and increasing your own mindfulness and nonattachment to things and desires, increase your capacity to experience ecstasy, particularly in relation to both the object and the process of inquiry.

A core, paradoxical notion of Buddhism is that following desires and attachment to ego, which would seem to lead to pleasure, actually leads to suffering, whereas giving up attachment to desires and ego leads to the higher, different sort of pleasure called *Nirvana*. Genuine inquiry can lead to ecstatic experience as part of taking one out of one's self. The impersonal part of it, that which has to do with flowing with the structure of reality, is part of what makes inquiry sometimes take on self-transformative, even spiritual properties. Note that this is related to hermeneutics's emphasis on letting new beings and new meanings appear in the "clearing" of Being. You may know of the legend of King Midas, who wished to be surrounded only by things of gold, only to find that these gold things did not lead to happiness but, instead, through their coldness, to misery. Part of inquiry is giving up our immediate impulses to have things be the way we think we want them to be, in order to discover the pleasure of otherness, of what is outside of our known desires. In the words of the ancient Greek philosopher

Heraclitus, "In searching out the truth, be ready for the unexpected, for it is difficult to find and puzzling when you find it" (1979, p. 14).

◼ Beyond Research Ethics to Mindful Inquiry

Research ethics typically is thought of as an avoidance of doing harm to human research participants. Universities have human subjects review committees. (The Fielding Institute, where we work, has a research ethics committee that is a step beyond the narrow framework for understanding the ethical ramifications of social research.) A broad concern for research ethics may begin with mindfulness of the effects of the research on those who participate in it, including the researchers. Ethics may be reconceived as mindfulness in the Buddhist sense. In a state of mindfulness, the higher self observes the various inquiring selves who engage in the thinking and doing that is research. The *overself* is the mindful self watching the other selves in the state of inquiry as discussed in Michael Weinstein's *Finite Perfection: Reflections on Virtue* (1985). Weinstein also discusses the way in which virtuous persons are cultivated. For a more philosophical discussion of an epistemology based on *phronesis,* or the ways of being and acting of the virtuous self, see Zagzebski (1996). Schutz (1973) has discussed dimensions of all possible lifeworlds, regardless of the historical position of any particular lifeworld.

In mindfulness, the researcher is in a state of care and acceptance. This attitude allows the Beings of the participants of the study to shine forward, to reveal themselves to the inquirer. The participants of an inquiry may be women, men, animals, work organizations, events, and so on. Such openness can only be allowed, not forced. In the absence of this kind of openness, all the inquirer can find out is what he or she already knows.

Unmindful (mindless in this sense) inquiry is a form of what Heidegger calls "idle curiosity." This is a form of finding out based on the preconceptions of the inquirer, who simply mirrors this inner, wished-for reality by imposing it on the outer world. Is it any wonder that when one looks in such a mirror-like inquiry one sees and multiplies, clone-like, one's own reflection?

The mindful inquirer engages in activities to prepare a space for the inquiry to occur. The preparation of the space invites the participants of the study to occupy it as they are becoming. Mindful inquiry is a creative act. It seeks not only to discover or to record what is there, but to allow what is there to manifest itself in a new way, to come forward in its "shining." This means that not only what is there, but the potential behind it, reveals itself. Let us say, for example, you wanted to study the potential of inner-city, low-income youth at high risk for delinquency. One way to study them would be to conduct in-depth interviews, then categorize the participants on the Minnesota Multiphasic Personality Inventory (MMPI) or according to the *DSM-IV* (1994). One could then know something about them and, if the study wished to be predictive, follow them up 10 years later to see how many get into trouble with the law.

Anderson (1998) has initiated an inquiry into what would happen were she to bring wonderful experiences and resources to bear on high-risk, urban adolescents. Her action research project is based on the theory of George Herbert Mead (1934), which speaks of the importance of the expectations of significant others and the community on persons' identities. She designed a project in which adolescents from four different ethnic groups, who are normally at odds with each other, will go together on a trip to climb Mt. Kilimanjaro in Africa. As a component of the project, the young people will receive physical endurance training and training in skills and knowledge related to the project. This form of inquiry allows untapped potential to come forward.

What emerges from mindful inquiry may be for ill as well as good, presenting an ethical challenge to the scholar–practitioner. One such result was reported by action researcher Don Bushnell in his work with delinquent gangs in Chicago and Philadelphia. Whereas one gang used the resources and personal support Bushnell provided through his project to develop a legitimate enterprise in cooperation with a rival gang, another used it to become more efficient at extortion and other illegal activities.

The preparation of the space invites the participants of the study to occupy it as they are becoming. Creating the space is, in itself, an inquiry. One may say that the research question of such a project is, "If I prepare a space for such-and-such kinds of beings to appear, will they do so? And in what form? And will they do so in a certain frame of time?" If they do not, the research becomes a description of the preparation for the coming of the beings that did not appear under that time and place.

Such a mode of inquiry is congruent with critical theory, particularly Habermas's notion of the necessity of preparing a place for communication that is not distorted by power relations in order for truth to be discovered in a discourse community. The researcher is watchful of herself or himself alongside the participants of the study.

Mindfulness requires care for the lifeworld in which the inquiry occurs. It questions the manner in which the inquirer enters the lifeworlds involved in the inquiry, taking care that they are left in a better state than they were before, and certainly not in a worse state. The mindful researcher will look at the possible effects of the inquiry not only on the lifeworld but also on persons in the lifeworld, on the self of the researcher, on the lifeworld of the researcher, and on potential future lifeworlds.

The setting for social sciences inquiry is then always the intersection between lifeworlds. *Lifeworld* comes from the German term *Lebenswelt*. This term was used by philosopher Husserl, the father of phenomenology, to mean "the world as experienced." A lifeworld involves the intersecting biographies of the persons in it as well as of their predecessors and imagined successors. The ways they have patterned relationships with each other include their understandings of their pasts, their longings, and their anticipations, hopes, and fears for the future. Such lifeworlds contain stocks of common knowledge, which are systems of typifications that allow for discourse and for practical actions to be accomplished. They are laden with meaning. The inquirer entering a lifeworld must be cognizant of possible disruption and violence to the meaning structures that may result from the intervention of the inquiry.

It is essential that research into a work setting takes into consideration its effect on that lifeworld. For example, if the aim of the research is to improve the communication between board members of a voluntary association, one may decide to administer a psychological test to find members' levels of creativity. One could find a standardized instrument, such as (hypothetically) the Charlesbeck Creativity Scale, and divide members into two groups—the creative and the uncreative. One could then make plans to counsel the uncreative to follow the ideas of the creative, or one could train the uncreative in mundane chores or find ways in which their activities would become so unfulfilling that they would leave the board to make room for creative types. However, it may be that this scale does not take into account that the uncreative types may have motives, intents, and potentialities outside the bounds of the way you score them on the scale. The act of taking the test and being so categorized may be enough in itself to cause some of them to resign. One way human subjects committees deal with such discomfort caused in their participants is to have them sign an informed consent form, which tells them that the researcher will supply a list of qualified psychotherapists to help them after the study is over!

The lifeworld of an organization will be affected by the research as persons in the organization have career paths that are affected by organizational change. Often, social research involves asking questions. The persons providing the answers may be prodded to expose aspects of their lives that they had not thought of before. This, in itself, may provide new direction to the organization.

■ Affinity of Mindful Inquiry to Non-Western Thought and Feminist Thought

With a few notable exceptions, the sciences and the social sciences that predominate in the world today arose historically within Western European cultures. We believe that critical social science, phenomenology, and hermeneutics, although coming from the Western tradition, incorporate elements of and are compatible with non-Western modes of knowing and feminist ways of knowing. Our approach to inquiry sets up a Buddhist-like framework for opening a space for contemplation in which research occurs. The quality of mindfulness requires a centering of the work on inquiry fully within the consciousness of the inquirer. Buddhist approaches to knowledge insist that truth lies in absence and that meditation leads to ever-deepening insight into self. The inquirer watches herself in the process, noticing the wake she makes as the boat moves forward or anchors for a while until a storm passes or the sun rises.

Our Western theoretical–philosophical positions, critical theory, hermeneutics, and phenomenology are fundamentally and radically critical of that tradition and even of themselves. They are the most open instances of non-Western/male modes of thought, and have been described as such. For example, phenomenology began and continues to be in dialogue with hidden philosophy, and critical of Western modes of thinking (Chattopadhyaya, Embree, & Mohanty, 1992). A core group of Japanese thinkers, coming from Buddhist and Zen perspectives, have embraced phenomenological sociology and have yearly conferences on phenomenology. Louise Levesque-Lopman has written that phenomenology offers a way to explicate women's experience, finding it congruent with feminist thought (1988), as does Iris Marion Young (1990).

Heidegger's depth hermeneutics lies in deep critical dialogue with Western metaphysics from which the social sciences have sprung. Heidegger listens to the speaking of the earth and the sky and, from this perspective, argues that science has covered up as much as it has uncovered. Heidegger's principles of hermeneutics seek to open spaces so that what has been covered up may again shine forth. Horkheimer's and Adorno's *Dialectic of Enlightenment* (1975), a major work of critical theory originally published half a century ago, anticipates many current critiques of Western civilization and its dominating, instrumental, imperialistic, masculine, egoistic, and racist modes of thought and action, whereas Marcuse's *Eros and Civilization* (1966a), another piece of critical theory, sketches out the basis of a new "reality principle" completely opposed to the Western "performance principle" and drawing explicitly on non-Western cultures for some of its ideas.

Fundamentals of Mindful Inquiry

There are some fundamental characteristics of mindful inquiry, regardless of which method, technique, or culture of inquiry you use. Mindful inquiry

- is framed by consciousness (in the tradition of Schutz and Husserl);
- is framed by the historical–political–social–psychological setting (Habermas);
- is framed by interpretation (Heidegger and Ricoeur);
- is interested in cause;
- is interested in meaning;
- is concerned with underlying experimental design;
- is connected to theory;
- is interested in sequences of events;
- is interested in prediction;
- results in typification or typology;
- makes comparisons; and
- cares for lifeworlds.

Different cultures of inquiry and research methods emphasize certain of these elements. Some research practices attempt to rule out one or more of these elements. However, we have found that, in the context of the lifeworld in which the research and the researcher exist, the missing element will still come into play. For example, a strict behaviorist denies the ontological reality of meaning. He focuses solely on observations of behaviors in sequential action. However, when speaking of the results of his research, the behaviorist is explaining to those in his lifeworld what the observations mean.

In a similar way, a historian who believes she is writing pure description of events without relationship to theory will still be asked why she wrote about a particular aspect of or period in history, why she used certain sources and not others, and so on. The explanation will undoubtedly reveal an underlying or implicit theory.

A phenomenologist or ethnographer may say she is not interested in prediction but only description. However, the reader of the description of a phenomenon of culture will tend to assume that, in similar circumstances, other human beings from other cultures may act as was forecast by implication in the description. For example, if one reads James Heap's (1982) phenomenological descriptions of getting into a depression, one expects that if one followed a thought pattern as described by Heap, one would likely also get into a state of depression.

■ Experiment and Typification in Everyday Life and in Social Inquiry

Everyday Experiments

Everyday we conduct inquiries as we accomplish necessary tasks and attempt to fulfill our goals. We may not be conscious of all the goal-seeking aspects of our behavior. Our behavior may be aimed at a purpose we are not aware of at the time.

Trial and error and imitation are primary ways in which we make inquiries in everyday life. By imitating others, we may quickly learn how desirable results may be obtained. Trial and error is a form of experimentation. Usually, we will already have accomplished something one way in the past. Then we add a new component and then observe that things go better or worse. It is like an experiment divided up into two or more points in time.

Learning in everyday life is also a process of observing typifications or patterns of objects and events. Birds learn to fly in certain ways, depending on and according to the way the sky typically looks in certain directions. Following these clues may sometimes be wrong, however.

Social scientists are in the business of categorizing the typifications made by persons in their lifeworlds and then making typifications of these typifications. For example, in this book, we typify certain kinds of research strategies under the rubric of cultures of inquiry.

Cooking Pasta

If our previous efforts at cooking pasta in a white enamel pan for 10 minutes resulted in a soggy consistency, we may decide to experiment next time and cook the pasta for 8 minutes. Then, if it is still too soft, we may try a different pan, an even shorter cooking time, or some other variation. After several more trials, we may have found our preferred way of preparing pasta. If we want faster results, we may want to do a classic experiment by matching groups. We may ask a number of friends to each cook the same pasta in different kinds of pots for different lengths of time. We will, if the payoff is big enough, get two matched groups and expose only one to the treatment. We will observe how the results differ and then be able to typify the cooking of pasta based on these experiments.

Even when findings are produced in the purest, double-blind experiments, we cannot always be sure that the findings, when applied, will work out the same way because they will always be used in a unique lifeworld setting. Even the most desirable results cannot escape the edict of Heraclitus: "One cannot step twice into the same river, for the water into which you stepped has flowed on" (Heraclitus, 1979, p. 14)

The Classic Experiment and Its Derivatives

The classic experiment comes from chemistry. A substance is isolated in a test tube. It is submitted to a controlled process in a laboratory. It may be mixed with something else or have a catalyst added to it that is designed to produce change. The resulting substance is measured and compared with the substance before the experiment. The whole process is guided by theories of the properties of matter that allow descriptions of the process to be put into equations that must balance as matter and energy before and after the intervention.

Social Psychological Experiments

Social psychological experiments involve putting persons in controlled situations, manipulating variables, and observing and reporting on changes in behavior. In a now famous study, Stanley Milgram (1974) employed volunteers as assistants in a research project. The volunteers were ordered by "scientists" to increase the voltage of electric current to persons strapped to seats behind glass walls. Milgram found that most of the research participants were willing to obey the "scientists'" orders to increase voltage, even when the persons behind the glass were showing signs of agonizing pain and the voltage was strong enough to endanger their lives. Those behind the glass were in truth paid actors, a fact that was not known to the participants of the experiment.

Historical Ex Post Facto Experiments

Max Weber, a great, turn-of-the-century (nineteenth to twentieth centuries) sociologist, devised a way to address causal questions at the level of social organization. Weber developed a method called the *ideal type* to get a handle on complex historical phenomena so that comparisons and contrasts could be made. An ideal type is a selection of elements of a pattern of social organization that allows the inquirer to distinguish it from others. For example, Weber was able to discuss the emergence of bureaucratic organization by making a list of characteristic components common to all bureaucratic organizations and distinct from other forms of social organization. Bureaucracies are hierarchical, with each office above being responsible for those below. Records or files are central to bureaucracy. Bureaucratic officers act according to specified rules and only within their designated area of responsibility. They act without favoritism, they make a lifelong, full-time career of their roles. Bureaucratic organizations, based on these findings, may be contrasted with patrimony, in which decisions are made by the patriarch or his designee based on favoritism (Weber, 1968a).

Weber had doubts about Marx's monocausal economic interpretation of history. He developed ideal types of the nature of Protestantism and capitalism gleaned from the writings of Protestant leaders and exponents of capitalism. Weber looked at societies in history that were at the forefront in the development of capitalism and found them to be Protestant countries. He was able to show, therefore, that cultural developments influenced economic ones (Weber, 1967a, 1967b, 1968b, 1992). Weber's work is so groundbreaking and important for all of the social and human sciences that it is imperative that everyone in these disciplines, regardless of how remote her or his primary interests are from Weber's, be familiar with his theories. For a clear and comprehensive discussion of Weber's thought, see Bendix's *Max Weber: An Intellectual Portrait* (1962); for a short one, see Collins's *Max Weber: A Skeleton Key* (1986).

Simmel: Formal Sociology

Simmel developed descriptive models of typical forms of interaction and typical kinds of individuals (1950). His way of analyzing social relationships was like a social geometry that also carried an element of experimental design. In his formal sociology, he described how numbers affect social life. Relations between two people, for example, change dramatically when a third party is brought into the picture. Simmel catalogued the effects of bringing a third party into a dyad much as a chemist describes the introduction of a catalyst to a compound. Simmel also developed several typical models of individuals in social situations, such as the *stranger.* Such types are not psychological types but types that exist because of certain social structural situations. The stranger is both confided in more intimately (because his opinions have little effect on the social order) and more distrusted. He is located in more than one psychological geography at a time. When the stranger becomes a fully accepted member of the community, Simmel argues, his personality also changes.

Survey Research and Experimental Logic

Survey research is used when information is needed to answer questions about a population. It dates back to the Roman Empire, when Caesar wanted information about the population in the empire in order to impose taxes. It has been institutionalized in opinion polls. The survey is not designed to expand or change the consciousness of the researcher, but only to give him information so that he may in some way control, explore, or "help" the population. Political and governmental bureaus and advertising and marketing agencies are primary users of survey research. The production and distribution of such research is, in itself, a mammoth operation. To save money and time, the technique of random sampling was devised in order to be able to generalize from a select group to an entire population. Questions of cause and predictability may be addressed by survey research with the use of sophisticated analysis techniques, such as path analysis (Blalock, 1964).

Tests and Measurements: Developing Types

Measurements have been devised to categorize persons according to attributes deemed important by the inquirers or those who pay them. These attributes include intelligence, learning style, and personality type. Such measures organize responses in such a way that the respondents come to be better understood and their behavior can be predicted. Such tests may be used to predict and control outcomes. Once so categorized, persons may be deemed qualified or disqualified, fit or unfit, for certain kinds of jobs.

Experts in measurement psychology may be able to explain and predict anyone's behavior based on knowledge of their type. For example, the Myers–Briggs Type Indicator, following Carl Jung's observations about introversion and extroversion tendencies, has developed four personality factors yielding 16 possible combinations in any individual (Myers, McCaulley, & Most, 1985). If one is an INFJ, for example, one is seen as someone who is introverted (I), bases actions on intuition (N) and feeling (F), and seeks closure on situations (J—judgment). Once so categorized, anything a person does or says may be said to be "according to type." For example, after sitting at a faculty meeting for 8 hours, 2 days in a row, a member of the faculty left, saying he felt exhausted and needed time to think and recuperate. An advocate of the Myers–Briggs said, "Oh, he is an INTP, that explains why he can't deal with this so well!" Such an explanation detracted from the fact that all of the attendants felt exhausted, but most were too polite or too frightened of losing face with the dean or their colleagues to say so. In such a way, political situations may be psychologized. This psychologization is a built-in hermeneutic stance in the use of such tests and measurements. In addition, the fact that human beings' attitudes and feelings are in flux are not taken into account by the tests. This is not to belie the possible usefulness of some tests. Reflection on what is known about behavior patterns and characteristics of others who took the tests could be helpful. However, a test score may be used as an excuse for not developing one's self in new and challenging directions.

Mindful inquiry looks at typification as an inherent aspect of social science research. The typification process is one of the primary ways lifeworlds operate and consciousness is constituted. By making this central, those practicing mindful inquiry are constantly aware of the dangers of reifying typifications and creating self-fulfilling prophecies.

■ Journalism Versus Social Science: Linking Theory and Research

How does human science research differ from journalism? Journalists (as well as police officers, insurance investigators, attorneys, etc.) investigate aspects of social and organizational life. Journalists interview witnesses or participants in events that are deemed newsworthy. Investigative reporters will, at times, become participants (overtly or covertly) in the activities they are inquiring about, as will police and governmental investigators.

Market research is opinion surveying that seeks to predict consumer behavior. In this sense, it borders both journalistic investigation and social science research because it tests hypotheses such as how age or socioeconomic status relates to buying patterns. Human sciences research does not just focus on the who, what, when, where, and how aspects of human behavior (even on the predictive hypotheses of market research), but it does focus on the why.

Theory guides all of our actions. Each of us carries an internal book of theoretical maxims that guide us in everyday life events. Phenomenologists call such theories typifications. For example, we may develop a theory of trash collection from observing what the garbage collectors leave behind. If the refuse they leave behind is troublesome to us, we may inquire about how to get them to pick it up. We may call the Department of Sanitation and discover that if we label the extra trash with a sticker sent for a fee, it will be picked up. We also learn from further investigation and hearsay from neighbors that the workers will pick up extra if you tip them.

Sociological, psychological, or economic theories are explanations about the causes of human events or the elucidation of their meanings. These investigations are based on known strategies and validated through the canons of acceptable evidence among scholars who share a discourse community. Theory is not static, but evolves and changes along with research as well as with the kinds of questions facing humans and organizations. Knowledge of the theoretical landscape gives one a road map that scholars have traveled as the social sciences developed. On these roads, there are well-known guides who have traveled them before, such as August Comte, the father of sociology (1974), and Emile Durkheim, author of *The Division of Labor in Society* (1947) and developer of a method of statistical correlation to investigate the causes of suicide. Such pathways also include highways built over battlegrounds on which armies of guides who disagreed about which way to go are still pulling out their swords.

There are many good books that describe the terrain of sociological theory. We recommend that you read one or two of them before engaging in social research, because they will help you navigate the frameworks of discovery and understanding in the social and human sciences. These texts will make you aware of the kinds of questions, concerns, and frameworks that have been developed for understanding human experience and in reference to which you will conduct your research. See Turner (1991), Ritzer (1992), Coser (1971), and Lemert (1993) for thorough treatments of sociological theory. Other social sciences also have reviews of theory that you should read if your research area is related to these social and behavioral science disciplines.

Prior to beginning your investigation you should, at the very least, know how your topic would be explained given several different theoretical perspectives. For example, say you are investigating a conflict between two inner-city youth gangs. A symbolic interactionist would view such conflict as a process of interaction between persons with different identifications using interpretations of meaning that frame each other as enemies. A structural functionalist would look at them as functioning to structure and solidify their groups in relation to the society as a whole, albeit in a socially unacceptable manner. A Marxist would look at them as victims of an oppressive system, the powers of which they do not ever address because they are too busy competing with each other. Researchers from each theoretical perspective would certainly approach their work in totally different manners and would probably reach different results.

■ Conclusion

We have reviewed some general principles of mindful inquiry, regardless of the specific research cultures, traditions, methods, and techniques you may use. All inquiry occurs in a lifeworld that is structured by circumstances. The consciousness of the researcher also affects the entire research process, from conception to results.

Mindful inquiry is related to theory and is interested in both cause and meaning. A primary logical structure of all research is the logic of the experiment. It is concerned with sequences, predictions, and comparisons of typical components of social life. Mindful inquiry is governed by a mood of gentleness and care.

The Scholarly Practitioner

*Facing the Loss of Identity
Through the Onslaught of
the Information Age*

M anagers in corporations, as well as professionals in law, health care, and education, find themselves faced with change and stress unique to postmodernism. Managers may no longer rely on outdated ways of knowing and management strategies from the past. There is turbulence at the workplace resulting from the pressures of the world marketplace, the movement around the globe of persons with different cultures and languages, and the pressure of population explosion. As world resources are diminishing (such as rain forests and uncontaminated water), population continues to increase. All of this turbulence causes suffering manifested in the form of downsizing, re-engineering, and redesign efforts that often result in massive disruption and loss of jobs.

Coping with the environment requires managers and professionals not just to learn better techniques but to become mindful inquirers. Each of us must strive to keep grounded and centered and to have a philosophical underpinning to our work. In this way, practitioners may successfully navigate these turbulent waters.

The cornerstones of mindful inquiry are crucial in that they focus on understanding the consciousness of one's self and others and on the accurate and deep interpretation of meanings. They focus on the alleviation of suffering with respect for the lifeworlds of all involved.

To us, a scholarly practitioner is someone who mediates between her professional practice and the universe of scholarly, scientific, and academic knowledge and discourse. She sees her practice as part of a larger enterprise of knowledge generation and critical reflection. If you are (or if you are intending to become) a knowledge worker or professional, you will most likely be a scholarly practitioner—that is, someone who is continually integrating professional practice and research. A purpose of this book is to help you navigate through the process of structured inquiry, or knowledge generation, in order to increase your competence as a scholarly practitioner. In an ideal outcome, it should help you absorb, evaluate, and find workplace applications for the knowledge that exists in the research literature. It also should help you use your work, your interests, and the questions to which they give rise as the starting place for knowledge that you can then contribute to scholarly discourse and to your profession. In this way, the book should also provide you with direction in beginning the process that will lead to your thesis or dissertation.

▀▀ The Role of the Scholarly Practitioner

The role of the scholarly practitioner involves a two-way relationship. It involves using professional practice and knowledge as a resource for the formulation and production of scholarly knowledge as well as for evaluating, testing, applying, extending, or modifying existing knowledge. It involves mastering procedures for generating knowledge, not only to create knowledge but, as important, to become aware of the limits of knowledge. This awareness of both the nature of knowledge and its limits is, we believe, part of the identity of a mature practitioner who is personally, ethically, and professionally responsible.

The enterprise of knowledge generation and critical reflection, in both its professional and scholarly forms, is devoted to answering questions about the nature of human beings and human systems organizations, groups, families, communities, and societies and their experience, behavior, patterning, and evolution. It is also concerned with intervention, action, management, and, in general, helping people to take account of the conditions that shape their lives so they can more effectively intervene to change those conditions. The questions that stimulate inquiry arise from both professional practice (What is a better way to run a meeting? Help a family? Design an organization?) and intellectual curiosity (How does spatial arrangement affect a meeting? How can we make sense out of a particular pattern of family interaction? How are organizational structures affected by the technologies they use?). The questions may arise out of purely personal experience and concern or out of a scholarly tradition of inquiry. Both professional practice and scholarly inquiry may contribute to answering these questions.

What distinguishes scholarly or scientific inquiry from more informal, everyday, intuitive sorts of inquiry is primarily the existence of rationally grounded procedures of creating knowledge that is accepted as reliable and valid within scholarly discourse. A secondary distinguishing factor is participation at some level in scholarly or research communities along with work and professional communities. This is not meant to disparage everyday informal inquiry. Inevitably, we use informal and intuitive methods to answer some of our questions much of the time, and scholarly and scientific methods have grown out of the types of inquiry in which we engage in everyday life. But as our society has moved increasingly toward being a knowledge-based society, structured inquiry of a scholarly kind has come to shape knowledge in every field.

Professional and expert practice, although drawing heavily on explicit and scientific knowledge, is often based, to a considerable extent, on tacit knowledge, intuition, habit, and flying by the seat of one's pants, as well as on prejudices and simple extensions of what has worked previously. Scholarly and scientific knowledge is shaped largely by making explicit knowledge claims and validating them through some public procedures that have been established as producing reliable methods of knowledge that have been widely criticized, analyzed, and agreed on by at least a significant number of scholars. There are a number of ways of carrying out inquiry that command broad assent among scholars and the public at large. We all know that if we want to find out what the public thinks about an issue, we are more likely to get a reliable answer by asking people chosen randomly from many locations than by asking our best friends, let alone relying on a hunch.

As we discussed earlier, there are major disagreements about what constitutes reliable knowledge and reliable procedures for generating such knowledge. Nevertheless, there are some broad traditions with solid intellectual foundations in our disciplines that tell us both what knowledge looks like and how to create it. These traditions will be discussed later in this book.

It is useful to realize that the existence of alternative ways of conducting inquiry does not mean they are merely reflections of opinions and preferences. Rather, these alternative traditions are part of an ongoing debate in the human sciences about what constitutes knowledge and what generates it. It is precisely because of this debate and controversy that we have reason to take these traditions seriously. In the world of scholarly discourse, it is precisely because ideas have stood up to criticism that they can lay claim to validity, even if it be a limited one.

Because the debate is ongoing, elements of personal preference, value commitments, and intellectual partisanship may enter into the choice of methods used to conduct inquiry. This makes the process of inquiry more exciting. It also places a greater responsibility on the investigator to be able to justify her choice of method, of the tradition(s) or culture(s) of inquiry that she chooses. That is why the study of inquiry requires some attention to the philosophical justification of different modes of conducting inquiry.

There are four primary functions of scholarly inquiry for the scholarly professional:

1. personal transformation;
2. the improvement of professional practice;
3. the generation of knowledge; and
4. appreciation of the complexity, intricacy, structure and—some would say—
   beauty of reality.

These functions may occur in isolation or in combination. Although the latter
objectives are generally self-evident, it is not always obvious that studying research can also have a profound personal impact. The following statement by
graduate student Linda Ford illustrates the many ways in which understanding
the diverse traditions of research can illuminate our personal understanding as
well.

> Since I started working on my independent study in research about two
> years ago, I've learned a great deal about lots of things. Much of that learning,
> while not directly related to research was absolutely essential to my ability to
> engage actively with the subject. The "learning" took many forms, some very
> personal and emotional and some more intellectual. And the "doing" also took
> many forms, some active and outwardly reaching and some more inwardly
> searching. While the product of that learning is represented in the paper I've
> written, it seems worthwhile to pause briefly to reflect on the process.
>
> First, I want to describe the emotional learning which had to take place to
> enable me to learn about research in a meaningful way. This entails changes
> in my self-perception, my attitudes and beliefs about reality and knowing, and
> in my feelings. While all of these are interrelated, I'll try to separate them
> somewhat to describe what happened. Also, they are all related to the more
> intellectual learnings I'll describe later.
>
> When I first attempted to work on the research paper, I would have been
> quite comfortable describing my approach as positivist (although I didn't know
> that was the word for it). Reality was what I could touch and feel. While each
> person could form a subjective interpretation of reality, I was quite sure that
> we all live in the same reality. The way we can know about that reality is to
> measure things that are objectively observable. Then we can explain, predict,
> and control things in the world. Through several personal experiences, conver-
> sations, and readings, I began to believe that such phrases as "the social con-
> struction of reality" might be meaningful, that an individual's experience of an
> event could be completely different from another individual's experience of
> the same event, that knowing could come from many sources, some internal
> to me and some external. This awareness led me to be more open to learning
> about research which explores things I can't see or touch. I began to read about
> research strategies which aimed at understanding, not explanation, at uncov-

ering meanings instead of observing behaviors, at exploring the person's experience of events instead of just the events. It became more important to me to consider the effect of the researcher on what she was observing or participating in and the consequences of the research results to those being observed.

I began to feel a sense of increased responsibility to use research in a socially responsible way—to want my research to empower and enable those who contribute to the research as subjects (or co-researchers in a collaborative inquiry). That feeling had its roots not only in my new approach to the personal nature of reality and its meanings for individuals, but also in my changed self-perception. Somewhere along the road, a gradual shift occurred in the mindset I had in reading research studies. Two years ago, I read studies as a student looking for "the answer." Now I read them as a peer, critiquing constructively, evaluating critically, and listening actively. Without that shift, I could not think in the first person about research. The key issues of values and ethics and meaning didn't come alive for me until I began to be able to think of "my" research. So, my relationship to the subject of research changed because my relationship to myself, to the nature of reality, and to the social system in which I live changed.

All of those changes opened the way for me to learn a variety of things related to research. I learned that learning and knowing are related but different. This definition isn't exactly *Webster's,* but, for me, learning involves taking things in from the outside, whereas knowing is what happens inside. I may know because I've learned or simply because I find what was inside all along. The intuitive or tacit part of knowing is now real for me in a way that it wasn't before. Connected to that is that I've begun to know that there are many ways to know, many ways to learn, many ways to create, and many frameworks in which to place all of that.

So, I guess I've collected a little philosophy and epistemology along the way. And, through all of that, I've learned a little about myself in the world. I now know that I'm a self-aware, self-reflective, responsible, empowered actor in a social arena. That may seem obvious, but for me, it was just a set of words with no personal meaning. Now I KNOW it. That is, it lives inside me. And, I learned that research is exciting, challenging, and dynamic. That it can be personally engaging and rewarding. And that I may have something to contribute to that someday.

■ Research as a Socialization Process

If you are a graduate student, your thesis or dissertation will be the central part of your contribution to knowledge while you are in graduate school. This knowledge is conceived as part of a socialization process into the scholarly community. If you are a professional carrying out a research project, this will be an important part of your job and will contribute to your expertise and possibly your professional status.

For better or worse, the conduct of inquiry in a graduate program, including the dissertation process, is a ritual of socialization into a particular community— the community of scholars. Like any socialization process, it involves mastering the procedures of a community and some of its roles so that one can function as a member of that community. These include certain methods of conducting inquiry with which one must be familiar in order to be able to claim competence. Unlike many other communities, the procedures of the scholarly community rest entirely on their claim to rational justification. Hence, in principle, a person can enter this community while criticizing its procedures and proposing alternatives, if she or he provides a compelling argument for doing so.

The word *community* does not adequately describe the cacophony of competing theories and methods within the human sciences. Derrida (1976) has argued that all texts "deconstruct" themselves when their own premises (whether acknowledged or not) are turned back on themselves. Horkheimer (1972) revealed the political ideology underlying cultural forms, and Foucault (1980) elucidated the relationship between power and knowledge. However, basic standards of investigation prevail in communities of discourse and within research traditions. Such discourse communities are international in scope. Underlying all of these are canons of evidence, logic, and continuing critique.

Socialization into the community of scholars consists largely of critically learning the types of inquiry and explanation used in one's discipline. Doing dissertation research is the critical test of this. When people evaluate your dissertation and, especially, your proposal, they will be looking to see whether you have mastered the modes of explanation or understanding appropriate to what you are studying, including their limits and inadequacies.

Because this socialization process is also socialization into a profession, your proposal and dissertation will also be evaluated in terms of your knowledge of the people and institutions who are the bearers of the knowledge and modes of explanation. Are you familiar with the main figures, journals, books, professional associations, and conferences in which the research tradition is carried out? Are you familiar with the main lines of development of a particular research tradition (e.g., who influenced whom?). Are you familiar with the main journals where your topic is discussed?

There are no universal modes of explanation or universal research methods. The only universal in scientific knowledge is a general commitment to using argument and evidence to arrive at conclusions recognized as subject to further revision. Appropriate research methods are contextual—that is, they depend on the key problems currently at issue in the discipline and the current state of the methods accepted as relevant in that discipline (including current critiques of those methods). For this reason, most textbook classifications and definitions of research methods and the labels attached to them are unreliable oversimplifications. They convert fluid, dynamic, interpenetrating approaches to research into abstract, timeless categories that have little to do with the way investigators actually go about the activity of inquiry. Hence, the first thing to learn about doing research is how to construct a valid map of one or more research traditions into which your research fits. This includes

- the theories that shape those traditions,
- the empirical findings they have come up with,
- their outstanding problems and questions, and
- the research methods that are used within or appropriate to those traditions.

■ Assessing Your Growing Competency as a Researcher

As one learns to become a musician, there are certain competencies one develops. They do not come overnight, but over time and with practice. One must first listen to music, then sing it, then dance it, then practice scales on an instrument, then learn to read music, then practice simple pieces on the piano, then play a duet with someone, then read a book about music, then study music theory, and so on. Along this road, one will play some wonderful music and keep on learning. Playing music in different styles is like becoming a researcher working from different cultures of inquiry, each of which requires a select repertoire of methods and techniques.

One way to look at your own development as a researcher is in relation to established competencies that skilled researchers possess. These competencies are acquired over time and by various means. The best way to achieve them is to get involved in research. Take advantage of opportunities to collaborate with skilled researchers in a number of different modalities. Volunteer to conduct a survey, or to gather qualitative data for your favorite organization, or to conduct telephone interviews to test the marketability of a new idea. Analyze a transcription of a telephone conference call using techniques of conversational analysis. Read books about various kinds of research, as suggested in our bibliography. Read books and articles of actual research and write reviews of them for journals. All of these practices over time will help you become a skilled researcher with many competencies.

In Appendix B, you will find categorizations of research competencies devised by the faculties of the Clinical Psychology Program and Human and Organization Development Program of The Fielding Institute. This is so that, as you are becoming a skilled researcher, you may be conscious of which skills you are developing along the way, and so that you may seek out opportunities to put other research skills into practice.

Getting Started

There are a number of complementary ways to get started in scholarly inquiry:

- Talk with faculty to explore your research interests, situating them within the context of your department and school, and building them into your graduate program of study.
- Familiarize yourself with research that is relevant to you.
- Learn about different approaches to conducting research, the language of research, and some of the philosophical issues about what counts as knowledge and valid ways of establishing it.
- Become acquainted with classic or major research studies in your area of interests.

Although the knowledge of the methods of scholarly inquiry overlaps with the knowledge of specific subject matter in individual disciplines, it differs from them in being essentially a set of tools for use in one's professional work in those disciplines and in the dissertation process. As a consequence, the following suggestions for getting started bear not only on research specifically but also on other aspects of your studies. You do not need to follow all these simultaneously. Because everyone has her or his own learning style and comes from a different background, pick the ones that make the most sense for you as a starter.

Familiarize yourself with research traditions and research that is currently going on in your areas of professional and intellectual interest, and incorporate reviews and discussions of this research into all of your graduate studies and papers.

To be a scholarly practitioner means thinking about one's professional work in a scholarly manner, keeping up with the research that is going on in one's field and incorporating its implications into one's practice, and, eventually, contributing to this research. In our program, we think of inquiry as an attempt to answer actual questions that arise from or bear on professional work. These problems can arise from your everyday experience at work or elsewhere, or they can arise out of a scholarly tradition. In either case, linking up to the research relevant to one's work and interests is a sensible strategy.

The following is a list of ways to locate relevant research traditions:

- Use the books referred to in this book.
- Speak with faculty and experts in your field. Even a telephone conversation with an expert is an excellent way to get oriented to current research about your interests.
- Attend conferences in your field at which research findings are being presented.
- Perform computer searches to locate articles on relevant topics, as well as to find periodicals that regularly publish on the subjects of your interest.

- Subscribe to one or two scholarly journals that regularly publish research relevant to your main interests and scan other related journals regularly at the library.
- Subscribe to and read some book review periodicals.
- Find out enough about the main cultures of inquiry and approaches to research in the courses you take to help you understand and reflect critically on the research studies you encounter and make choices about the approaches that seem most appealing or stimulating to you.
- Read interesting, important, or classic research studies in the human sciences—journal articles, books, and dissertations—to get a concrete sense of options available for research as you learn more about the subject matter of the human sciences. Make sure that most of your scholarly papers include current research from scholarly journals and discuss them as part of your work. For this purpose, it will be essential to review some of the major scholarly journals that cover the discipline or subdiscipline in which you are working. See what scholars are arguing about, what research they refer to, and their criticisms of research in the area. Part of being competent in an area of knowledge is being able to report on and critically evaluate some research going on in that area.
- Start engaging in research about your professional activities and context. This can be part of your work in courses and papers. It can also contribute to professional publications and presentations and can become part of your dissertation. An excellent short and simple introduction to the practice of research is the book by Robson (*Real World Research: A Resource for Social Scientists and Practitioner–Researchers* (1993). This book tells the basics of what you need to know to start researching settings of your own choosing (including your workplace), and covers everything from taking notes and dealing with your fears to analyzing your findings and writing them up.
- Read some introductory works on inquiry and research in our bibliography.

Inquiry is not a mechanical technique but part of the larger process of reasoning, argumentation, and critical thinking. Every piece of research is essentially an argument that something is the case, or that something can be explained in a particular way, or that something is better than something else, or that something can best be understood or interpreted in a particular way. The obstacles to having a dissertation proposal approved are frequently flaws in argument or in critical thinking. One way to enrich your conceptual framework for engaging in inquiry is to sharpen your critical thinking and reasoning skills. Our bibliography includes some useful works on developing these skills.

Argumentation and critical thinking are sedimented in scholarly writing, and the practice of scholarly writing is not only the primary form for expressing the process and results of inquiry but a primary way to develop the thinking skills for doing it.

Regardless of one's chosen method of inquiry, research libraries are an essential component in the practice of research, for it is in them that research traditions are embodied in physical and electronic forms. Familiarizing one's self with the culture of information as it is embodied and organized in research libraries is an important part of the process of developing the framework and context for inquiry. Thomas Mann's *A Guide to Library Research Methods* (1986) is an excellent place to get started.

For most students, a principal focus of their inquiry and research activities is their thesis or dissertation. Most general books about research are concerned with scientific research in general. But as a socialization process and as a personal and interpersonal process, dissertation research has features that set it apart from research in general.

Entering a Research Tradition

People approaching research without prior experience tend to think of the results of research as a collection of certified knowledge, "approved" by "science," which can be then relied on without hesitation, as when people say, "Research shows that . . . " or "research proves that. . . . " From this perspective, the enterprise of science and scholarship is like a big sausage grinder that takes in ignorance and unclarity and, through research, turns out absolute certainty—"nothing but the facts."

But this view of research is both naive and refuted by the entire history of science. As a little reflection on the history of knowledge will show, neither ordinary human beings nor scientists can ever know "the truth" in any direct, guaranteed, or stable way. People used to think that ghosts were facts, just as people used to think that living forms emerged from spontaneous generation. For centuries, scientists believed that the sun revolved around the earth. Until recently, some scientists asserted that women are "by nature" inferior to men in certain kinds of mental functioning.

The kinds of methods and procedures used to establish physical and biological knowledge have changed significantly over the course of the past generation. At any point in time, there are standards for what counts as knowledge and for the procedures of establishing it. Indeed, these standards are not uniform even at a single point in time, for the scientific community is often divided over them. Even standards that are widely accepted often have unstated assumptions and opinions built into them—that is, they themselves reflect the untestable worldviews of the community of scholars that adheres to them. This, in turn, is reflected in differences in research methodologies.

Given all that has been said, how is one to enter a particular research tradition, mastering it sufficiently for the purposes of advanced research, such as a doctoral dissertation? There are usually three main questions that must be asked as one evaluates a research proposal as acceptable:

1. Is the research question a clear, unambiguous, legitimate, and researchable one whose answer will fit into existing knowledge and extend it in a significant manner?

2. Has the question been situated in the context of surrounding and related knowledge, theories, facts, and questions in a way that shows you have adequately taken into consideration the relevant background material, as well as alternative ways of looking at your subject?

3. Is your proposed method for examining and answering your question (i.e., your "research design") appropriate for your purpose?

These questions imply other, more general questions about research that have to do with the nature of the knowledge that is being produced.

■ What Makes Something Count as Knowledge?

Epistemological questions include the following:

- What will make my dissertation count as knowledge, rather than merely a statement of my belief or opinion?
- How does a piece of research acquire legitimacy as reliable knowledge?
- Under what circumstances does something count as evidence for a truth claim or factual assertion?
- Am I concerned with making statements of fact, with showing causal relations, with making judgments of value, or something else?
- Are my methods primarily inductive (drawing general conclusions from "the data"), deductive (drawing logical conclusions from general principles), or abductive (making creative leaps)?
- How do my ideas bear on existing theories? How are they derived from existing theories?
- How do I know that my proposed research approach is adequate to my research concerns? Will it likely yield results that can shed light on my research question(s)? What are the chief defects of my research method, and how might they be compensated?

As we said earlier, there are presently significant debates over the nature of knowledge and the types of knowledge that are appropriate to providing useful "scientific" understanding. One's epistemological stance will usually have a major impact on what one considers a meaningful or productive form of inquiry. Choosing a research method necessarily requires one to make conscious choices about the assumptions underlying inquiry. One must, in other words, take responsibility for one's approach and its consequences. An important goal of work in this area is to foster such responsibility through providing sufficient understanding that one's choice can, in fact, be made consciously.

Difference Between a Generating and a Validating Idea

This section deals with two major questions. The first—"Where do scientific ideas come from?"—refers to the creation of theories, hypotheses, models, and abstract constructs. For instance, I may have the idea that people are motivated by forces of which they are completely unaware, that unconscious motivation plays a major role in human behavior. Where does such an idea come from? How is it generated within scholarly discourse?

Once an idea has arisen, whatever its source, it must be validated. The second question, then, is simply, "How can I verify this idea?" There are as many means to verification as there are cultures of inquiry; in fact, in a sense, one of the most important characteristics of a culture of inquiry is its standard of verification. In some traditions, verification is usually taken to mean prediction. To "test" an idea, I derive some consequence that must follow if it is true, construct a means to measure that consequence, and then see if my prediction is supported. In the other traditions, the standards of verification are much more broadly defined. In all cases, however, as we have noted previously, only those ideas that will stand up to rational argument count as valid.

Where Do Scientific Ideas Come From?

In the early social sciences tradition, it was widely believed that *truth* (defined as unequivocal knowledge of "the facts") was best achieved by letting the facts speak for themselves. Methodologically, this entailed purely inductive procedures, drawing impartial conclusions from supposedly unbiased observations. The starting place was to be the facts themselves; the task of the scientist was observation, experiment, and description.

This simple view is no longer held by all researchers. Following the seminal ideas in Thomas Kuhn's celebrated *Structure of Scientific Revolutions* (1970), it is now widely accepted that a scientific community of discourse shares a set of beliefs and assumptions that helps to shape their observations. Pure, unbiased observation is not possible: All observation is guided by a mixture of explicit theories, implicit assumptions, and often even pure hunch. Kuhn termed this complex of concepts a paradigm, a framework or worldview that helps guide the hands of a community of scientists as they proceed. One of the defining characteristics of a community of scientists is its widespread acceptance of a single paradigm.

The notion of paradigm provides a partial answer to the question, "Where do scientific ideas come from?" Such ideas seldom come from the facts themselves; rather, they typically come from the minds of scientists. This source is often guided by the prevailing paradigm, which will suggest useful avenues of inquiry, point out unsolved issues, and identify questions that have previously proven to be intellectual dead ends. Socialization into a paradigm is highly important, and is achieved by studying a particular tradition of inquiry.

Although knowledge of a paradigm is important in helping the researcher to frame questions, there is an important ingredient that is purely personal as well: the creative, perceptual, cognitive, emotional, and motivational state of mind of the researcher. The importance of the "aha" experience of discovery in the development of scientific knowledge cannot be understated. Ultimately, it is the creative genius of the researcher that converts a mundane piece of research into a truly extraordinary work of discovery. Inspirational ideas, in a sense, may come from anywhere; their source has little bearing on whether or not the research that follows from them will stand up as scientific.

This leads us to our second concern: the scientific validation of ideas, whatever their source. First, scientific ideas are open to exploration. The scientist holds them up for scrutiny rather than acclamation. Disconfirmation, rather than proof, is the prevailing mood within the scientific community. This requires that scientifically framed ideas must be stated in such a way that they are capable of being investigated by persons other than the original researcher, and thereby be disconfirmed by others interested in the same problem. Scientific ideas are public, not private.

The statements scientists make of their ideas and the descriptions they provide of their methods ideally are not only precise and systematic but also as explicit as possible concerning their underlying premises and assumptions. This entails several precautions. I may devise a method that makes it difficult for me to operate out of my own bias systematically. On the other hand, I may describe these biases for the benefit of other researchers, so that they can evaluate what impact my bias may have had on my findings. By precise and systematic description, we mean that the scientific community should be able to understand exactly what the researcher has done. In this way, other researchers should be empowered to see where the method might be applicable in better understanding other related phenomena or where the reported outcome might be replicated.

Over the past two decades, it has been repeatedly demonstrated that researchers most often find what they expect to find. It has been found, for example, that when teachers were falsely informed that certain students were either gifted or slow, those students, in fact, performed in accordance with their teachers' expectations on supposedly impartial tests. Even rats were found to learn to negotiate mazes more quickly when researchers were falsely informed that they were genetically "maze bright." Such demonstrations have reinforced the belief that pure objectivity is unattainable. Therefore, the best a method can hope to do is to clarify the researcher's own beliefs and values insofar as they may distort the results.

It is obviously critical that the scientist be able to discriminate between her or his own values, beliefs, opinions, and more data-driven support for his or her ideas. Whether that support comes from the examination of experience (phenomenology), the collection of empirical data, the interpretation of text or verbal evidence, or the outcome of an action project, the scientist proceeds in the spirit of inquiry rather than persuasion.

In the course of your research work, you will, we hope, have a great many creative ideas about various subjects of interest to you. It is important that you discover how to state your ideas precisely and how to clarify your own values and beliefs about those ideas. We hope you will begin the process of understanding how to design a method of verification that is well suited to an idea, how to carry out that method in a fashion as free from bias as possible, how to make your remaining biases and assumptions explicit, and how best to evaluate the results of your efforts.

■ Gaining Mastery of Research Competencies to Maximize Creativity as a Researcher

Selecting a Method

We referred to research competencies earlier. The mastery of the first level of competencies is essential for all evolving researchers. This is because you cannot feel free to select which methods and techniques you will employ for a project without the skill and understanding to appreciate the power and limitations of the range of practices being employed in the communities of scholarly discourse. This is very much like a musician learning to play scales in every key, as well as learning to read and interpret music in different styles. Only then can the musician feel confident in executing a particular piece of music in a manner adequate to the task. (See Appendix B.)

Some good questions to ask yourself as you select a method include the following.

- Will the method allow me to discover what I want to know?
- Will my results using this method be convincing to the consumers of my research? (Remember, the consumers are not only the members of the scholarly discourse who are likely to read your work, but the members of the larger community who experience problems the research may seek to ameliorate.)
- What journals or potential publishers of my research do I have in mind?
- What good or harm may come from this project to myself or others?
- What changes in my life or the lives of others may occur as a result of this research?
- How will my skills as a scholar–practitioner be enhanced by this research?

Selecting a Topic

Although, in many academic departments, choice of topic and method is restricted by the interests and ongoing research endeavors of the faculty, a successful project is one in which your unique focus, question, or concern drives your process of inquiry.

Selecting a good topic follows from a play between deep personal needs, the structure of the field of inquiry, and the opportunities one has (makes). Students often select their research topics because of an unresolved problem or struggle in their own work or personal lives. There is nothing wrong with such a base, for such experiences are also often experienced by others. C. Wright Mills points out that one of the goals of sociological research is to connect the personal troubles we experience in everyday life with social issues (1959). The need to resolve such troubles can provide the energy and focus that will take one through the trials and tribulations of the process. However, it is usually useful to be aware of the drives that lead us to a topic. With such awareness in hand, we can creatively relate the internal drive to the contributions we wish to make to our professions through the research work. The first topic that comes to mind may be too strongly influenced by either personal drives often arising from pains we have experienced or by a feeling that we must accept external demands. Neither extreme is likely to provide good guidance. One method of gaining perspective on selection of a topic is to study the biographies of creative researchers and leaders. Another is to study work that explicitly deals with the process of gaining such balance. An excellent source is Peter Reason's *Human Inquiry in Action* (1988).

Personal Growth and the Selection of Research Approach

Different research methods require different kinds of skills and capacities of the inquirer. One's capacity includes prior experience, knowledge, attitudes, and personal drives or ambitions. It may be interesting for you to learn more about what various measurements of personal proclivities say about the probability that you will be either comfortable with or challenged by different research processes. For example, the Myers–Briggs Type Indicator will help you find out that you tend to act according to your feelings if they are in conflict with your reason or vice versa, or that you are more comfortable when you have a lot of interaction with others as opposed to working alone in your study (introvert vs. extrovert). However, you may want to use the opportunity of exploring a more "introverted" research method, such as historical or theoretical research, if you score as an extrovert on the Myers–Briggs, because you may desire to stretch yourself. Other such indicators include the following.

Learning Style. A scale like the Kolb Learning Style Inventory provides a classification of your mode of learning–inquiring. By reflecting on your learning style in conjunction with the characteristics of the different cultures of inquiry, you may get some clarity about which cultures of inquiry will provide the most challenge.

Energy Level and Pace. All research takes an immense amount of work, but methods require different pacing. Examine your own work history to find the best pacing.

Control Needs. There is more certainty in what will be expected of the inquirer in data gathering and analysis in some styles of research than in others. For example, once you have designed your quantitative study, you can be fairly certain what process you will go through in analyzing your data. However, you still will not be able to predict exactly how long it will take to obtain your data and all of the secondary analysis that may be necessary to thoroughly elucidate your findings. Doing social research as a mindful practitioner challenges you to accept the unexpected and unknown and relinquish your need for control. You can have a well-managed project and still be open to the unexpected and to opening the space for new insights and true growth in your own knowledge and being to occur.

Social Support Needs. The stereotype of theoretical or historical research is that it is an activity for loners or introverts, and ethnography for extroverts and lovers of group activity. In truth, all forms of social sciences inquiry are collaborative processes that challenge your skills at negotiating and working in teams. However, each of them also challenges your ability to think creatively and independently.

It is important to think carefully about who your collaborators are on any specific research endeavor. The quality and scope of insight of your collaborators will affect the outcome of your work significantly. There are many levels of collaboration involved in a successful research project. It is helpful if you think about these ahead of time. It is like getting your crew set up before beginning a sail across the ocean. Here are some examples of collaborators to consider:

- your research participants;
- the principal theorists related to the topic;
- experimental researchers in the field;
- critical readers to review your manuscript;
- co-researchers; and
- support personnel, such as librarians, consultants, and granting officers.

Perhaps the best way to attune your style is through practice and sharing—practice, by doing small pieces of research along the way, and sharing, by openly discussing your style with others, both on the conduct of inquiry and the feelings of being the inquirer.

Attunement With the Environment
and Available Resources

Knowledge is formed from a web of contributions. Without tying into the fabric of the times, a piece of research is lost, through being either redundant or disconnected. Attunement comes from contributing to the net of knowledge or facilitating change. One can achieve this by knowing what has happened in a field, knowing the struggles that have led to the current authoritative positions and important questions.

Inquiry is, by definition, open ended and unpredictable. Only the most mundane investigations can be expected to follow a well-established path and thus use only those resources—time, money, skills, data—that were originally anticipated. Research should be carefully planned, even if our hope is not to develop certainty but to escape from it. We find the unexpected by being explicit about how and what we expect to find.

A list of optimal resource planning might include:

- time—the task must be done within personal and other constraints;
- money—information should be gathered on what costs are likely to be incurred and probable sources of financing;
- skill—what skills are required to gain access to the information by exploring, manipulating, imagining;
- data processing—what tools are required, such as audio or video equipment or computers and appropriate software, access to databases and appropriate places on the Internet; and
- expertise—some sources will be incomprehensible, some techniques will require long experience to perform; therefore, it may be critical to gain access to leaders in the field of the investigation, and the willingness to track them down and converse.

As a professional, a significant element of the conduct of inquiry is how to plan for the resources needed for the methods chosen. An informative piece on this topic is the lead article in M. Patricia Golden's *The Research Experience* (1976).

In this chapter, we have given you more questions and things to think about than we have given you answers. That is precisely because a mark of competence and expertise in any field, including research, is knowing what things to think about and what considerations are relevant. We believe that the scholarly practitioner must be aware of the questions that need to be asked and answered for a piece of work to count as scholarly research.

Cultures of Inquiry and Research Traditions

I n Chapter 1, we pointed out that a major source of confusion and overload in the human and social sciences today is the proliferation and overlap of disciplines, philosophical orientations, theories, methods, research traditions, and so on within which a researcher must situate herself and among which she must choose.

■ Disciplines, Cultures of Inquiry, Theories, Methods, and Techniques

Inquiry in the social sciences takes place at the intersection of disciplines, cultures of inquiry, theories, methods, and techniques. A *discipline* is an established field of social sciences knowledge that has, over time, developed standing and recognition within the academic community and the world at large. Until the late nineteenth and early twentieth centuries, universities were divided into the fields (faculties) of philosophy, medicine, theology, and law. Philosophy was divided into natural philosophy and moral philosophy. Natural philosophy turned into the disciplines of physics, chemistry, biology, astronomy, zoology, and so on. In the nineteenth century, moral philosophy, which had come to include social and political philosophy, turned into the disciplines of history (which is at the boundary of the humanities and social sciences), economics, psychology, sociology, government (which later became political science), and anthropology. Later, other professional fields that drew on the knowledge and research in the social sciences developed, including business, communications (which also drew from literary criticism and the humanities), education, graduate nursing, and social work.

A *culture of inquiry* is a chosen modality of working within a field, an applied epistemology or working model of knowledge used in explaining or understanding reality. Persons from various disciplinary backgrounds may work within the same culture of inquiry. In fact, in all of the disciplines except anthropology and history, probably the majority of researchers work within the culture of inquiry of quantitative and behavioral science. However, in most departments, there are some who work in cultures of inquiry outside this mainstream. Departments of anthropology consist mostly of persons working as ethnographers, because this method was developed and perfected within that discipline. However, increasingly persons from outside anthropology are using ethnographic methods. There are phenomenologists from various departments, including sociology, education, nursing, political science, and psychology. Hermeneutics is concentrated in history and communications departments, although some scholars in sociology, psychology, and other departments are using hermeneutics.

Theories of social organization and of human behavior cluster in various disciplines, but they also overlap. Some of the major theorists, such as Marx, Weber, and Durkheim, spanned several fields within the social and human sciences. In addition, it is important to note that the term *human sciences* was developed in order to detract from the idea that persons in these disciplines all worked within the quantitative and behavioral science culture of inquiry. Each discipline in the social sciences frames its own history largely in terms of the development of the theories of the social sciences in relation to their discipline and in relation to the research traditions that developed within them.

In addition to overlapping theories, disciplines overlap in their orientations to methods. *Methods* are ways of understanding and interpreting data. For example, within each culture of inquiry, there are several methods of approaching the work. Within phenomenology, there is the method of describing typifications within social lifeworlds and the method of describing the essences of discrete phenomena. Within quantitative and behavioral science culture there are experimental methods, survey methods, path analysis methods, and so on. However, at times, some methods will be used in several cultures of inquiry.

Finally, specific research techniques are used to implement methods. To conduct survey research, for example, one must master the techniques of questionnaire design and data analysis. In phenomenological research, one must learn how to bracket aspects of an experience in order to fully describe remaining aspects.

Any culture of inquiry or research method, even our three primary cultures—phenomenology, hermeneutics, and critical social science—may be carried out mechanistically or superficially. One may ritualize them or their procedures and hence not carry out research in these traditions in a mindful way. For example, there are researchers who know they wish to avoid mathematical and statistical techniques. They find out that some phenomenological studies involve interviewing a small number of persons and transcribing these interviews, looking for themes. They decide this method is palatable. They design a study, using this method to learn about a particular aspect of social life in a particular setting. They do not immerse themselves in the phenomenon or in the kind of discipline and consciousness required to become a phenomenologist. The result is a shallow study leaving the reader wondering what it all means. The same hollow process can be carried out within any culture of inquiry. This is like going into a culture without learning the language, asking your way around with a beginner's dictionary and reporting that you then have conducted research on that culture's way of life. Although you may be able to impress outsiders with the results, those who live there may find your study to be ludicrous.

A cartoon image comes to mind. A young person in an expensive business suit knocks on the front door and asks the person opening it, "I am conducting a sociological study of lower middle-class life. May I plug in my tape recorder?" Even if the homeowner let him in, one is not convinced that, even with sophisticated techniques of analysis, he will get the point. By a similar token, a researcher may think it appealing to be an ethnographer, because, on the surface, it seems as if it means getting involved in a setting that intrigues you and taking notes that you later glean for information. Becoming an ethnographer really requires immersion in a setting over a considerable period of time and use of a number of techniques. In order to properly carry out a culture of inquiry, you should be prepared to become a participant in that culture, interacting with other scholars in that culture by attending conferences, exchanging papers, taking classes, and so on.

To become a skilled inquirer within any culture of inquiry, you should

- read research written within that approach, both articles and books;
- read works on the theory of the approach, including its epistemology and methodology;
- write reviews of such work;
- attend conferences at which such work is presented;
- become involved in collaborative projects within the approach;
- do exercises using the method or aspects of the method; and
- collaborate with skilled practitioners in the culture.

In one sense, research methodologies may be looked at as tools an inquirer may pick up and use at his or her convenience. However, like any good tools, they cannot simply be picked up and used without developing the skills for using them. Anyone may pick up a bow and arrow and try to shoot it; not everyone is an archer. And many archers do not aim properly, or have sufficient range or endurance to hit a bull's-eye with their arrows.

Terms and Their Connotations

By *cultures of inquiry* we mean general types of inquiry based on differing paradigms of knowledge, such as phenomenological, ethnographic, quantitative and behavioral, historical, or action research. An alternate, in some ways preferable, term would be *working epistemology, epistemology in practice,* or *applied epistemology,* but we will use *culture of inquiry* to emphasize that learning an applied epistemology is not a purely conceptual matter but involves being socialized into the values, norms, and practices of the community of inquirers who work within that epistemology. It is important to bear in mind that research is a human enterprise, carried on by communities of scholars and practitioners who learn their craft by way of both formal study and informal example. Within a particular community, researchers will serve apprenticeships, read one another's studies, exchange unpublished papers, publish articles in journals refereed according to community standards of scholarship, and, in general, acquire similar languages with which to understand their common research endeavor. Research, in other words, must be understood as much as a social process as it is an engagement with an object of study. One is socialized into a particular culture of inquiry both by reading studies regarded (within a particular community) as exemplars and, eventually, by conducting one's own research.

Nevertheless, we use the word *culture* with a caveat. These types of inquiry do not grow out of groups of tightly knit collaborators. There are ongoing conflicts and controversies within each of them. Most social science researchers would shrug their shoulders and wonder what you were talking about if you asked them, "Which culture of inquiry do you ascribe to?" In normal usage, *culture* implies shared values, norms, and language. This is to some extent true of these cultures of inquiry, but remember that cultures also contain subcultures and deviant and rebellious members.

A culture of inquiry or working epistemology is not the only, or even the primary, context that shapes a research study. Equally important is the *research tradition* in which it is situated, that is an evolving body of inquiry into a particular topic using a particular method. We shall go into research traditions in some detail below. Here we emphasize the epistemological dimension because of our belief that researchers need to be conscious of their philosophical and epistemological assumptions.

To what extent can a culture of inquiry be regarded as "scientific"? The answer to this question hinges on the meaning of science. As we will argue later, the model of science popularly associated with the natural sciences—cool, detached observation; highly mathematical modeling; quantitative measurement; predictions—seldom adequately captures what goes on in the human sciences. Human beings, unlike atoms and molecules, talk back. They think, they live in a world where "things" have symbolic rather than fixed meanings, and they are capable of reflecting on their world (including the "findings" of social scientists) and altering their behavior as a result. As a consequence, whenever you see the term *science* in this book, you should put mental quotation marks around it. By "science" we mean nothing more than a commitment to using rational procedures and arguments to bring about results that achieve broad agreement among a community of scholars. Although the goal of science is understanding, the nature of that understanding will vary according to the particular culture of inquiry. The scientific attitude entails a strong desire for understanding, a spirit of inquisitiveness, and a willingness to subject one's ideas and results to the critical scrutiny of others.

For many people, the word *research* conjures up a wealth of specific associations: people wearing white coats in laboratories or survey researchers conducting interviews over the telephone. Although many of these associations can, in fact, be traced to particular methods of inquiry that derive from the natural sciences, the human sciences use many other methods of inquiry that bear little resemblance to these. From their inception in the nineteenth century, the social sciences have investigated human phenomena through a wealth of techniques

- analyzing texts and documents to understand more about historical events, social change, or what a society or social group is or was like;
- observing and talking with members of specific societies or social groups in order to understand more about their cultures and their experiences;
- observing, communicating with, and taking notes on clinical patients and clients;
- participating in social action and analyzing its consequences;
- undertaking a fine-grained analysis of one's own and other people's subjective experience;
- interpreting the meaning of literary, artistic, and musical creations;
- formulating the rules that underlie language, communication, and interaction.

New techniques of inquiry continue to be formulated. In fact, some of the most interesting lines of research currently being undertaken in the human sciences use methods that did not even exist 25 years ago (conversational analysis and social network analysis are two examples).

These methods are major forms of human science research. Yet none of them occurs in a laboratory, and few of them rely primarily or even significantly on statistical data analysis. Few of them follow the sacred "scientific method" that most of us were taught in high school and college: Make some observations, develop a hypothesis about the observations, then test the hypothesis. This method is used for only a narrow set of problems in the human sciences.

So, it is not at all the case that there is something like a unified "scientific method" that governs all intellectual inquiry in the human sciences, and every one that has ever been proposed has been soundly attacked immediately on its formulation. Research need not involve experiments, statistics, computers, or hypotheses, although it may. It may involve interacting with human participants, but it may not if it is based primarily on documents or analyzing demographic data.

Method and Technique

In the context we are presenting, *research* simply means structured inquiry—trying to answer some question or questions using some appropriate method likely to produce generally valid and reliable knowledge. In most cases, this will mean using a method that already exists and has already been used by other investigators, although it may need to be tailored to specific circumstances. The method will need to have been chosen because of its suitability to the question being asked.

A research method is not primarily a technique. It is, rather, a coherent way of going about answering a question and may resemble a guideline more than a recipe. Many researchers, for example, who do qualitative, ethnographic, or historical research, do not use research "techniques" at all, at least not in the narrow sense of laboratory procedures or statistical data analyses. Rather, they gather material from or about human beings and look for patterns of coherence, often using a combination of previous knowledge, intuition, and creativity to find patterns. Of course, because they are trained in their field, they know the kinds of patterns that have been found by other investigators. This gives them a foundation on which to proceed; it is a method. They may use techniques as part of their method. For example, a person looking for correlations among census data may analyze them with a particular kind of statistical procedure. A person looking for patterns of meaning in transcripts of people that he or she has interviewed may use a particular numerical code to classify the material. But those are not research methods. It is the method that dictates the use of a technique, but the technique is not the method. The method is a way of answering a question by selecting, approaching, and making sense out of information and fitting it into a wider intellectual context.

The quantitative–qualitative distinction is used in much social science literature. Although we occasionally have used the terms *quantitative* and *qualitative* in this book, we have generally avoided using them as primary classifications of cultures of inquiry or research methods. This is because a too rigid use of the terms may distort genuine similarities and differences among different kinds of inquiry and tend to encourage people to make a priori choices about research methods based largely on whether they involve the use of numbers rather than on other, usually more relevant, considerations.

Within the social sciences, a large number of cultures of inquiry have developed over time, each with its own assumptions about the nature of knowledge and the appropriate methodology for obtaining correct understanding. During the past two decades in particular, there has been a fertile discussion among research practitioners over the nature of knowledge itself. Many of the old beliefs and methods have been called into question by new approaches with radically different viewpoints. There is no universally right or wrong culture of inquiry; each has its own strengths and limitations, providing a spotlight that illuminates a particular facet of reality.

A culture of inquiry is not a research method in the usual sense of that concept. A research method is an actual way of going about observing, describing, and understanding phenomena; often, it is a set of rather precise procedures for doing so. A culture of inquiry is a general approach to studying the world that may include a number of different research methods. But it uses a more or less consistent set of methods employed to obtain knowledge about some feature of the social world.

For example, within the cultures of inquiry discussed next, we have included ethnography, phenomenology, hermeneutics, and historical cultures of inquiry. But each one of these includes a variety of research methods, sometimes dozens of them. Ethnography, which studies the culture and life of groups, organizations, and societies, includes methods that focus on the conceptual categories used by a group, on the group's rituals and symbols, and on the material practices of the group. It may use description of what is observed by the ethnographer or draw on in-depth interviews with the research participants. It may attempt to eliminate the observer's role and produce a neutral description, or it may give a significant place to the ethnographer's subjective reactions to the people studied.

The ethnographic culture of inquiry is a family of related research methods, not a research method in itself. In some cases, advocates of a particular research method within a culture of inquiry may reject another method within that culture and consider it fallacious, misleading, primitive, or worthless. A culture of inquiry is more a family of research methods than a method itself. It is simply a way of grouping approaches to knowledge according to a few relevant similarities.

The same is true of every other culture of inquiry. Phenomenological methods differ according to the level of experience on which they focus—cognitive, psychological, or social—as well as according to whether their data are of consciousness or of communication. Cultural historians differ in their methods from political and intellectual historians.

Scholars working on particular problems will often draw on disparate methods to aid them, sometimes leading to important cross-fertilizations or syntheses among different research methods or cultures of inquiry. In the multidisciplinary context of the social sciences today, this is as much the rule as the exception. For example, some historians today are increasingly using approaches that derive from ethnography, and others are drawing on quantitative–behavioral methods. Interpretive approaches integrate phenomenology into hermeneutics.

Triangulated Research Design

Although we discuss each culture of inquiry as if it were distinct, some of the most interesting social research occurs when researchers use methods from several distinct cultures of inquiry to get a richer understanding of the phenomenon. The idea of *triangulation* is that different theories, cultures of inquiry, methods, and techniques will elucidate and cover different aspects of a situation. A design is "multiple triangulation" (Denzin, 1989) when you triangulate at several levels—for example, by using several theories, methods, techniques, and researchers on the same situation. Triangulated design is well suited for mindful inquiry, because it requires that the researcher be the clear center of the process, weaving together and describing the results from each point of the triangle.

The results from different aspects of the same research project may not be the same. For example, I (Valerie) conducted a study of Midtown Manor, a halfway house for men who were diagnosed with chronic alcoholism or schizophrenia. I worked with a group of students. I was interested in exposing what I thought was an inadequate and exploitative facility.

The study involved a student who worked at Midtown Manor as a nurse's aide and whose research role was as an ethnographer–participant–observer. Two female students acted as ethnographers, but in a different sense. They were informal visitors who got to know the men as if they were friends or relatives. One researcher was a graduate nurse who gave physical exams and checked medical records. A team of male researchers designed and executed interviews with each of the 55 men in the facility. I reviewed all of the results and also interviewed the director and the staff and looked at available records. The results from the different sectors painted divergent pictures of the men and their true circumstances. The nurse and participant–observer found them to have inadequate medical care and psychological and social services, poor diets, and inadequate recreational activities. The interviewers found them to be very satisfied with the Manor. The ethnographic visitors described them in such a way that they did not seem to belong in such a facility. The point here is that any one of the methodological approaches to understanding this situation alone would have been quite misleading.

My ethical dilemma as a researcher at the end of the project was that if I wrote up and made publicly available the results, the facility might be closed by the state. The men then would have nowhere to go but the streets or back into a large hospital, which they abhorred. (The participant–observer found out in conversation with the men that they thought the interviewers were working for the manager and that if they said anything critical about the Manor they would be asked to leave. Their dread of going back to the hospital motivated their praise.) Instead, I consulted with the owner (who was once the janitor there), and he made some positive changes, including hiring the nurse researcher to run the facility.

Wolfe (1984) conducted a triangulated study of a lesbian motorcycle club in Dallas. She happened to be the psychotherapist for several of the club members. She also did ethnographic research by hanging around in their bar and going with them on a bike trip, taking field notes. She distributed a questionnaire to all of them. Putting all of these data together, she was able to describe the way progress in the therapy of several of the members coincided with radical changes in their relationships with others in the group as well as in their presentation of self.

Mosley studied an African American family cemetery in Texas and its impact on the mental health of family members (1991). Her study consisted of a survey including a mental health scale, distributed by mail to the large extended family. She also did ethnographic observations and conducted in-depth interviews with family members at several family gatherings at the cemetery. She interpreted historical records of the cemetery that dated back to the antebellum days when her great-great-grandmother, who was the wife of a white Confederate general, was buried there. The levels of this triangulated design together gave a complete picture of this family and the role the cemetery played in their individual and shared lifeworlds.

■ Situating Yourself Within
Research Traditions

A research proposal would be quite incomplete if it merely situated itself within a culture of inquiry. This would be like answering the question, "Where were you born?" by naming the country but leaving out the city. At the stage of a concrete research proposal, the researcher will need to choose the exact methods to be used based on their appropriateness to the particular question being asked and the existing research relevant to that question. The researcher will want to situate herself in one or more concrete research traditions, which would be like adding the city to the country.

If a *culture of inquiry* is a broad family of approaches within a certain epistemology, that is, a conception of what knowledge is and how it is generated, a *research tradition* is something more concrete. It is a body of research on a particular subject that has evolved over time, carried out within either a particular culture of inquiry or using a particular research methodology, often within a particular theoretical framework. Thus, for example, research about gender roles carried out within the ethnographic culture of inquiry is a research tradition. So is the study of psychopathology within the phenomenological culture of inquiry. The study of organizational change within the culture of action research is a research tradition. And so is the analysis of the global economy using world-systems theory. In each of these research traditions, knowledge evolves or accumulates. Individual research studies build on previous research, respond to it, and critique it.

The notion of a research tradition includes that investigators within a tradition actually experience and think of it as such. That is, they refer to each other's work and to the same paradigmatic studies, and they discuss and define their methods within an evolving body of knowledge. Often, researchers within a common research tradition use the same terms and concepts, publish in the same journals, and may attend the same conferences.

Practical Tips on Creating
a Map of Research Traditions

(This section is by Paul Bundick, a graduate student.)

After reading the book by Randall Collins on *Four Sociological Traditions* (1994) and an excerpt from Stephen Toulmin's *Human Understanding* (1972), I selected a topic that (a) had a direct bearing on my professional work at the time and (b) had an established literature. I then set off to the library to scan the card files and periodicals. I spent about two or three days reading parts of books and articles and taking notes. I suppose one tip is not to get caught in the details of the various studies but to try and understand some of the underlying assumptions, theoretical frameworks, and key research questions.

What generally emerges quickly from your study is the broad outline of the dominant research tradition in a given area. Often, as in the case of cultural diffusion research, there are a few major research figures that help define the field. To better define this tradition, however, it is useful to go to the "alternative" literature. Every dominant tradition has its critics, and there is nothing like criticism to help define the boundaries of a research tradition with its implicit assumptions and often unconscious biases. These are better clarified by those outside a tradition. By moving back and forth between the mainstream and the alternative literature, one can begin to piece together various approaches.

One of the problems students will likely encounter is tracking a given subject matter through different disciplines—for example, social psychology, sociology, psychology, anthropology, communications, cross-cultural studies, and so on. Often, research in one discipline is isolated from another, not by difference in philosophical orientation but rather by the sociological barriers of a fragmented academia. The subject matter may even have a different name for the same basic phenomenon. Scanning basic textbooks in these different fields can give one clues to follow up in the card catalog. Journals are extremely valuable in following academic debates between members of a research tradition or identifying battles between research traditions. Bibliographies can be very useful in tracking down new sources.

A good way to map out a plan is to write down key words, concepts, approaches, assumptions, major figures, and so on, for each basic approach and develop a short profile for each tradition. A chronology is useful to order the events in time.

Constructing a map of research traditions is essentially the same exercise one should go through for a survey of a given discipline or subdiscipline. After all, a survey is really drawing a map of the various theories, identifying major questions, getting acquainted with leading researchers and theorists in a given area of knowledge.

Following are two examples of possible approaches to selecting diverse research traditions for a particular research interest (both by Jeremy):

Case 1: Electronically Mediated Sexuality

I am interested in the way in which electronic media—principally electronic mail, but also the telephone—affect the sexual and erotic experiences of people who engage in sexual communication, encounters, or interaction via those media. Here are some possible research traditions:

- phenomenological studies of communication and of sexuality (phenomenological culture of inquiry);
- psychoanalytically oriented studies of sexuality based on case histories (hermeneutic culture of inquiry);
- studies of the impact of media on experience and culture, of which there are examples that fall into both the comparative–historical and ethnographic cultures of inquiry;
- phenomenology and hermeneutics of technology and how it mediates our relation to the world and to others;
- reading general literature about phenomenology, hermeneutics, cultural studies, semiology, and historical research or ethnography, and looking at the strengths and weaknesses of these approaches for gaining understanding of my topic.

Case 2: Social Impact of Computer Technology

I am interested in a number of aspects of the ways in which computer technology is affecting our society and culture. At the level I want to study, my interest does not narrow down to a precise research question. But I want to explore the subject in depth as well as understand more about the cultures of inquiry. Some possibilities for research traditions include the following.

- the tradition of studying the labor process: Here, I have a number of theoretical choices, ranging from Marxian theory to sociotechnical theory, and cultures of inquiry ranging from comparative–historical to ethnographic or field research to quantitative and behavioral science research. As in other areas, there are strong links between particular cultures of inquiry and particular theories, but most major theories have connections with a few different cultures of inquiry.
- the effect of underlying metaphors in shaping culture: For example, there are comparative–historical, hermeneutic, and phenomenological methods of looking at the ways in which the underlying tools of a culture shape experience in that culture.
- Recent research about how people experience their interaction with computers or other tools and media that could be ethnographic or phenomenological.

■ Looking at Cultures of Inquiry

What follows will help you to understand the major cultures of inquiry that have proven fruitful within the scholarly community of the human and social sciences. It is not our purpose to express a preference for one over another but rather to help you choose cultures of inquiry and research traditions adequate to your research topic and compatible with your personal style. The cultures that shape the vast majority of work in the human and social sciences are first summarized and then discussed at length.

Although any delineation of cultures of inquiry is bound to be somewhat arbitrary, the following distinctions are commonly made and cover the vast majority of research designs. The principal cultures of inquiry can be identified as falling into the following categories:

- Phenomenology
- Hermeneutics
- Critical social science and critical theory
- Ethnography
- Quantitative and behavioral science
- Historical research
- Theoretical research
- Action research
- Evaluation research

Each of these will be briefly characterized in turn, paying special attention to four primary sets of questions:

1. What are the principal sorts of problems and concerns typically addressed within each tradition? For example, do studies generally concern themselves with aggregate patterns of human behavior or with detailed accounts of individual variations and nuances? Is the concern with identifying underlying social processes or with understanding the meaning of situations to participants? Are the major problems generally found at the level of individuals, groups, and organizations or whole societies, or do they cross-cut these distinctions? Are problems in the literature ultimately traceable to concerns arising out of ideas and theories or out of more tangible social concerns? Do writers in the field seem primarily concerned with the growth of pure knowledge and understanding, with changing the world, or with some combination of the two?

2. What are the underlying epistemological assumptions concerning the sources of knowledge? How do we know something to be "true"? Are truth claims taken as nonproblematic once certain safeguards are taken to ensure "objectivity"?

Or is such objectivity regarded as inherently impossible, rendering all truth claims subject to change in future research? Is there a single reality to which all research has access, provided it is properly done? Or are there multiple realities such that no particular study can claim to have discovered a universally valid truth? To what extent is the research itself regarded as helping to construct the reality it studies? What is the optimal outcome of the tradition? For example, do researchers consider a problem "solved" once they have successfully made predictions on the basis of their findings? Or are problems regarded as more open-ended, with explanation instead consisting of successfully influencing (rather than predicting) outcomes? Or does explanation consist of dispelling myths and misunderstandings about social processes that are taken for granted? You may find you wish to work within a culture of inquiry that makes different epistemological assumptions than those implied by mindful inquiry. Here is where it is important that you contextualize or bracket the work you do in this culture so that you may keep your center while you do the work. The process is similar to visiting a culture very different from your own, learning the language, and learning how to get along and accomplish your work within that culture. At the same time, you keep your identity with the original culture to which you return. Of course, there is a possibility that you will like the experience, perhaps so much so that you adopt these assumptions as primary. This is a process that anthropologists have experienced and that they term "going native."

3. What is the relationship between the researcher and the subject of research in each culture of inquiry? Is the researcher primarily a detached, dispassionate observer, or a fully engaged coparticipant? Is the researcher actively in charge or passively observing? Does the research entail manipulation of the subject, facilitation, or disengagement? Does the ideal study see itself as leaving the subject unchanged, or does it view such an outcome as an impossibility? A mindful inquirer will be able to function in different roles, bracketing prior assumptions in order to get a new insight from a different perspective. As a mindful inquirer, you will learn more about yourself as you take different stances and strengthen your ability to keep your center and focus. To accomplish this, it will be necessary to practice meditation or other centering techniques.

4. What is the nature of attunement between one's personal style and the culture of inquiry? Previously, we noted that all research involves some form of hands-on activity that requires a great deal of the researcher's time. Is this a "people" method, involving intimate contact with your research participants? Or is it more remote and detached, requiring instead that one spend long hours manipulating data in the privacy of his study or office? Are you more likely to be dealing with flesh-and-blood people, with numbers, or with both? Do most studies in the tradition seem to require outgoing, direct engagement with the setting and participants, or indirect contact and less interaction? Does most research seem to you to be focused and bottom-line in orientation or divergent and

open-ended? Is research typically grounded and concrete or abstract and theo-retical? Most important, how comfortable would you be if you were to person-ally conduct the studies that are a part of the culture of inquiry? Can you see yourself in the role of principal investigator?

In discussions of the different cultures of inquiry later in this book, we have followed up the idea that certain cultures of inquiry may be most suited to, or congruent with, people of particular personal characteristics. It does seem, on the face of it, that, independent of contents, an individual may be attracted to a certain mode of interacting with people, phenomena, or ideas. For example, it seems likely that a person who likes to read more than to converse will prefer historical research to fieldwork, and that, inversely, someone who thrives on interaction may prefer participant observation to either phenomenology or the analysis of census data.

A word of warning is called for. People of every personal interaction style have worked within every culture of inquiry, sometimes driven by the problem they are trying to solve and sometimes desiring precisely to extend themselves in new and unfamiliar ways of interacting. For example, a student we worked with who was terrified of using quantitative data analysis as part of her research but eventually did so because of the nature of her research questions ended up confessing to her committee, "I love statistics." Introverted researchers have discovered that immersing themselves in fieldwork was not only challenging but exciting, because it led them to discover hidden parts of themselves. All of the cultures of inquiry involve some mixture of subjective engagement with a particular research question and subject matter and the ability to be detached, critical, and reflective.

Do not let yourself be deterred from a research method because of your self-definition. Inversely, and more important, it would be a serious mistake to choose an approach to research purely on the basis of your current concepts of your personality without exploring what method makes the most sense for the research questions you are asking.

Phenomenological Inquiry

P henomenology is used to obtain knowledge about how we think and feel in the most direct ways. Its focus is what goes on within the person in an attempt to get to and describe lived experience in a language as free from the constructs of the intellect and society as possible. At its root, the intent is to understand phenomena in their own terms—to provide a description of human experience as it is experienced by the person herself.

"To the things themselves!" was the maxim of Edmund Husserl, a founder of phenomenological philosophy.

Phenomenology thus provides the irreducible datum of that human behavior that is logically prior to all social behavior. In ideal circumstances, the researcher, as self-observer or participant–observer, gains direct knowledge of the feelings and images of the research participant or subject so that the first conceptualization is as close to the experience as is technically possible. For example, the researcher may achieve this by an extended conversation organized around the phenomena of interest. Or a study might begin with an attempt to imitate the movements or facial expressions of another person doing a task related to the research. Ultimately, the researcher's report would be of his own personal understanding of the phenomena of interest.

Phenomenologists argue that such an understanding must precede research on such human concerns as fear, anxiety, the forms of motivation, and the processes of learning, creating, and deciding. They further argue that social scientists provide poor grounding for organizational theories or the conduct of research if their constructs have not been based in a phenomenological understanding of the ways in which feelings and thoughts are made public.

In classic usage, the term *phenomenology* means "the study of appearances" (from the Greek word *phenomenon,* "meaning appearance"). In current usage, introduced by Husserl, it means studying the ways in which things appear to consciousness and, therefore, also the way in which consciousness is structured such that things appear to it in the ways that they do. According to Husserl's phenomenology, consciousness is always "intentional" (Husserl, 1962). That is, it is always consciousness "of" something. Even a diffuse feeling of anxiety involves specific mental contents and a consciousness of objects as they present themselves within a horizon of anxiety. Inversely, everything that we know, we know as the object or correlate of some kind of consciousness. There is no such thing as a tree, pure and simple; it is always a tree-as-perceived, a tree-as-remembered, a tree-as-dreamed, a tree-as-conceptualized, and there are identifiable differences among all of these "trees."

Phenomenology attempts to rid us of ideas, which we sometimes take for granted, that we have about things in order to grasp them in their most essential nature, as they appear to consciousness prior to the constructs, ideologies, and myths that we make about them. It shares with most other forms of inquiry the calling into question of so-called commonsense and taken-for-granted ways of describing and defining things. But phenomenology, more than any other form of inquiry, attempts to get behind the most elementary experiences of everyday life to look at their inner structure and how the mind makes them what they are. It is a sort of intellectual X-ray vision. According to phenomenology, our experience of the world does not just happen to be the way that it is. Rather, it is constituted as such by our consciousness (Husserl, 1977).

The term *phenomenological research* is sometimes used loosely as equivalent to naturalistic research, or any research that pays attention to people's subjective experience. In a strict sense, this is an error. Whereas "naturalistic" research attempts to capture the way in which people in natural settings experience and describe their lives and the meanings that are part of them, phenomenology aims to get beneath the ways in which people conventionally describe their experience to the structures that underlie them, which may be quite different from everyday consciousness. In everyday life, for example, I do not pay attention to the differences between the structures of reality of waking and sleeping life. If one tree appears in my dream and another in my waking life, I refer to both of them, naturalistically, as trees and usually do not analyze the differences, phenomenologically, in the ways in which these trees present themselves to me. The confusion between these two modes of relating to experience arises partly out of phenomenology itself. In Husserl's later work, he introduced the concept of the lifeworld to refer to the cultural assumptions built into people's underlying ways of experiencing reality (Husserl, 1970).

The primary tool of the phenomenologist is the inquirer's own consciousness. Therefore, one can pick up a technique or two of the phenomenologist; however, this does not make one a phenomenologist nor does it make the results of one's research phenomenological. Because phenomenology is the study of objects of consciousness, and the foundational way to study consciousness is through studying your own consciousness, one must first become a phenomenologist in order to do phenomenology (Van Manen, 1990). To become a phenomenologist requires immersion in the writings and language of phenomenology.

In addition to reading phenomenology, the budding phenomenologist must write phenomenological descriptions of his own experience of phenomena. Phenomenologists search for essential or fundamental structures underlying experience. To locate these structures, one must be able to manipulate components to find out what must be there in order for such experience to occur. This variation in the structures of experience is usually done imaginatively—that is, within the consciousness of the phenomenologist. For example, if I am trying to describe the essence of fear, I may describe several memories of fear and look for what is common between them. I may find that all my fearful experiences involve a sense of loss of control, loss of breath, and other elements. I may also discover what aspects of any of those experiences are not necessary for there to be an experience of fear.

■ Typical Problems and Concerns

One uses a phenomenological approach when one wishes to understand, to gain access to the meaning of human phenomena as expressed through an individual. The occasion to use phenomenological methods arises, for example, when there is no established understanding of the phenomena and nothing closely related enough from which to make valid inferences, or there is a distrust of the prevailing description or explanation of some behavior of interest, a situation often arising when there has been a change in the prevailing culture that calls into question our old ideas and assumptions (e.g., our understanding of the conditions that lead a person to enter into the stages of mid-life change).

The overall research question that starts a phenomenological study could arise anywhere there is a concern for human behavior and meaning. One investigation compared the phenomenology of auto racing with playing the financial markets; another, the mentality of professional torturers. One famous study is of the personal experience of criminal victimization; another is of learning to use one's hand to play jazz piano. Phenomenological methods are not appropriate when one is trying to establish the pervasiveness of an attitude or behavior or to compare situations in order to predict or control.

■ The Raw Data of Phenomenological Research

The basic datum of phenomenology is the conscious human being. That datum, and the wealth of data of which it consists, is revealed by paying detailed attention to the structure of one's own consciousness or that of others. To the extent that phenomenological inquiry focuses on others, it involves listening to, watching, and generally engaging in empathic understanding of another person, although much phenomenological research does not involve interacting with human participants at all. Phenomenology draws on the most subjective of all data, so much so that the empirical and behavioristic sciences have even rejected the meaningfulness of a personal statement about internal states and, until very recently, denied the scientific usefulness of such information about feelings or memory. Such highly personal data are by nature not quantifiable in the raw form, for quantification relies on a social agreement process.

To the greatest degree possible, the observer must act to prevent the data from being prematurely structured into existing categories of thinking—a task made difficult by the typical scientific training of the researcher. One approach is to protect the data in their primitive state by using a recording device, doing as little editing and censoring as possible, and offering a clear psychological and linguistic critique of one's own perceptual and cognitive biases.

■ Phenomenological Methods of Gaining Understanding

The phenomenological position, fundamentally, is that any analysis will delimit the meaning of an observation. One gains understanding of an experience through empathy, coming to understand as the other with the aid of various tools that bring to consciousness the related elements of an idea, feeling, or situation. Understanding can be gained by a study that includes empathic immersion, slowing down and dwelling, magnification and amplification of the situation, suspension of belief, the employment of intense interest, turning from objects to their lived meaning, and questioning directed by the researcher to her own judgment (e.g., "How am I understanding this phenomenon such that this statement reveals it?"). Data analysis involves a deconstructing and reconstructing process somewhat similar to grounded theory analysis. Through imaginative variations, the researcher asks if all constituents, distinctions, relations, and themes could be different, or even absent, while still presenting the participant's psychological reality. The researcher is thus regarded as the cocreator of the transcribed narrative, generated through interviewing or through an experimental situation. Once the basic record is created, the material may be treated as a public document and handled accordingly. It could be subjected to quantitative analyses or hermeneutic interpretations. It becomes the raw material on which other scientific research can be based.

■ The Nature of Explanation and the Nature of Knowledge

Phenomenology is not ultimately interested in explanation. The question typically asked by a phenomenologist is not, "What causes X?" but, "What IS X?" In other words, it is interested in the essential features of types of experience or consciousness. For example, a phenomenologist will be interested not in what causes anxiety, but on what anxiety is; not in why middle-class people behave in certain ways, but in what the experience of being a middle-class person is really like. Most important in the phenomenological work is the acceptance of mentation and intentionality; people are regarded as having internal awareness and preferences on which they base decisions and choices. Behavior is not simply a stimulus–response loop, nor is it the output of a cybernetic machine. Also of importance is that meaning is constructed both in internal conscious and unconscious processes and in interpersonal exchanges through which the meaning is made social. Phenomenology does not explain, but rather it creates understanding among the set of observers and observed. In this sense, it is not a research procedure but a means of cocreation that makes public and manageable the lived experience.

■ Forms of Analysis in Phenomenology

Textual Phenomenological Analysis

Some inquirers have found it useful to take techniques of textual analysis developed from the analysis of phenomenological protocols or descriptions. Such analyses are little different from standard content analysis procedures used in quantitative research. The psychological phenomenology of the Duquesne school is known for the development of these procedures (Giorgi, Fischer, & Von Eckartsberg, 1971). It is ironic that such techniques may further separate the analysis from the lived experience.

Cultural–Social Phenomenology

Another form of phenomenological work is cultural or social phenomenology as developed by Alfred Schutz and his followers (Schutz, 1970). Schutz took Husserl's concept of the lifeworld and developed an analysis of the essential structures of any lifeworld (Schutz & Luckmann, 1973). For example, all lifeworlds are based on "stocks of common knowledge" that are shared by members of the lifeworld. Each lifeworld has multiple realities within it, as members participate in differential fashion. Persons orient themselves to each other based on systems of typifications—that is, ways we have of knowing and relating to each other. Even in what Schutz called a "we–relationship" with our close intimates and companions, these typifications change over time, sometimes radically. Helmut Wagner, who wrote an intellectual biography of Schutz (Wagner, 1983a), gives an example of a man radically changing his typifications of his wife. After 20 years of a marriage, in which every now and then she would say she was leaving but actually stayed, she one day said she was leaving, packed her suitcase, left, and did not return. Wagner's typification of her was radically altered. For an insightful analysis of marital and intimate relationships that draws on this phenomenological tradition and is not only intellectually valuable but can also help one think in a new and constructive way about one's own intimate relationships, see the article by Berger and Kellner (1970).

Political Phenomenology

Leo Strauss brought phenomenological critique into the world of political science. Strauss argued that the positivist turn taken by political science could lead to moral nihilism (1959). Hwa Yol Jung offers a profound critique of behaviorist (positivist) political science, which he says fosters a "crisis of political understanding." The parsimonious logic of political behaviorism is no guarantee that objective truth is obtained. As Jung said, "The behavioralist self is not the human being, not the human body or human soul, but rather the scientific subject, the limit of the world—not a part of it" (1979, p. 108).

Ethnomethodology

Ethnomethodology is a research approach that developed directly out of phenomenology. The term *ethnomethodology* was coined by Harold Garfinkel. It means "the study of folk methods for making . . . [one's] own culture make sense" and to allow one to accomplish one's tasks. Garfinkel studied how a man who had a sex change operation managed the task of changing his identity to that of a woman (Garfinkel, 1967). He and his students also studied how juries make decisions, how astronomers negotiate the announcement of scientific discoveries, how mathematicians create new concepts, and how doctors make diagnoses.

Conversation Analysis

Others in this tradition have developed and refined techniques of analyzing transcripts of conversations in order to uncover universal patterns of relationships. For example, there is a limited number of ways in which we enter and exit conversations, greet each other, and insult each other. Don Zimmerman and his students are conducting research using conversation analysis methods to study the ways police and medical emergencies are handled by dispatchers (Clayman & Zimmerman, 1987; Whalen & Zimmerman, 1990a, 1990b). Conversation analysis is covered in George Psathas's *Conversation Analysis: The Study of Talk-in-Interaction* (1995).

■ Relationship Between Researcher and Subject Matter

The phenomenological researcher becomes the instrument of articulation. To become so requires that there develop as deep an empathy between the researcher and the relevant topics as is possible. In some work, the researcher is also the subject, as in David Sudnow's *Ways of the Hand: The Organization of Improvised Conduct* (1978), a study of his experience of learning to play jazz piano. In other work, where there are separate research participants, the researcher may prepare for the interviews by immersing herself in experience that matches or approaches that of the participants. The research must create an in-dwelling awareness.

Personal Characteristics of the Researcher

This research mode is as thoroughly experiential as any that is possible, so the researcher must have the qualities that will allow him or her to let data come, losing one's self in the pacing and the language of the other. Yet it is not a passive nor even a purely reflective task because it calls on the observers, if they are studying human participants, to cocreate and test with the observed persons the understandings they articulate. It requires the patience to make detailed recordings and validate both them and any interpretations with the source. It also calls for skills in social interaction and a pervasive empathic manner. At the same time, it is one of the most resolutely analytical modes of inquiry, requiring a willingness to engage in dissection of and reflection on the nature of consciousness and meaning.

■ Critique of Phenomenology

Some criticism of phenomenology has been that the phenomenologist focuses on the consciousness of the inquirer as the central point of study and that, therefore, it is "solipsistic." *Solipsism* is a philosophical school of thought that holds that all one can know is one's self. Phenomenological work, however, as all scholarly work, takes place in a community of fellow scholars. For example, when Levesque-Lopman presented her work on the phenomenology of childbirth, she described certain essential aspects of the experience as glorious. Other phenomenologists in the audience found that to be totally outside their experience. After further investigation, it was discovered that the word *childbirth* describes several distinct kinds of experience with some essential features. Another way in which phenomenological experience, when shared, yields new insight was when Moynihan (1996) shared her descriptions of "walking the mystical path with practical feet." Her description included an example of how she was capable of harboring murderously aggressive feelings. By contrast, McLane (1996) presented an analysis of the consciousness of an attorney who brutally murdered his wife and children. By comparing the descriptions, it was found that Moynihan and the murderer had much in common, except that the murderer did not reflect on his murderous and aggressive side and, in fact, thought himself justified and blameless in his actions.

Examples

Over the past few years, there has been a flurry of publications of phenomenological studies done in a very disciplined way, often with results delightful to read. Kockelmans's *Phenomenological Psychology: The Dutch School* includes descriptions of a hotel room, driving a car, and falling asleep (1987). Casey's *Remembering: A Phenomenological Study* is a major work of a central cognitive function (1987), as Clifton's (1983) *Music as Heard: A Study in Applied Phenomenology* is of musical experience. The classical sociological phenomenologist was Schutz, whose studies, such as "The Stranger" (1976c) and "Making Music Together" (1976b) are gathered in his *Collected Papers* (1976a). The ethnomethodological school founded by Garfinkel attempts to synthesize phenomenological and ethnographic inquiry. See Garfinkel's *Studies in Ethnomethodology* (1967) as well as Heritage's *Garfinkel and Ethnomethodology* (1984). Castaneda's *The Teachings of Don Juan* (1968) is a famous, although controversial, example of this approach. Davis's *Smut: Erotic Reality/Obscene Ideology* (1983) applies phenomenology to the study of sexual experience.

Some of the most interesting phenomenological studies are those carried out by phenomenological psychiatrists and clinical psychologists, including the existential analysts whose work is derived from phenomenology. See, for example, Binswanger's *Being-in-the-World* (1967); the collection *Existence,* edited by May, Angel, and Ellenberger (1958); and Fischer's *Theories of Anxiety* (1988), which explicitly compares a phenomenological theory of anxiety with those of other psychological schools; and Laing's brilliant *The Divided Self* (1965).

Phenomenology is by no means primarily a study of personal or psychological experience. Because it sees all objects as objects for consciousness, and all consciousness as consciousness "of" something, rather than "bare" consciousness, phenomenology is interested in the world as much as it is in consciousness, or, perhaps more accurately, it is interested in the relationship between consciousness and the world. As a consequence, phenomenology discovers, appropriates, and analyzes new objects in response to the historical situation. In his important recent study, *Technology and the Lifeworld: From Garden to Earth* (1990), Ihde develops a general phenomenological theory of technology with direct policy implications for the social and political management of technology in today's world situation. In a similar way, the growing awareness of the importance of the human relation to the environment is reflected in emerging phenomenological studies of place, space, habitat, and the environment. Casey has recently published *Getting Back Into Place: Toward a Renewed Understanding of the Place-World* (1993), a major, thorough analysis of the nature of "place," a realm of experience and being that is increasingly important in our world. Studies by phenomenologically oriented geographers, architects, and urban designers and planners can be found in *Dwelling, Place and Environment: Towards a Phenomenology of Person and World* (Seamon & Mugerauer, 1989) and *Dwelling, Seeing, and Designing: Toward a Phenomenological Ecology* (Seamon, 1993). The phenomenology of place and space can help us to appreciate and design our habitat and environment in a meaningful way. Finally, a major contribution to the analysis and understanding of one of global society's most important problems—racism and ethnic, cultural, and religious hatred—is a phenomenological study, Sartre's *Reflections on the Jewish Question,* published in English as *Anti-Semite and Jew* (1976). Sartre uses existential phenomenology to understand anti-Semitism not as a set of ideas, beliefs, or feelings but as a way of being-in-the-world.

To paraphrase, to believe that phenomenology is focused primarily on the personal experience of the researcher or her subjects or on subjective experience cut off from the real world is a mistake. Although phenomenology may focus on personal experience, one of its primary goals is to understand the real world. It simply recognizes that the real world is given to us in consciousness. Phenomenology is not, as it were, "gazing at your own navel," but gazing "through your navel" at the world that is given to you, for consciousness is part of the umbilical cord that attaches us to the world.

Doing phenomenology means that the researcher will have a philosophical outlook, with keen awareness of the flavor and style of phenomenological writing. In general, phenomenological work requires that the researcher become a phenomenologist in that the work requires a unique approach to seeing and understanding the world and writing about it. Writing rich descriptions of phenomena and their settings is an important skill for phenomenologists. It is ironic that there is a tendency in some of the literature to equate the technique of in-depth interviewing, transcribing, and searching for themes with true phenomenology. Some of this work is actually done in a mechanistic manner, outside of the spirit and epistemological assumptions of phenomenology.

Hermeneutic Inquiry
and Ethnography

The term *hermeneutics* simply means "the art and science of interpretation." The term derives from the Greek god Hermes, messenger of the gods, who was killed for bringing unwelcome news to the community. (The phrase "don't kill the messenger" comes from this.)

Hermeneutics was brought into broad usage by theologians, such as Schleiermacher, to interpret the Bible. As the conditions of modern society and culture differed so considerably from those of the Bible, the need for interpretation of the text in order to discover and apply its meaning in the modern context became increasingly clear. For people living within a Christian frame of reference, this need for interpretation was essential if they were to be able to live a Christian life, especially as they became increasingly conscious of the historical gap between our time and the time of Jesus. Hermeneutics originated as a way to meet this need.

A concrete, familiar, secular example of the practical employment and relevance of hermeneutics in contemporary life is the ongoing process of interpreting the U.S. Constitution. At one level, because the Constitution is a brief document containing general principles, an act of interpretation is necessary to apply those principles to the details of social and juridical life. What does "freedom of speech" really mean in a concrete situation? Because things have changed since the time of the framing of the Constitution, a second level of interpretation is needed: How can the Constitution be translated into today's terms? How, for example, do we apply the concept of freedom of speech to speech broadcast via mass media that did not exist in the eighteenth century? How do we apply the concept of freedom of assembly in a world in which an assembly might include a million individuals? Answering these questions requires a third level of interpretation—when they created the Constitution, what did the authors intend? A person's intent, especially when it involves application to an unexpected or unprecedented situation, cannot be discovered merely by inspection. Knowing a person's intent in everyday life often involves taking into consideration not only her words but her tone of voice, gestures, and actions. So we must bring into our interpretation of the Constitution the wider context of the authors, their lives, their political actions, their religious beliefs, and their relationships with their fellows.

This brings us to a fourth level of interpretation—the level of history. To understand the wider context, we need to know something of its history. Interpreting the concept of freedom of speech requires us to learn, for example, what "freedom" meant in the eighteenth century. This means investigating the historical, cultural, and political traditions of thought about freedom: Where did the notion of freedom of speech come from? When we carry out this historical investigation, however, we discover a fifth level, namely that our understanding of this history is itself shaped by our own point of departure in the present. Because the impact of speech is changed by new media, every new medium makes us see the speech of the past in a new light. For example, with the invention of the radio, a person could sit in a room, talk into a microphone, and have his speech transmitted instantly to a group of people on the other side of the world. This made people perceive speech prior to radio in a new way. We could suddenly see all of the invisible, taken-for-granted limitations of pre-radio speech. Now, with the advent of computer networks, we see communication in ways that differ from radio, which means that we will probably also gain a new retrospective understanding of the eighteenth century and its notions of freedom of speech. So understanding the historical context is not a one-time act independent of the context of the knower. Our own ongoing history makes us continually reinterpret the past.

We see that it is not even possible for the authors to have had intentions, in the everyday sense of intention, regarding future things that they could not have even imagined. Does it really make sense to say that Thomas Jefferson had an intention regarding computer networks? Can we say that we in the present can have intentions regarding the quality of life during space travel to distant stars? Whatever intentions we discern in the eighteenth-century authors regarding certain aspects of the present are not only interpretations, they are in effect constructions. But these constructions cannot be arbitrary or fantastic. We need them to ensure the meaning and continuity of our own lives in the present. They need to be as compelling and "objective" as we can make them. Hermeneutics makes us aware that, in a reciprocal interpretive process, the present is interpreted in terms of the texts of the past and their historical context, although those texts and that context are themselves interpreted in terms of the present.

Going back to Hermes, his other areas of responsibility, such as invention and cunning, perhaps testify to the power of interpretation to change the course of events. The search for new meanings occurs when problem events challenge the routinized patterns of life, when the taken-for-granted aspects of the life-world are not happily accepted. New meanings are elicited at historical times in which accepted ways have become problematic for a group in power or a group that challenges that power. Mannheim, in *Ideology and Utopia* (1985), wrote of such conflicts of interpretation. *Ideologies* are interpretive frameworks that support the status quo. *Utopias* are those that support alternative structures of power.

Hermeneutics may be viewed as relevant to many levels of the research process. As discussed earlier, hermeneutics is a way to view the overall process of any research project, regardless of what methods and techniques may be used within the project. Reason and Rowan, in *Human Inquiry: A Sourcebook of New Paradigm Research* (1981), noted that hermeneutics is just one example of an everyday process through which persons make sense of their world. All understanding is hermeneutical, taking place in time, history, and culture, and to a very large degree determined by our finite existence. Modern hermeneutics argues that we cannot ever totally transcend our historical position, our viewpoint; therefore, the prejudgments that we bring to our understanding are largely culturally predetermined. Once this is realized, it is clear that we must distinguish between some notion of an objective understanding and an interpretation that is valid for all people who share the same worldview at a given time in history.

Hermeneutics is a reverse epistemology from research processes devoted to the prediction and control of the behavior of others. The hermeneutic inquirer is the object of change. (This does not preclude that there would be change in the object of interpretation as well.) Hermeneutics involves a movement back and forth between looking at the object of inquiry—texts—and analyzing their meaning. As it has become recognized that all social science investigations involve interpretation, the idea of what "text" is to be interpreted has been expanded (Brown, 1987; Ricoeur, 1981), although the limits of what can be regarded as text are controversial (Giddens, 1986). Texts include conversations, classroom interaction, and even clothing and fashion.

■ Strategies for Analyzing Texts

There are various hermeneutic strategies for engaging in textual analysis. It is important to be aware of them because they yield different results. Also, there may be particular affinities between texts and certain interpretive strategies (Bentz, 1993).

In contradistinction to the ideal of distance from the object of study promulgated by positivist science, hermeneutics contends that the closer you are to the object, the better you are able to interpret the meanings accurately. The best example of this is the way baby talk, which is sometimes incomprehensible to outsiders, is readily understood by mothers. The closer you are to the source of the text, the more valid your interpretation is likely to be. This doctrine was promulgated by the nineteenth-century hermeneutic theorist of history Johann Gustav Droysen. Understanding can be seen as a fusion of two perspectives— that of the phenomenon itself and that of the interpreter. This is an ancient approach to research and understanding. It was once limited to the study of ancient religious texts that needed to be reinterpreted in light of modern language and culture, but in the nineteenth century, its traditions were borrowed to provide a sound methodological basis for historical research and for the humanities at large. Its present form can be traced back to Wilhelm Dilthey and Martin Heidegger.

Droysen's Hermeneutics

Droysen's classification is helpful because it helps to clarify which level of interpretation persons in a situation and analysts of the situation (from news reporters to experts to researchers) have used. For example, Andrew Cunanan allegedly killed several homosexual men in Minnesota and noted designer Gianni Versace in Miami. Cunanan was known to be gay, thought to have had relationships of some sort with these men, and to have had an incredible memory for persons' names. It is instructive to look at media commentary about the event in relation to Droysen's modalities: (a) Interpretation of the immediate consequences—when former friends and partners of Cunanan were interviewed by the media, they said they were worried that they might be on his hit list. It was said that Cunanan had AIDS and was trying to get revenge by killing those who may have infected him. (b) Psychological interpretations of motives—deeper explanations were sought in interviews with his former schoolmates and teachers, who described him as being a loner, a social climber, and insecure, seeking to curry favor by displaying signs of wealth that he did not possess. His father said that he could not have done these things because he was raised a good Catholic and was an altar boy. (c) Social and cultural interpretations—Cunanan grew up in a single-parent family (his father left when he was young) and in poverty. He felt unaccepted by his peers in high school. The cultural climate is one in which there is little support for the mainstream integration of a gay person who is also an immigrant. (d) Moral and ethical interpretations—we did not find this level of interpretation in the media reports we read.

Droysen contended that social scientists must offer all four levels of interpretation for a complete hermeneutics. The example points out the ultimate connection between theory and hermeneutics. Forms of interpretation are dependent on the type and level of theory used. One could add to Droysen's frame economic, anthropological, biological, and other levels. Each social science discipline is itself a range of hermeneutic strategies represented by the body of theory available in that discipline. For example, sociology includes symbolic inter-action, conflict, phenomenological, exchange, evolutionary, socioeconomic, and other interpretive strategies. Anthropology includes theories of culture, kin-ship, and change.

Ricoeur's Hermeneutics

Paul Ricoeur's hermeneutics brings in the element of the analysis of the' uses of language within a text (1981). Texts have peculiar structures, such as sentence length, grammar, syntax, and rhetorical dimensions. Ricoeur also en-courages one to look for the world implied but beyond the text itself. Because modern hermeneutics arose in the nineteenth century as part of the process of interpreting the text of the Bible—a text written in an ancient culture, from the perspective of the present, and at the same time using its interpreted meaning in the present—it was natural for this process of transcultural, transhistorical, tex-tual interpretation to be described as a process of transmitting divine messages. The term has been extended to cover all processes of interpretation that mediate between and incorporate different cultural and historical meanings and traditions through the analysis of texts and symbols in their cultural and historical context with a view to applying or extending the meanings and traditions. In other words, the interpreter is concerned with the "objective meaning" of ideas or symbols and with what they have to say to us. A hermeneuticist sees his culture and self as the product of a tradition that he is both perpetuating and changing through the act of interpretation.

■ Typical Problems and Concerns

The chief concern that leads one to hermeneutics is the need to have an enriched understanding of the context of a piece of data, the setting that gives it meaning and out of which it arises. The purpose of hermeneutics, according to Barrell and others, is to provide contextual awareness and perspective (Barrell, Aanstoos, Richards, & Arons, 1987). It may serve as a step toward a more formal investi-gation along more objective lines, spiraling in on a topic with newly discovered meanings to aid in formulating the analytic questions. It is intended to give meaning to a fabric of data, rather than predict or control some particular event. So it might be used to interpret the events in the life of an organization or indi-vidual in order to contribute to a theory of leadership or of social transformation.

Hermeneutic research interprets data considered to be so essentially embed-ded in their context that the assumption of the natural science model of inde-pendence of events from the specific time and place will not lead to under-standing. Thus, one may use a hermeneutic approach to understand a historical event, make sense of an artifact, analyze the origin of language, or extract from a mass of data a question that merits formal research. Research questions might be: What were the social foundations of scientific management? What can be learned from the use of toys by autistic children? What did Freud really mean by "unconscious"? What is the meaning of bathroom graffiti in an office environment?

Although hermeneutic work is sometimes done in a context in which the subjects cannot validate the interpretations, it is, in principle, oriented toward understanding the meaning intended by research participants, even when the researcher lacks direct interpersonal contact with them. The researcher must, according to the canons of the work, follow two contradictory paths—that of maintaining the autonomy of the subject of research while achieving the greatest possible familiarity with it. In extreme opposition to the canon of natural science, the researcher must show the meaning of the phenomena in a way intelligible to both herself and to the participant's sociocultural frame of reference. Dilthey highlights the separation by indicating, "We explain nature, but we understand human beings."

■ The Raw Data of Hermeneutic Research

The data of a hermeneutic project is anything that is recognizable in a context. It is based on things said, interviews, biographical or personal accounts, objects, historical records, texts, artworks, tapes, or data coming back from Neptune. In one well-known study, the data was everything the researcher could relate to the phenomenon of anxiety. It is objective data in the sense that the records on which the work is based are public. However, in most studies, hermeneutics is fundamentally nonobjective (in the standard "scientific" sense of studying independent "objects") in that it assumes the observer is part of the stream of understanding within which the phenomenon is to be understood. Observer and observed are both embedded in historical contexts through which any interpretations must be conducted.

A study by Packer (1985) gives information on the hermeneutic process, suggesting why it is not an easy method to follow. A further unique characteristic of hermeneutic inquiry is its openly dialogical nature—the returning to the object of inquiry again and again, each time with an increased understanding and a more complete interpretive account. An initial understanding becomes refined and corrected by the work of interpretation; fresh questions are raised that can be answered only by returning to the events studied and revising the interpretation. This dialogical character means that we must generally employ some way of recording what we are studying, audio- or videotaping it, or at least making detailed field notes, so we can return to it to check and correct our interpretation. Developing a new interpretation will often change the very form of the facts with which we are dealing. We view our recording in a new way as fresh aspects of the conduct leap to the foreground. Both rationalism and behaviorism, in contrast, so constrain the way their data are approached that, although formal and causal explanations can be attempted after the fact to explain the various phenomena, the actual discovery of these phenomena is unlikely, perhaps impossible, within their objectivist frameworks.

■ Hermeneutic Methods of Gaining Understanding

The hermeneutic route to understanding is through the iterative use of patterns, metaphors, stories, and models to amplify understanding. We "dialogue" with the phenomenon to be understood, asking what it means to those who create it, and attempt to integrate that with its meaning to us. That is, by building an image of the phenomenon and matching the image and data, we identify the aspects that are out of synch. Then, using the phenomenon, we improve the model, reflecting back and forth to create the most powerful understanding. An old term that covers a part of hermeneutics is *idiographic* (describing or understanding concrete individuals), in contrast to *nomothetic* (seeking general laws). Hermeneutics is an exploration that assumes a deep connection to the whole of our culture and tradition; it draws its conclusions based on formal cause rather than efficient cause, as the quantitative and behavioral sciences do. Dilthey has characterized hermeneutic understanding as "moving with the order of event so that it keeps step with the course of life" (Müller-Vollmer, 1988, pp. 195–196). As Bernstein has emphasized (1978, p. 145), we are continuously ordering, classifying, and interpreting our ongoing experiences according to various interpretative schemes. But in our everyday life, these interpretative schemes are themselves essentially social and intersubjective. Intersubjectivity lies at the very heart of human subjectivity. The analysis of behavior and action leads to a realization that we are continuously endowing our lived experience with meaning. In order to do this, we must choose interpretative schemes. But these schemes themselves, which come to be and pass away, are not intrinsically private—they are essentially social or intersubjective. For all the fancy company it keeps, the hermeneutic method is the most commonly used form of inquiry. It is our first mode of (cognitive) understanding, initiated as we learn the contexts of things, ideas, and feelings. Its common use begins with asking people what they mean and how they make sense of their cultural environment and its themes and symbols, including its metaphors (analogies), stories, models, and archetypes.

■ The Nature of Explanation
and the Nature of Knowledge

The aim of hermeneutic analysis is to reveal the meaning of human expression within a contextual awareness and perspective (Aanstoos, 1987). It does not so much explain as it develops an interchange of the frames of reference of the observer and the observed. Thus, we come to know the observed. It is a dance in which, through repeated interweaving, the observer comes to be entrained with the observed. The concept of proof or validity is not clearly stateable in this viewpoint, for there is no starting point that forms the hypotheses, nor is there a final answer. Rather, it is a spiral of guess and validate and continual resetting of the boundaries of the investigation as the researcher works back and forth between the part–whole relationship of the data and its setting and the context in which it is interpreted. (See Heelan, 1983, for an explicit development of the hermeneutic circle of premise and conclusion, and Shklar, 1986, for a critical discussion of this concept and its use in the social sciences.)

The hermeneutic approach assumes the interconnectedness of all aspects and elements of the intersubjective world. There are no natural limits to a phenomenon. The question of the reality base is not raised because the world is defined by the webbing of the observer's world with that of the observed. It does not matter if things are "real" in the sense of having a factual existence independent of our perception and experience, for things are understood only in the context of all other things. For example, reality cannot be determined by tests involving measurement, because the measurement is itself a part of the contexts. Conversely, a dream or fantasy is treated as real if it has an impact on intersubjectively accepted data. The reality is in the strength of the web.

■ Relationship Between
Researcher and Subject Matter

Hermeneutics is founded in the belief that researchers are embedded in a context of explanation that intrudes into the context of the data. You cannot get away from being involved. That is both a problem of validation and the basis for validation. The researcher's job is to bring to bear on the data all he knows about his present context in order to understand the context of the data. For in the long run the validation is the ability to make sense of the relations between the two contexts. This makes the question of arm's-length honesty difficult. Because both the present context and the data's contexts are practically infinite, the researcher can select elements from both sets to produce the appearance of understanding and, thus, of explanation. The concern needs to be met by the way in which the researcher reports the process of search. The total trail of inquiry should be recorded, indicating means by which sources were sought out and material extracted. With such an involvement, it is unlikely that the researcher would remain dispassionate about his topic, as the idealized model of natural science would seem to call for. Rather, like the actual scientist, the researcher should come to know as much as possible about the topic so that the essential aspects have been explored and presented in a structure that can be judged by the not-so-impassioned critic.

■ Deep Hermeneutics of Heidegger and Gadamer

Heidegger's deep ontology brought with it a major break in the hermeneutic tradition. To Heidegger, interpretation comes not by forceful analysis, an act of aggression, but by allowing an opening or clearing to occur. In this clearing, new "beings" may appear that were in hiding during the previous era of interpretation. One cannot force such beings to appear but can provide the space in which they may appear by making a pathway as a mindful inquirer. One may leave the clearing and enter another pathway, then return and find the clearing empty. Or one may wait and find it full of a new emergent insight. Such a process was actually experienced by Ann Clancy in her dissertation on the phenomenology of time. She began her dissertation years before her discovery of Heidegger. She allowed herself the time and the space to think about her problem of the theory of time in a new way, and then the resolution—which bridged the internal experience with the external sense of time—emerged, and she wrote an outstanding dissertation.

Gadamer sees hermeneutics as a form of play that is an encounter between traditions. Prejudice is rehabilitated in the recognition that we always bring foreknowledge and typifications from the past into the new ones in the present. The purpose is to bring that which is far away near. Mary Lou Michaels carried out doctoral research in which she explored the texts of fundamentalist women on school boards, for she, as a liberal Jewish woman, had seen them as her political enemies with worldviews she did not understand. She was able to see some fundamental similarities and concerns she shared with them as a result of this interpretive process.

Gadamer views the hermeneutic space as a place where one reaches out to someone who is a stranger. The "stranger," in Gadamer's sense, may even be one's friend, neighbor, or spouse, but as seen from a position of distance. Gadamer sees no method in the search for truth, but rather an attitude of openness coupled with curiosity, which he characterizes as "serious play" or "playful seriousness." Gadamer conceptualizes the process as bringing together the horizons of different traditions. This requires the inquirer to rehabilitate her or his own prejudices, in the literal meaning of *prejudice* as prejudgment. All human action, interpretation, and understanding occur within traditions that guide tastes, points of departure, concerns, and patterns of interaction. It is impossible to approach something one is trying to understand without any culturally shaped prejudgments or biases. The hermeneutic encounter is one that, when done mindfully, prompts the interpreter to reflect on her prejudices, understand them, attempt to justify them as rationally as possible, and to go beyond them through what is encountered.

Personal Characteristics of the Researcher

Interpretive work is a divergent task, requiring a style open to exploration and free from the need for specific and certain answers. It is hard work and flows more from passion for understanding than from pragmatics. It is methodologically open and ambiguous, thus requiring a confidence that one has done sufficient exploration to present an understanding. The work is likely to produce new ideas, but one always runs the risk that she will eventually uncover what is already widely understood. If the work is to produce succinct, useful findings, the inquiry needs to be continually guided and focused toward that which will be understood broadly. That is, the study must be strategic as well as thorough.

Examples

An outstanding recent example of hermeneutic inquiry is Bloom's *The American Religion: The Emergence of the Post-Christian Nation* (1992). In order to understand the nature and meaning of Christian religious fundamentalism in the United States today, Bloom created a model hermeneutic dialogue between the present-day fundamentalist movements and their founding texts, most of which date from the nineteenth century. In so doing, Bloom interpreted the present situation in the light of those texts, which are themselves interpreted in turn in the light, or horizon, of the present situation.

Another sort of hermeneutic study is Stein's *In Midlife* (1983), which uses Homer's *Odyssey* as the archetypal source for understanding mid-life changes in contemporary men. Polkinghorne (1988) contains other examples. Much of contemporary literary criticism is hermeneutics. A classic study is Auerbach's *Mimesis* (1953), which interprets major works of Western literature, from Homer and the Bible to Virginia Woolf, as stages in the history of the Western representation of reality.

Hermeneutics is often blended with other cultures of inquiry. So, for example, much of the critical theory of society consists of the interpretation of works and traditions of literature (Adorno, 1991c, 1992b; Lowenthal, 1957, 1961), music (Adorno, 1973, 1991b, 1992a), and philosophy (Adorno, 1993; Habermas, 1971; Marcuse, 1954) in order to improve our understanding of issues in contemporary society, culture, and thought. Hermeneutics is often blended with phenomenology. Texts are interpreted in order to arrive at structures of consciousness or of existence, as, for example, in Binswanger (1967) or Laing (1965).

Another example of a hermeneutic approach is the work of Carl Jung. Jung used amplification to describe a phenomenon by setting it in the larger context of an archetypal, mythic perspective. A masterpiece in this tradition is Zimmer's *The King and the Corpse* (1993). The clearest cases are critiques of a life or a body of work—psychodynamic biographies, analyses of a major writer's or scientist's corpus, studies of the meaning of a piece of art or architecture. In practice, the researcher builds a case for the interpretation so that we begin to see how it relates to and interpenetrates the totality of existence (Barrell, Aanstoos, Richards, & Arons, 1987). Specific tools include text analysis, etymological study (of central terms in a text), statistical trend analysis, and detective work—that is, finding the obvious connections among aspects of a context.

Narrative

There is a lot of recent hermeneutical work that comes under the rubric of narrative analysis. Narrative analysis is not in itself a culture of inquiry but rather a range of techniques for interpreting the meaning of texts with the structure of stories. Narrative form implies that something happened to particular subjects in a given lifeworld. Mechanical use of narrative in social research may lose sight of the true roots and purposes of narrative, as well as the assumptions that underlie the narrative form itself.

Some research traditions are linked to specific theoretical frameworks that are applied to all texts. For example, archetypal literary criticism applies Jung's and Joseph Campbell's mythical archetypes to all literary works. In the same way, psychoanalytic interpretation involves the translation of life events into the Freudian and neo-Freudian theoretical framework. On the macro level, much work in social theory involves the mapping of leading interpretive theories to empirical data. This is what Marx did in developing his materialist interpretation of history.

Semiology

Although it does not usually describe itself as hermeneutic, there is an entire interpretive tradition focused on the hermeneutics of nonverbal, usually visual, languages of signs encoded in the objects of everyday life. We are familiar, for example, with the concept of someone making a "fashion statement." That is because we recognize that articles of clothing and the way that they are combined convey meanings. A particular outfit of clothing may transmit meanings having to do with social propriety, class membership, social status, work orientation, sexual availability, or links to particular periods of time. In other words, clothes and many other domains of signs can be studied as though they were languages.

This branch of hermeneutics is known as *semiology* or *semiotics* (the study of signs), and semiologists have studied many sign domains, from clothing (Barthes, 1990) to advertisements (Williamson, 1978) to Disneyland and shopping malls (Gottdiener, 1995). Semiology has grown in importance as modern life is increasingly shaped by the production of commodities, objects of consumption, mass media, information, and advertisements, many of which convey meaning through signs that may express important social ideologies (Shapiro, 1970; Williamson, 1978). These meanings and ideologies have become the mythologies (Barthes, 1972) of industrial, consumer, and postmodern culture, which have been studied by semiologists and other hermeneutic scholars. For example, McLuhan, in *The Mechanical Bride,* produced a classic study of the "folklore of industrial man" (1967). Good introductions to semiology can be found in Barthes's *Elements of Semiology* (1968) and Gottdiener's *Postmodern Semiotics* (1995).

Cultural Studies

There is a tradition of research that studies popular culture, applying a range of theories and hermeneutic approaches. In the 1980s and 1990s the field called *cultural studies* developed, drawing on symbolic interactionism, psychoanalytic theory, Marxism, postmodern theory, critical theory, semiology, and literary criticism in the interpretation of films, popular music, television, and other products of the mass media in current lifeworlds. (See Collins et al., *Media, Culture, and Society: A Critical Reader,* 1986; Fiske, "Audiencing: Cultural Practice and Cultural Studies," 1994; and Grossberg, Nelson, & Treichler, *Cultural Studies,* 1992, for introductions to cultural studies.)

In concluding our discussion of hermeneutic inquiry, there is one thing that we would like to call to your attention. In everyday parlance, the word *interpretation* is often used to imply something subjective or arbitrary. "Oh, that's only your interpretation!" The idea behind this is that there is an "objective" reality, independent of interpretation, and then a "subjective," perhaps even whimsical, interpretation that is laid on top of it. This implies that when you are interpreting something, you can interpret it any way you want. This point of view is what philosophers call *naive realism,* the notion that reality is simply given to us independently of any interpretation. Interpretation then is seen as a subjective distortion of that objective reality. Hermeneutics is really based on the opposite view: Language, symbols, and meaning, even the most simple statements of everyday life, require interpretation for understanding to be reached. Therefore it is only interpretation that makes it possible for us to arrive at an objective understanding or view of a human reality. All of us have had the experience of trying to interpret what other people are saying in order to arrive at what is "really going on" (objectively) with those people. The point is that hermeneutical inquiry does not give you license to interpret things any way you want. To the contrary, it means striving for objectivity in understanding and using interpretation to do so.

■ Orientation to Ethnographic Inquiry

We use the term *ethnographic inquiry* (literally, "description of a group") to include not only the kind of cultural and behavioral description typically associated with anthropology, but also the various forms of inquiry usually referred to as naturalistic research, field research or studies, participant–observation research, and grounded theory. They all have in common the immersion in, participation in, or direct observation of the life, behavior, attitudes, and concepts of a particular cultural or social group by the researcher. The researcher usually also interviews members of the group to obtain more detailed descriptions, explanations, or interpretations of members' ideas, values, meanings, concepts, and behavior. Ethnographic inquiry is located on a continuum that extends from pure description to the use of such descriptions for theoretical models and explanations of features of organizational, cultural, and social life.

Like most forms of inquiry, the methods used are not independent of the theories that inform inquiry. No matter how open-ended ethnographic inquiry may be, it always operates with some model of the relevant features of what is being studied. Hence, the ethnographer will pay attention to different things, depending on whether she or he sees the cognitive structure of reality, the structure of conversation, material culture, symbols and myths, or kinship and group structure as the most relevant features of the setting being studied.

While all cultures of inquiry aim to some degree to comprehend "mysterious," "alien," or "hard to understand" features of human existence, from its beginnings ethnography has been focused on the "otherness" of human beings, especially people in "other" cultures. From Herodotus' descriptions of Egypt in the ancient world to the travel reports of explorers and missionaries in early modern Europe to the analysis of "primitive" cultures by 19th century anthropologists to recent ethnographies of urban subcultures, ethnography has tried to understand human phenomena without reducing them to the conventions and assumptions of the researcher's own environment. The more the cliches of advanced industrial, commercial, multimedia culture wash over the entire globe, the more difficult it can become to grasp anything different or "other" than the dominant culture and the more important becomes this focus on the uniqueness of diverse cultures, whether in our midst or in other parts of the world.

■ Typical Problems and Concerns

Ethnography is concerned with capturing, interpreting, and explaining the way in which people in a group, organization, community, or society live, experience, and make sense out of their lives, their world, and their society or group. It attempts to answer questions about specific groups of people (e.g., a particular town, a particular organization), about specific aspects of the life of a particular group (e.g., how women in American corporations handle gender roles), or about human beings in general. It pays special attention to the relative and constructed nature of all forms of behavior, moral and social rules, and systems of ideas, and it attempts to undercut common sense and ideological understandings by looking at how people really do things and experience their world.

■ The Nature of Explanation and the Nature of Knowledge

Ethnographic knowledge takes three interrelated forms: (a) description, (b) interpretation, and (c) explanation. A particular study may focus more on the description of the life and practices of a group, the interpretation of its symbolic systems, or the explanation of features of social life. The particular focus depends on the question guiding inquiry.

The nature of explanation is highly dependent on the theoretical framework and tradition in which the inquiry is carried out (e.g., functional, cultural, psychological, ecological). It is also influenced by whether a particular research study is primarily inductive or deductive. In the deductive approach, the ethnographer carries out a study within an established theoretical framework.

Margaret Mead, in *Coming of Age in Samoa,* deduced the functionality of multiple premarital sexual relationships among adolescents (1973). Her value-neutral approach supported the then widely accepted anthropological notion of cultural relativism. In the inductive approach, the ethnographer develops theory out of the process of description and interpretation. Colin Turnbull, applying a more inductive and critical theory-based approach, studied a mountain tribe in Africa (1972). A traditional functionalist anthropologist, such as Kroeber or Malinowski, would have accepted the practices of this group uncritically. The group sent their 3-year-old children out to fend for themselves in gangs and accepted the practice of stealing food from elderly sick persons. Turnbull interpreted these behaviors as signs of cultural decline. He also drew explicit parallels to aspects of contemporary U.S. suburban and inner-city life.

■ Relationship Between Researcher and Subject Matter

Although the ethnographer or field researcher is immersed in her subject matter, living in it or with it, she must have maximal detachment from this same subject matter. Like the phenomenologist, the ethnographer takes nothing for granted, and turns the most conventional background aspects of human experience and behavior into "phenomena." Hence, ethnography is one of the most difficult forms of inquiry to apply to one's own environment. In everyday life we take for granted, hence rendering invisible, the very things that would be relevant to the ethnographer. That is a primary reason that the training of anthropologists usually includes fieldwork in a totally different society, so that the researcher can attain the sort of detachment that is difficult in one's own society. This is also why ethnographic research requires rigorous note taking and rich familiarity with other studies and is often helped by having colleagues with whom to talk over the interpretation of one's material.

Personal Characteristics of the Researcher

The ethnographic or field researcher is fascinated by human beings—their behavior, interactions, values, culture, and everyday life. This does not mean that the researcher is necessarily extroverted, sociable, or gregarious. Rather, the ethnographic researcher must be willing to experience the fear, discomfort, and embarrassment of being a novice and an outsider. He must be willing and able to be detached, to look at everything as a "professional stranger." And he must be interested in detail—willing to pay attention to and record a vast amount of it. The concept of participant–observer sums up the prerequisites of this sort of inquiry. In general, the ethnographer or field researcher will be interested in and acquainted with a wide range of studies of different social phenomena.

Examples

Ethnographic and field studies in the human and social sciences are legion. Major studies include the works of Goffman, such as *Asylums: Essays on the Social Situation of Mental Patients & Other Inmates* (1961), the work of the grounded theory school (especially Anselm Strauss), such as Strauss and Glaser's *Anguish: The Case History of a Dying Trajectory* (1977), and studies by the ethnomethodological school associated with Harold Garfinkel, such as Garfinkel's own *Studies in Ethnomethodology* (1967), which we have already referred to in our chapter on phenomenology. Some noteworthy examples include Cicourel's *The Social Organization of Juvenile Justice* (1977); Sudnow's *Passing On: The Social Organization of Dying* (1967); Burawoy's *Manufacturing Consent* (1979); and Weppner's *Street Ethnography: Selected Studies of Crime and Drug Use in Natural Settings* (1977).

Since the publication of Edward Said's work *Orientalism* (1978), anthropological ethnography has been in a state of crisis. Said pointed out the Western colonial bias underlying the entire field of anthropology. Cultural evolutionary theory posited that cultures with labor-intensive, small-village, and nonindustrial ways of life were evolutionary throwbacks as reflected in the use in reports of terms such as *primitive* and *native*. The assumption of traditional anthropological ethnography was that the anthropologist could deliver a deeper and more true rendition of the cultures than the persons who are members of the group. The crisis was heightened when another anthropologist refuted Mead's long accepted interpretation of the behavior of adolescents in Samoa. The crisis in ethnography is well captured in Marcus and Fischer's *Anthropology as Cultural Critique: An Experimental Moment in the Human Sciences* (1986).

Contemporary cultural anthropologists such as Hamabata (1986, 1991), Kondo (1985, 1990), and Visweswaran (1994) bring the anthropologist's experience to the center of the ethnographic process. In the meantime, organizational managers and consultants have discovered the concept of culture in a big way and are beginning to write case studies of cultural change in organizations.

Quantitative and Behavioral Inquiry, Action Research, and Evaluation Research

I nquiry in the quantitative and behavioral tradition is most broadly characterized by a concern with explanation, and explanation is conceptualized in
a manner similar to the natural science model (although, in fact, there is considerable diversity among the methodologies of the natural sciences). That is, researchers look for general laws and lawlike relations among phenomena as the
key to causal relations. That is why this culture of inquiry places emphasis on
measurement, estimation, and, in general, the quantification of phenomena—not
as an end in itself, but because mathematics is a rational and elegant way of
expressing relationships and regularity in relationships.

■ Orientation to Quantitative and Behavioral Science Research

The natural science model remains concerned with precision in measurement,
with reducing all phenomena to that which can be somehow counted, because
this precision makes it possible to arrive at agreed-on facts and standards for
analyzing facts and especially to discern relations among them. This approach
plays a major role in virtually all disciplines in the social sciences.

The quantitative and behavioral culture of inquiry has both an empirical
and an analytic component. Hence Habermas (1971) called them "empirical-

analytic." The word *empirical* derives from the Greek word for experience and simply means "experiential" or "based on experience." Its significance lies in the fact that modern science differentiated itself from medieval natural philosophy and theology by restricting itself to what could be derived from experience and observation rather than basing itself on a priori reasoning about the world or on religious ideas. The concept of *analysis* (also from the Greek) means breaking things down into discrete parts. Thus, quantitative and behavioral science construes knowing the world as breaking things down into discrete parts derived from observation and discovering the regularities in relations among these observed parts. Actually, however, all cultures of inquiry are empirical and analytic in some ways. Each of them purports to directly observe, intuit, record, or report on aspects of direct experience. In the same way, each of them analyzes data to see what patterns of connection, sequencing, and relationships exist in them.

Quantitative and behavioral inquiry involves mathematics as a developed set of tools for expressing relations and regularities. Both factual relationships, such as correlations, and causal relationships can be clearly and elegantly expressed in mathematical form.

Scales are created constructs about certain attributes of individuals, groups, or societies. Be aware that if you use a preconstructed scale, the consciousness and purposes of the organization and the research results of those who already used it are the predetermined meanings that will emerge. Know and critically accept that consciousness if you use a scale.

Know that the logic of the system of numbers applies to the results; for example, that the distance between 1 and 2 is assumed to be equal to the distance between 2 and 3, and so on. Know that the same person cannot be scored as both 3 and 5 or as any two numbers at the same time. However, most meaningful human relationships are characterized by ambivalence, which means that the answer to any question could change from one day to the next. For example, your responses to a marital satisfaction scale would be very different on the day following a major argument than on a peak day. Or persons may feel ambivalent about the president of the United States. Opinion surveys are likely to tap random sides of this from one day to the next. One hopes that, statistically, this will balance out.

▇ Typical Problems and Concerns

At the micro level, quantitative research methodologies study psychological or social–psychological processes primarily through experimental or quasi-experimental designs. In these approaches, artificial and highly structured settings are created that permit the researcher to experimentally manipulate variables thought to be important. Often, these situations are created in laboratory settings (experimental design), although sometimes field settings can be manipulated as well (quasi-experimental). In either case, the researcher is looking not so much at individual behavior as at aggregate differences between groups or classes of individuals. Therefore, the principal problem or concern is with average effects rather than with individual differences. For example, the researcher may want to know if males differ from females in terms of preference for a particular style of leadership, or if groups perform differently according to their prevailing Myers–Briggs types.

The same is generally true of macro-level studies that rely on quantitative methods. The goal is to identify general patterns rather than account for the subtleties of individual behavior. At the macro level, quantitatively based research methodologies typically entail the use of survey, census, or other questionnaire-type data. These data may be gathered through instruments specially constructed for the research at hand, such as survey questionnaires, or they may depend on the secondary analysis of data gathered for other purposes (e.g., business employee records, government census data). In any case, the primary problem or concern is with identifying patterns that underlie individual differences. For example, because of the large number of visibly mentally impaired individuals living on the streets of most major cities, one might conclude that the rise of mental illness is a chief cause of homelessness. A random survey of all homeless people would reveal, however, that, in fact, the "real" underlying causes have more to do with shifts in the economy and rising housing costs. Although the importance of these factors might not emerge from case studies of particular homeless individuals, a large-scale quantitative study conducted over time could reveal the relationship between increases and decreases in homelessness and changes in the larger economy.

In sum, at both the micro and macro levels, quantitative research tends to be concerned with aggregates rather than individuals. Its explanations are, therefore, likely to be couched in terms of group properties and general tendencies rather than in terms of the nuances of individual behavior and attitudes. The advantage of such methods is their ability to "get beneath" individual differences and identify common patterns or processes that can then be tied to causal explanations that emphasize the importance of more-or-less persisting structures—be they structures of the mind, properties of the group or organization, or features of society as a whole. The principal shortcoming of such methods is their inability to account for the extremely complex and subtle features of individual behavior, which, some have argued, simply cannot be reduced to numbers.

■ The Nature of Explanation and the Nature of Knowledge

In this culture of inquiry, explanation is equivalent to prediction and control. If one can predict the outcome of a study by controlling its salient features, one has explained the phenomenon being studied. This, in turn, assumes the existence of a determinate or causal universe. For example, in the experimental tradition, one might determine whether or not exposure to violent images on television leads to violent behavior among children by randomly assigning children to groups receiving different levels of exposure. If, in fact, degree of violent exposure predicts subsequent violent behavior, one would have successfully explained the relationship.

This version of explanation is not limited to experimental situations. In survey research, information is obtained for a variety of variables that are then used to predict other variables. In the example cited, instead of assigning children to different experimental groups, one might interview a large number of children regarding their television-viewing habits, peer and parental influences, age, number of siblings, and any other factors that might possibly influence violent behavior. One would then construct a causal model, with some measure of violence the dependent (or outcome) variable and other factors independent (or causal) variables. The model would then permit the researcher to predict the level of violent behavior as a function of differences in the other variables.

This example points to something very important about quantitative and behavioral science inquiry—like every culture of inquiry, it can be used trivially or significantly, and it can be used for humanizing or dehumanizing purposes. There is currently an antiquantitative vogue in some quarters, asserting or implying that quantitative research is necessarily alienating, positivistic, dehumanizing, and not "spiritual." In fact, it is clear that using quantitative methods to identify causes of human and social problems and suffering can be of immense practical, human, and emancipatory significance, and they are not necessarily positivistic in orientation. For example, quantitative methods are currently being used in the analysis of statistics to help identify the principal causes of rape. Baron and Straus have analyzed police records on rape quantitatively to look at the relative roles of gender inequality, pornography, gender cultural norms about violence, and social disorganization in causing rape (1989). Clearly knowing the relative contribution of these factors in causing rape would be of great significance for social policy, economic policy, the law, socialization, and the criminal justice system, and it is difficult to see how one would arrive at compelling conclusions about this without quantitative analysis. Of course, this research, like much research, is subject to critique. For critical discussions see LaFree (1990), Warr (1990), Foglia (1990), Talarico (1991), Bart and Kimball (1992), Snyder (1993), Chafetz (1995), and Ellis (1995).

To take another example, some people believe that it is possible for individuals to influence the time of their deaths. There are many everyday or folk beliefs about the effect of mental, spiritual, or subjective forces or factors on the bodily or physical realm. But this area is also one in which wishful thinking, illusion, and superstition can play an important role. How would one go about scientifically demonstrating the validity of such a belief? Phillips and Smith did so using quantitative methods. In their study of the "postponement of death until symbolically meaningful occasions" (1990), they analyzed mortality statistics of Jews and Chinese before and after certain major holidays and found that the death rates fell before those holidays and rose right afterward. In other words, people were postponing their deaths until after the holidays. It is hard to imagine how this could be convincingly demonstrated without the use of quantitative methods.

Finally, both quantitative and experimental methods have been used for the purposes of critical social science (see Chapter 11), which is to comprehend fundamental social problems and analyze and criticize prevailing ideologies in a way that can contribute to structural social change and the alleviation of human suffering. Two excellent examples are Adorno et al., *The Authoritarian Personality* (Adorno, Frenkel-Brunswick, Levinson, & Sanford, 1950) and Lerner, *The Belief in a Just World: A Fundamental Delusion* (1980). *The Authoritarian Personality* is a study of a key question in contemporary society: How is it that individuals in a "rational," "scientific," modern society come to hold authoritarian and racist beliefs and come to support antidemocratic, ethnocentric, and fascistic social and political movements. Developing and administering instruments to measure the extent of individuals' democratic or authoritarian orientations was a key part of this study. At the same time, the results were analyzed in the context of large-scale social, economic, and political trends. *The Belief in a Just World* is an attempt to understand, using social–psychological experiments, how it is that individuals come to deny the existence of social injustice in the world around them, blame the consequences of injustice on its victims, reject either compassion or support for these victims, and form the belief that they live in a just world in the face of evidence to the contradictory. This belief in a just world is a key ideological component of the status quo, and understanding its mechanisms is important to social change efforts. From these examples it should be clear that quantitative, experimental, and behavioral science methods can be of great value to humanistic and critical social and political theory and practice.

In what is sometimes called *cliometrics,* quantitative methods are being used increasingly in historical inquiry to identify historical patterns, forces, and structures.

■ Relationship Between Researcher and Subject Matter

The researcher is to be uninvolved with the subjects of his study—whether they consist of other people, groups, or larger social institutions. Because objectivity is the ideal, it is argued that any departure from a detached position may lead to "contamination" of the research results on the part of the researcher. Such contamination can come from two sources. First, the researcher may have beliefs or biases that influence her perceptions, the study design, and the collection or interpretation of data. One study, for example, found that when graduate students studied the length of time it took rats to learn their way through mazes, the rats that had been (falsely) labeled as brighter somehow learned more quickly, suggesting that the experimenters unknowingly manipulated the rats in keeping with their preconceived notions of the rats' abilities (Rosenthal, 1976). Second, the researcher may influence the outcome of the study itself. A poorly constructed questionnaire may bias the responses; a carelessly designed experiment may reveal the experimenter's intentions to the participants, who then alter their behavior accordingly; a researcher who belongs to an organization he or she is studying may wittingly or unwittingly act in ways that change the behavior of other members of the organization.

Although most philosophers of science no longer claim that perfect objectivity is possible, the metaphor of objectivity is still regarded as useful for the conduct of research. In other words, the researcher should strive to be as objective as possible, revealing all biases and other influences that might detract from this goal. The best researchers will study a problem as if there were an objective reality, while acknowledging that, in fact, their own research tradition is partly constitutive of that reality. Observations partly reflect paradigms and theories, instruments, and, in general, the values of the scientific community.

Part of the concern with objectivity in the quantitative culture of inquiry stems from one of the fundamental requirements of quantification—accurate measurement. In order to quantify an object of study, one must first be able to measure it. That, in turn, leads to a fundamental concern with accuracy and precision of measurement. Although objectivity is often believed to be the consequence of precision in measurement, it should be remembered that the very notion that social phenomena can be measured at all implies that a set of operations can be specified by which one maps the phenomenon onto an accepted scale. Persons may be categorized as "tall," "medium," and "short," with each category designated by a number. To use more sophisticated statistics, one could specify a height in inches or centimeters, using a ruler or other instrument to determine—within some acceptable margin of accuracy—the precise height. In the same way, instead of describing a leader simply as "good" or "bad," one would try to specify the components of leadership and measure the leader's performance on each one, perhaps combining several into a single scale. Although such operationalization of variables permits the prediction and modeling of many phenomena, critics have argued that it also provides a false sense of objectivity, leading us to confuse our artificially constructed variables with the more complex social realities that underlie them.

Personal Characteristics of the Researcher

Because this type of research often requires that a great deal of time be spent in constructing questionnaires, operationalizing variables, and computer analysis of data, the researcher should feel at home in working at arm's length from the subject matter, at least for extended periods of time. The very nature of this approach requires the ability to conduct appropriate forms of statistical inference. Although off-the-shelf statistical packages have made it possible for non-statisticians to access highly sophisticated statistical programs, even the most user-friendly software requires a basic knowledge of the methods being employed. One should be able to intelligently defend one's choice of method and statistical measurement as well.

Examples

A study of homelessness that shows both the strengths and the weaknesses of this method is Rossi's *Down and Out in America* (1989). Much of this book consists of a sample survey of Chicago-area homeless people, conducted in the streets and shelters of that city. Ropers's *The Invisible Homeless* (1988) contains a similar study of skid row residents in Los Angeles. Wilson's highly controversial book on the origins of the underclass, *The Truly Disadvantaged* (1987), is based largely on secondary analysis of statistical data.

■ Orientation to Action Research

Action research is less a separate culture of inquiry than it is a statement of intention and values. The intention is to influence or change a system, and the values are those of participation, self-determination, empowerment through knowledge, and change. Although different models of action research call for somewhat different sets of steps, the following sequence is generally common:

1. identification of a problem area about which the individual or group is concerned and wants to take action;
2. formation of a hypothesis or prediction that implies a goal and a procedure for reaching it (each of these two aspects—the goal and the procedure—is very important);
3. careful recording of actions taken and the accumulation of evidence to see the extent to which the goal has been achieved;
4. inferring generalizations from the evidence regarding the relationship between the actions and the desired goal; and
5. continuous retesting of the generalizations in the situation.

■ Typical Problems and Concerns

The origins of action research can be traced to two independent sources—Kurt Lewin, a person of science, and John Collier, a person of practical affairs. Lewin

(1946) developed the action research approach as a way to deal with and learn to solve social problems, or to create social change. He argued that realistic fact finding and evaluation are prerequisites for any learning. His approach was composed of a spiral of steps, each of which was composed of fact finding, planning, and action. Collier (1945) stressed the requirement for cooperation among the administrator, the scientist, and the layperson. He argued that taking effective action required research directed at important practical problems and that solutions must be relevant and feasible.

Early studies in action research were more concerned with changing the behavior of persons or organizations in a specific direction than in using action research as a means of participative problem solving. The elements of self-determination and empowerment were missing. For example, Lewin's initial studies were aimed at convincing homemakers through group discussions to use less meat in wartime. Coch and French's (1948) study aimed at increasing productivity in a pajama factory. Neither study empowered participants, although both used methods in which participants discovered for themselves the merits of a specific change.

Paulo Freire developed a form of inquiry he called "participatory" action research, which is exemplified in the work of Peter Park and his associates (Park, 1993). As a participatory researcher, you act as a facilitator of a process of inquiry involving as many stakeholders in the situation as wish to be involved. Ideally, these stakeholders will be involved in the research design, data gathering, data analysis, and implementation of action steps resulting from the research. For example, Susie Veroff (1986), in her doctoral dissertation, involved a group of Inuit high school students in Montreal in a study of the impact of leaving the reserve on their own identities. The students participated in deciding how they would gather data themselves to document the changes they were undergoing. Lois Sculco (1997) involved a group of African American women college students in participatory research on their experiences as a small minority in an Eastern college. Both efforts resulted in improved situations for the participants.

■ The Nature of Explanation and the Nature of Knowledge

Action research can use any of the methods discussed in this book. As a model or guide, action research is an application of the scientific method to practical problems requiring action solutions. The outcomes of action research are (a) solutions to immediate problems and (b) a contribution to scientific knowledge and theory. It should be noted that most of the work performed under the heading of action research during the past 10 years accomplishes only the former of these two goals and is, therefore, not action research in the more traditional sense of the term. Organization development is a prime example.

■ Relationship Between Researcher and Subject Matter

As opposed to traditional research values of neutrality ("let the chips fall where they may, we are simply producing knowledge"), action research proposes to help the system by helping it gather the information it needs in order to change or to, at least, explore the need for change. Thus, it plays a facilitative role rather than a neutral one. There is the general and implicit assumption that a system is more likely to change if it gathers its own information about its problems, its potential, its future direction, and so on.

The role of the researcher in action research is somewhat different than in traditional research. The researcher helps the system plan its actions and design fact-finding procedures so it can learn from them, become more skillful, set more realistic objectives, and discover better ways of organizing. Thus, a particular action research project is at least partially designed and conducted by the participants rather than the researcher. In one sense, it is the participants' topic, hypothesis, method, and conclusions. Yet action research can be seen on a continuum running from issues and topics that are completely participant-determined (in which the researcher plays a completely facilitative role) to issues and topics that are largely researcher determined.

At its best, the action research process becomes embedded within the participant system. Thus, it can be said that successful action research builds into the system (i.e., the organization, the person, the society) an ability to identify and solve problems, to select goals and evaluate movement toward these goals; successful action research builds a learning capacity into the system.

Personal Characteristics of the Researcher

Because action research can draw on most of the other cultures and methods described in this book, it calls for an openness to cross-cultural understanding and skill. In addition, action research calls for a person who is action oriented, who is not simply satisfied with understanding, explaining, or predicting something, but is also willing and wanting to do something about it. The action researcher will be concerned with social and organizational issues and will have values that reflect democratization and humanization of communities and organizations. Specifically, the action researcher will want to use his research skills to empower people in communities and organizations, to help them discover their common needs, and to help them organize to act on these needs through enhanced and shared information. Finally, the action researcher will tend to play a facilitative role rather than a directive role in this research–change process.

Examples

Excellent case studies using action research are available. See particularly Lewin, "Group Decision and Social Change" (1952); Pasmore and Friedlander, "An Action Research Program for Increasing Employee Involvement in Problem Solving" (1982); and Whyte's *Participatory Action Research* (1991). Reason and Rowan's *Human Inquiry* (1981) cites many fine cases, for example, Elden on participative research in improving sociotechnical systems, Maruyama on prison systems, Tandon on organizing peasant communities in India, Brown and Kaplan on participative research in a factory, Torbert on collaborative inquiry into voluntary metropolitan desegregation, and Whitehead's use of action research in educational research. Park's collection, *Voices of Change: Participatory Research in the United States and Canada* (1993), gives a good sense of what is going on today in participatory action research.

■ Orientation to Evaluation Research

As with several cultures of inquiry (e.g., action research), evaluation research is less distinguished by its epistemological assumptions and more defined by its purposes. It is a form of inquiry most concerned with effects, whether these are general outcomes of educational programs or the effectiveness of social programs in delivering services, or more fine-tuned determinations about which aspects of an intervention contribute most to its success. It is a form of research that uses many social science research methods—traditionally and most often, those described in the quantitative and behavioral science culture, although often in combination with others, such as ethnography. Evaluation research is an action- and context-oriented approach to inquiry; often, those within it find themselves struggling between the definitions of rigor found in traditional approaches to research and the "real life" needs and circumstances of the subjects of their research.

Under certain conditions, evaluation research can lead to the generation of knowledge. However, all too often, it does not make use of relevant theory and focuses exclusively on experience. Students seeking the PhD must be aware of this danger and meet the challenge of incorporating theory into their research in a meaningful and appropriate manner.

■ Typical Problems and Concerns

Evaluation research is a familiar form of inquiry in the public and nonprofit sectors. Those who make and implement policies ask or are asked to produce evidence of their effectiveness. Social service agencies compete for limited resources and need to document whether they are achieving their goals. Colleges and universities are called on to assess how well they are meeting institutional objectives. Within programs, efforts at distinguishing what is working well from what is not help to maximize success. At its base, evaluation research is concerned with change. A program of action has been put in place, and someone has been called on to systematically inquire about its effects. The most common effect of interest is the goal or outcome. Occasionally, however, evaluation research is also concerned with describing the process itself.

A person outside the program, agency, or school is often hired as a contractor to conduct the evaluation. There usually are also elements of evaluation built into the delivery of services, but the design of these indicators is frequently in the hands of outsiders. Evaluation research can be viewed as an exercise in holding people accountable, and it is often used as a tool for eliminating an activity as well as for improving it.

■ The Nature of Explanation and the Nature of Knowledge

The central assumption in evaluation research is that the goal of a particular activity is clear, specific, and measurable. Inquiry is constructed as a rational, objective, and systematic enterprise. The goals of a program are grounded not only in past experience but also in theories or models that help to predict success. Evaluation research, then, seeks to compare what is happening with what ought to be happening.

Often, these assumptions are problematic for service providers who find it difficult to adequately operationalize the desired outcomes of their programs. Or they discover that their measures of success are different from those of legislators or funding sources. Their response can be the setting of minimal goals or agreeing to goals they have no hope of meeting in order to obtain resources. Thus, in the forms of evaluation research that focus on outcomes, decisions about what those outcomes ought to be and how they will be measured assume greatest importance.

Evaluation research can also be process oriented. In this form, it is usually descriptive, includes qualitative approaches, and is inductive in its approach to theory. Often, this form of evaluation research includes an interest in how participants understand the situation. This latter form of evaluation research is usually formative in its interest in improving activity through ongoing sharing rather than exclusively summative (i.e., concerned with outcomes). One should not assume, however, that descriptive and qualitative approaches must be restricted to process observations; they could be applied to outcomes as well. These kinds of decisions are circumscribed by how persuasive the data will be to decision makers.

■ Relationship Between Researcher and Subject Matter

The political aspects of research are most evident, perhaps, in evaluation research. The results of this form of inquiry are used to make decisions, often about allocating resources. Those sponsoring the research are different from those conducting the research, who are often different from those implementing the program. The researcher must be able to understand and appreciate the perspectives of all those concerned, including sometimes those on the receiving end of services!

It is common in evaluation research for investigators to work in teams. These teams can either divide responsibility for assessing the situation from various client perspectives (e.g., one researcher works with administrators and another with teachers) or can duplicate each other's activity in order to obtain multiple researcher perspectives of the same outcome.

Evaluation researchers, of necessity, spend most of their time on the turf of those they are studying. They learn from those whose work they are evaluating. Depending on who has contracted for the research, limits may be placed on what the researchers may see or with whom they may speak. Again, depending on the initial contract, the data may belong to the program, the decision maker or funding source, or the researchers. Clarity at the outset of the evaluation research process about roles, relationships, access, data ownership, and dissemination of results seems most advisable.

Personal Characteristics of the Researcher

In addition to the usual theoretical and technical expertise required of all researchers, those who do evaluation research must also be politically sophisticated and socially skilled. They should be comfortable functioning in an environment of multiple allegiances, while at the same time behaving with integrity in their individual relationships.

Often, the research questions of evaluation research are those of someone other than the researcher—the decision maker, the program staff, the program clients, political groups, activists, and so on. One must have the skill to negotiate an appropriate purpose to the research project and then, when the questions have been agreed on, follow through on gathering the evidence needed to formulate answers. A further challenge to all concerned in evaluation research is that circumstances are often fluid. Personnel change, the context shifts, decisions are reversed, crises arise. Researchers must be comfortable with a changing context for their inquiry.

Examples

Because evaluation research is so closely tied to context, different professional arenas offer varying, useful, and illustrative examples of how it is actually done. Using participant observation as her primary method, Suransky (1982) did a comparative evaluation of five day-care centers. She was able to discern structural arrangments in centers that were most beneficial to the children's emotional and intellectual development, depending on their class and ethnic backgrounds.

Comparative–Historical Inquiry and Theoretical Inquiry

C omparative–historical inquiry attempts to understand organizations, institutions, cultures, or societies by focusing on unique features that differentiate them from historical predecessors or current alternative structures. At the
same time, comparative–historical inquiry may strive to find cultural universals
or social, political, or economic patterns across time and geographic distance.
Sometimes this search for the unique and the general are part of the same inquiry.

▆ Orientation to Comparative–Historical Inquiry

An exemplar of such inquiry, at the most macro level, is the work of Max Weber.
In his *General Economic History* (1961), Weber identified general features of
the modern capitalist economy, the modern "rational state," and the modern
capitalist spirit by comparing modern Western societies with one another and
with the civilizations of China and India. Pitirim Sorokin's masterpiece, *Social
and Cultural Dynamics* (1937), attempts to demonstrate that societies tend to
shift according to their underlying philosophical outlook. Societies that are
highly motivated by material and immediate goals, such as the twentieth-century
global corporate culture, are *sensate*. Those motivated by transcendent values,
such as Europe in the Middle Ages, he termed *idealistic*. Sorokin found that
societies tended to shift emphases from one extreme to the other, rarely finding
a balanced state governed by enlightened reason, which he labeled *ideational*.

In an influential modern classic, *Social Origins of Dictatorship and Democracy* (1966), Barrington Moore, Jr., using a comparative–historical approach, studied industrialization in a number of nations, including the United States, France, Russia, China, India, and Japan, to determine under what conditions it led to democratic governments, dictatorship of the left, and dictatorship of the right. Daniel Chirot, in *Social Change in the Modern Era* (1986), influenced by, but critical of world-system theory (e.g., Wallerstein, 1976), identified principal features of social change on a world scale from 1500 to the present. In *Jihad vs. McWorld* (1995), Benjamin Barber looked for common patterns underlying the resurgence of religious fundamentalism in different parts of the world. And in *A Pattern Language: Towns, Building, Construction* (1977), Christopher Alexander and his colleagues surveyed architecture, the layouts of streets and buildings, and the details of dwellings to isolate fundamental patterns of human habitation. Because of the way in which individual and local cultures have been drawn into the swirl of a global economy and culture, a stimulating cross-fertilization is currently in progress between ethnography and comparative–historical inquiry, as anthropologists study the interaction between global and local cultures. The works of Appadurai (1996) and Hannerz (1992) are stimulating and valuable examples.

On the micro level, Carl Jung and his disciple, Joseph Campbell, researched similar patterns in the psyches of the human species in different times and cultures (Campbell, 1968; Jung, 1960). As discussed earlier, these patterns they labeled *archetypes*. A more up-to-date, philosophically rich, and scholarly archetypology is to be found in the work of Gilbert Durand, which still has not yet been translated into English (Durand, 1969). It should be noted, however, that the current climate of thought is highly skeptical of any cross-cultural or trans-historical generalizations. Two symbols, ideas, or meanings that may appear similar to a superficial or outside observer may really be quite dissimilar once you understand their cultural or historical context.

Lest the beginning comparative–historical researcher be intimidated by the knowledge required to carry out macro analyses that involve looking at entire cultures or historical periods or a set of them, some of the richest and most interesting studies have been done on quite delimited and discrete phenomena. For example, in *Medieval Technology and Social Change* (1962), Lynn White studied the stirrup in great detail. And Michael Miller studied the history of a single Parisian department store, the Bon Marché (1981). In each case, however, the individual phenomenon, no matter how "small," is used to understand a larger social trend or social structure. White's study of the stirrup is a contribution to the understanding of how feudalism developed. The European feudal system was based on the allocation of political power to mounted warriors. The stirrup, by making it difficult to dislodge a warrior from his horse, gave mounted warriors military supremacy. Miller's study tells the history of one individual store and the family that founded and developed it and also examines its role in the spread of modern patterns of mass consumption and a consumer society.

■ Typical Problems and Concerns

History is conventionally thought of as a study of the past. In this primitive, everyday conception, things become the object of historical inquiry as they sink behind us, while human events that surround us in the present are the object of sociology, psychology, political science, management science, and economics. Although many historical studies do, in fact, concern themselves with people and events prior to the present moment, this is not what is distinctive about historical inquiry. Two book titles of the past quarter century point us in a better direction, *The Present as History* (Sweezy, 1962) and *The Future as History* look at history and see it not necessarily as past, but rather, as a unique configuration of action and circumstances in time, whether that time be past, present, or future. Historical inquiry investigates what is unique in human organizational and social life, identifying its uniqueness, both in terms of its circumstances in time and its distinctive differences from other configurations, whether past or present. In this way, historical inquiry can lay claim to being the queen of the human sciences, both epistemologically and ontologically. For this reason, too, the study of the future is part of historical inquiry, because it is the study of the possible shape or scenario of a future period of historical time.

Anything can be studied historically—individuals, organizations, social movements, ideas, schools of thought, research methods, whole societies, public parks, the use of information technology, the representation of women in advertising. What makes the inquiry historical are such questions as, What is unique about this phenomenon? How did it emerge or come into being? What was the context of this emergence, and what was it about that context that made the phenomenon emerge as it did? How does this phenomenon resemble and differ from other, analogous phenomena (e.g., other lives, revolutions, organizational structures)? What actions, ideas, and forces gave rise to this phenomenon? What have been the developmental tendencies of this phenomenon? What choices were, or will be, present in the way people acted, act, or may act in relation to this phenomenon?

Weber, for example, sought to answer the question of how societies stay together, or "How is social order and the authority necessary to maintain it achieved?" By comparing types of social organization from ancient China and India through modern Europe and North America, he found three major forms of authority on which social order rests: traditional, rational–legal, and charismatic. Traditional authority is based on rule by custom over time. The British monarch was one such order. Since the establishment of parliamentary democracy (rational–legal authority), the crown took on a ceremonial function. In the late twentieth century, this function has changed to a celebrity one meted out in daily doses by the global mass media. A charismatic leader is able to effect change or possibly even act as a catalyst of revolution in rational–legal or traditional orders. Martin Luther King, Jr., and Mahatma Ghandi are two extraordinary twentieth-century examples of the power of charismatic authority.

■ The Nature of Explanation and the Nature of Knowledge

From an epistemologic standpoint, what has been common to both ancient and modern science and to both natural and human science has been the identification of knowledge with the general and the universal. What knowledge looked like to Aristotle, Newton, and Einstein, and to most modern physicists, chemists, psychologists, sociologists, and systems theorists, was the search for general principles that hold in all circumstances. In this view, there is no knowledge of the individual but only of the general, even though the general may account for the individual. Both the experimental methods and phenomenology agree that inquiry consists in the search for the most general and invariant features of their objects. This has been called *nomothetic* inquiry, from Greek words that mean "establishing laws." The examples of Sorokin, Jung, Campbell, and Weber are in this tradition of historical inquiry.

Historical inquiry, to the contrary, searches for precisely what is unique. Thus, in comparison with nomothetic inquiry, it is *idiographic,* from the Greek words for "describing the individual." Even though the historian may invoke general principles of individual behavior or social organization in her or his attempt to understand or explain a present or past historical phenomenon, a piece of historical knowledge will always have the form of an account of something individual, whether that individual be a person's life, or a period thereof; a particular event or process, such as the introduction of quality circles into American management practice; a social or cultural movement, such as humanistic psychology; or a large social trend, such as the computerization of society. Thus, historians can argue that they, even more than most psychologists, are really concerned with the individual. A case history sees a person primarily as an instance of some general patterns, such as the Oedipus complex, archetypes, or recurrent existential issues. A biography, on the other hand, sees the individual as a one-time event in the entire course of human history.

Historical inquiry can claim primacy and superiority over the other human sciences and cultures of inquiry on ontological as well as epistemological grounds, because all other cultures of inquiry come and go in history. They are a product of their own historical circumstances. For example, both phenomenology and hermeneutics can be seen as part of a romantic reaction to the march of the natural sciences and of societal rationalization. Paradigms come and go for intellectual, social, political, and cultural reasons. At any particular point, prac-titioners of a culture of inquiry tend to be unaware of its historical origins and limitations. Instead, they tend to see its principles as universally valid. Because all human phenomena, including cultures of inquiry, are historically unique, only history, it can be argued, can study them in their true nature.

Indeed, a distinctive feature of the current postmodern situation is the way in which all cultures of inquiry and intellectual disciplines are increasingly per-meated by historical consciousness—an awareness of the historical limitations and fragility of their concepts, assumptions, and procedures. In the new philoso-phy of science that has arisen from the work of Kuhn, Toulmin, Lakatos, and Habermas, all of science is understood as part of the history and evolution of the human and social knowledge enterprise. The scientist functions not as a disem-bodied, timeless mind but as a member of a community of investigators that has its own history. Thus, just as being a citizen of any community includes facing its problems and crises and acquiring enough historical perspective to under-stand and react to them appropriately, so a citizen of the scientific community requires historical awareness to respond appropriately to the state of her or his own discipline. History can contribute to both the objects and subjects of all inquiries.

There is one other feature of historical inquiry that should be stressed. It is commonly observed that the form of history is a story, a narrative. But what is the essence of a story? We have already observed that a story is about unique individuals in unique circumstances. But what makes individuals in circum-stances become a story is their actions. Action is the central category of historical inquiry. It plays the same role here as do intentionality in phenomenological inquiry, meaning in hermeneutic inquiry, and causality in quantitative and be-havioral science inquiry. We are satisfied that we have a piece of historical knowledge when it portrays understandable actions of unique individuals at unique moments in time with their surrounding circumstances. Thus, one of the axioms of historical inquiry is Karl Marx's assertion that human beings make their own history, but not in circumstances chosen by themselves.

History is a form of hermeneutic knowledge, but not only because it in-volves interpreting subjective meaning across boundaries of time and culture. History is hermeneutic also in that it is a form of self-understanding. That is, historical inquiry is shaped by the inquirer's point of departure and under-standing of her or his own situation. Problems of the present structure our under-standing of problems of the past. That is one important reason why history con-tinually has to be rewritten. Although the discovery of new facts and documents is a contributing factor to the rewriting of history, the predominant one is the ongoing reinterpretation of the present in which we live. Classic examples of this are the continuous rewriting of the histories of the scientific, French, and Russian revolutions. Because these events helped found the modern world in which we live, our continually new experience of that modern world affects our understanding of its origin.

Historical inquiry, like other forms of inquiry, is itself historical. That is, it is altered on an ongoing basis and enriched not only by current events but by the impact on it of other disciplines and modes of inquiry. For example, historical inquiry in the twentieth century has been decisively influenced by modern psychology in its efforts to understand the motivation and action of historical figures, and the field of psychohistory has come into being to merge historical and psychological ways of understanding. Eric Erikson's *Young Man Luther: A Study in Psychoanalysis and History* (1958) is a classic example of such psychohistory.

Some recent trends in historical inquiry involve influence by, or focus on the disciplines of anthropology, postmodernism, media, feminism, and ecology. Recent historians have been drawing from anthropology in analyzing culture, symbols, and the fabric of social relationships. Postmodernism has augmented a traditional historical focus on the historical origins of modes of thinking, feeling, and seeing. The increasing importance of media in our own society has stimulated historians to look at the role of media historically. Feminism has influenced historians not only to look at women's history and the role of gender (Collins, 1990) but the deep ways in which gender structures and power influence all aspects of society (Fraser, 1989; Irigaray & Whitford, 1991). Ecological consciousness has impelled historians to look at the natural environment as a factor in human history.

Comparative–historical inquiry looks for patterns in circumstances. And, because any human phenomenon, when its context and prehistory are included in consideration, has an almost infinite number of components and characteristics, this kind of inquiry requires the researcher to make choices regarding relevance. In its mode of explanation, it draws on all the social sciences. However, the explanatory models have to be relativized for the specific context. For example, psychological and economic factors in a twentieth-century market society may not operate in premodern society. The general principles of the social sciences may be altered as they enter into unique historical configurations.

Historical inquiry has the task of balancing and integrating "subjective" human agency and motivation on one hand and "objective" trends and structures on the other. Probably the best introduction to the nature of historical explanation is David Hackett Fischer's *Historians' Fallacies: Toward a Logic of Historical Thought* (1970). By looking at fallacies found in the work of historians, Fischer alerts the reader to underlying principles of historical explanation and analysis. For a statement of historical method by one of the major historians of our time, see Fernand Braudel's *On History* (1980). Braudel's works, such as *The Mediterranean and the Mediterranean World in the Age of Phillip II* (1972) and *Capitalism and Material Life 1400–1800* (1973), are modern classics of history informed by the social sciences. For a summary of this approach to history, see Stuart Clark's essay "The *Annales* of Historians" (1985). Frederick A. Olafson's *The Dialectic of Action: A Philosophical Interpretation of History and the*

Humanities (1979) is a thought-provoking and illuminating discussion of the philosophical foundations of historical inquiry.

■ Relationship Between Researcher and Subject Matter

Comparative–historical inquiry requires that the researcher form a relationship of subjective understanding (if not empathy) of the subject or object of inquiry with an objective, detached stance toward this subject or object.

Personal Characteristics of the Researcher

The ideal comparative–historical investigator would be fascinated by human life and behavior in general, and otherness in particular; empathically enter other cultural and temporal worlds; aesthetically enjoy form and pattern; be able to tolerate complexity; be able, conceptually and personally, to comprehend the dialectical relationship of subjective and objective forces in human affairs; and possess the imaginative ability to construct the unique in its context. The skills of writing and of recording meticulous documentation and the ability to read texts in original languages are all important to historical work.

Examples

A recent, large-scale comparative–historical study of a topic of general, current interest is Paul Kennedy's *The Rise and Fall of the Great Powers* (1987). James Beniger's *The Control Revolution* (1986) placed the development of information technology in the context of the history of industrial society, and Shoshana Zuboff, in *In the Age of the Smart Machine* (1984), did a comparative–historical study of several firms to look at patterns in the human impact of the implementation of information systems. For a biographical historical study, Erikson's *Young Man Luther* (1958) has already been mentioned.

■ Orientation to Theoretical Inquiry

Theory is a distilled form of existing knowledge in the social and human sciences. It brings into coherent form the concepts and principles used in the explanation and conceptual organization of reality. In a sense, a main purpose of all inquiry is the validation, revision, renewal, or creation of theory. Of course, theory is and should be related to practice; however, without theory, any given practice is lost to history without becoming a part of the cumulative wisdom embodied in theory.

Theoretical inquiry attempts to generate new knowledge through the analysis, critique, extension, and integration of existing theories and empirical research. After identifying limitations of, and contradictions within and among theories or between theories and empirical research, the researcher attempts to eliminate these and arrive at more consistent, comprehensive, and powerful theories. Like most other forms of inquiry, theoretical inquiry is an attempt to develop broad understandings of human beings and society. But, whereas other methods of inquiry go through a cycle of taking existing theories and refuting, modifying, or extending them through interaction with phenomena, or developing a theory out of phenomena, theoretical inquiry attempts to develop, critique, or modify theory on theoretical grounds, through logical or ideological analysis, consideration of other theories, or the use of existing empirical research that reflects on theories. Most cultures of inquiry are actually theoretical in that they seek to contribute directly or indirectly to the development of valid theories about people, institutions, and society. Theoretical inquiry is distinctive in being explicitly about theory and using theory as raw material.

■ Typical Problems and Concerns

Theoretical inquiry addresses itself primarily to concerns with the truth, validity, consistency, application, or limitations of the linked ideas, propositions, and explanations of the discipline. It is driven by awareness of inadequacy of a theory for explaining things; awareness of contradictions in a theory; awareness of historical or ideological limitations of a theory; observation of patterns linking or underlying multiple theories; wanting to provide improved grounding for a theory; wanting to extend a theory to areas where it has not been applied before; and awareness of limitations of existing theories brought to light by new empirical or historical phenomena. Theoretical inquiry is also often a locus of interdisciplinary cross-fertilization or integration. That is, theories from different disciplines or fields are linked, blended, or integrated to account for something in a fuller way than can explanations or understandings based on work within a single discipline.

■ The Nature of Explanation and the Nature of Knowledge

Like many forms of inquiry, theoretical inquiry aims to produce or expand theoretical knowledge. What it produces is either theory or the critique of theory, using primarily the tools of conceptual and logical analysis, synthesis, and evaluation. Theory within social science exists within every culture of inquiry and research tradition as well as within each discipline. Though the radical behavioral researcher may deny the relevance of theory and seek to "let the facts speak for themselves," the possibility of doing so is itself a theory.

■ Relationship Between Researcher and Subject Matter

In theoretical research, the subject matter of the inquiry is theory, concepts, analysis, and argument. The researcher relates to this subject matter in the mode of theoretical reflection, even though she or he may be deeply personally engaged with the relevant theoretical issues.

Personal Characteristics of the Researcher

Because theoretical inquiry draws on logical analysis, empirical knowledge, and personal experience, it draws on a range of personal characteristics. To be a theoretical inquirer, however, one must be keenly interested in the truth, validity, coherence, and explanatory power of theories. The logical status of theories must seem important for one to go through the work of analyzing, critiquing, refuting, or expanding them. Theoretical inquirers tend to love the aesthetics of form and totality, to appreciate the elegance of a theory's ability to explain or interpret a wide variety of phenomena through a small number of basic principles and the architecture that holds these principles together. In general, theoretical research requires that the inquirer be aware of the assumptions behind theory and research. Often, the researcher will need to have a philosophical bent, because philosophical analysis can illuminate both the foundations and the logical structure of theory.

In the human sciences, theories often have moral, political, social, and occasionally religious implications. Classical examples are Freud's theory of religion as the expression of infantile fantasies and fears, or Marx's assertion of a necessary connection between an accurate theory of capitalist development and a commitment to abolish capitalism. Hence, the motivations for theoretical inquiry are often ideological, political, or ethical. Theoretical investigators may want to establish, enrich, or demolish a theory because they believe that the consequences of their efforts will advance an ethical, philosophical, or political position they hold. What this means is that even though the method of theoretical inquiry consists largely of logical analysis, it may, and often is, driven by strong pretheoretical, prelogical commitments and emotions.

The theoretical investigator may be passionately attached to a particular theory or set of principles. At the same time, she or he must have a logical mind that is bothered by contradictions and inconsistencies and that can see the implications of a theory. She or he must be able to see and formulate what difference it would make to the understanding of some phenomena or what practical difference it would make to the world if a particular theoretical proposition were true or false. Thus, the theoretical investigator must also have considerable imagination because she or he must be able to perform intellectual experiments. In an intellectual experiment, the investigator–researcher may construct an imaginary case that reveals unstated assumptions of existing theories, or imagine how reality would "look" different if a different theory were true, or imagine what states of affairs would falsify existing theories and then either look for them or generate them through a concrete experiment.

Because theories, regardless of how abstract and scientific, are always the product of specific people in specific cultural and historical contexts, the theoretical researcher is aided by the capacity to enter into the minds of other theorists and the ambiance of other cultural settings in order to understand theorists' intentions and assumptions. Thus, the theoretical researcher will often need to have a historical bent—at least regarding the history of inquiry in her area, and often regarding its social and cultural context, in order to arrive at a new level of theoretical understanding.

In any case, the researcher must be well versed in the relevant theoretical traditions and their underlying concepts, arguments, strategies, and assumptions. She or he must also be familiar with current theoretical debates and the principles and arguments used in them.

Examples

It is interesting that there are very few guides to conducting theoretical inquiry in the human and social sciences, and most research textbooks contain no material about the logical structure of theories, let alone about theory building proper. This may reflect the empiricist bias that, ultimately, theory is a by-product of empirical research and thus has no logic of its own. It may also reflect the idea that scholars should engage in theoretical research only after a career of empirical work. In any case, the theoretical researcher is usually left to her own devices, and she must draw on exemplars of theoretical research in order to learn how to perform the work. Fortunately, Arthur Stinchcombe's *Constructing Social Theories* (1968) is an excellent point of departure for theoretical inquiry, not only because it focuses on the logical structure of theories but, in addition, has as its goal that the student become an active theorist in her own right.

Theoretical studies have been quite important and influential in the human sciences, because they have often been the starting point and inspiration of what are called *research programs*—that is, research traditions that have been undertaken to establish the validity of a particular theoretical synthesis or to use the concepts of that synthesis in empirical inquiry. A major example is Talcott Parsons' *The Structure of Social Action* (1949), the foundation of two decades of American mainstream sociology. Parsons analyzed and synthesized the theories of Weber, Durkheim, Freud, and Pareto to come up with a comprehensive systems theory of society, culture, and personality. A contemporary example, Habermas's *Theory of Communicative Action* (1984, 1988), attempts to do much the same thing from a perspective that reflects recent experience of the fundamental contradictions in and problems of modern society as well as recent research and theory about the nature of communication and meaning. It adds to the Marxian synthesis theory, the symbolic interactionism of G. H. Mead, Parsons's systems theory, and the critical theory of the Frankfurt school. Another such recent venture is Anthony Giddens' *The Constitution of Society* (1984).

Theoretical inquiry may overlap with hermeneutic and historical inquiry. For example, Norbert Elias, in *The Civilizing Process* (1994), uses historical material on manners to develop an explanation of aspects of everyday life in current society, such as using a handkerchief to blow one's nose. Foucault (1975) uses historical inquiry to formulate a theory of how modern medicine has placed the body under analysis, control, and restriction. In that it involves a reinterpretation of the meaning of, and intentions behind, prior theoretical work, theoretical inquiry is essentially hermeneutic. It always involves the interpretation and evaluation of existing theoretical or textual evidence for the generation of new theory.

Following are some stimulating examples of recent theoretical inquiry: In *Understanding Computers and Cognition: A New Foundation for Design* (1986), Terry Winograd and Fernando Flores draw on the existential ontology of Heidegger, the biological theory of cognition of Maturana, and the theory of speech acts of Austin, Searle, and Habermas to criticize current theories of artificial intelligence and computational rationality and to lay the foundation for a new model for the design of computer and information systems. In *The Listening Self: Personal Growth, Social Change, and the Closure of Metaphysics* (1989), David Michael Levin draws on Maurice Merleau-Ponty's phenomenology of perception, Freudian and Jungian theory of ego process, the critical theory of the Frankfurt school, and the philosophy of Nietzsche and Heidegger to reconceptualize the development of the self in terms of the development of the capacity for listening. In *The Mode of Information: Poststructuralism and Social Context* (1990) and *The Second Media Age* (1995), Mark Poster draws on the recent postindustrialist and poststructural theory, especially the work of French theorists Jean Baudrillard, Michel Foucault, Jacques Derrida, and Jean-François Lyotard, to identify the unique characteristics of a culture based on electronic communication and to conceptualize the "mode of information" as a basic dimension of society. And in *The Bonds of Love: Psychoanalysis, Feminism and the Problem of Domination* (1988), Jessica Benjamin integrates feminist theory, classical psychoanalytic theory, object-relations theory, and critical theory to provide a new understanding of the interaction of domination and gender in personality and society.

One potential problem of citing major syntheses as examples of theoretical inquiry is that it could lead the beginning researcher to set her sights impossibly high. Typically, a theoretical synthesis is the result of years of scholarly work, often including many prior publications. We cite them here only as examples of the kind of thinking involved in pursuing theoretical inquiry, not as examples of the scope that should characterize a piece of research. Usually an initial theoretical inquiry will be a critique or analysis of existing theories, or an elaboration or improvement of part of a theory or of one of its basic concepts, rather than a new theory or theoretical synthesis. Examples of such work are most easily found in journals, both general social science journals and those that specialize in theory, such as *Theory and Society.*

■ A Note on Grounded Theory

Glaser and Strauss (1967) refined the inductive method of developing theory about particular situations from observation and structured interviews. Grounded theorists search for different forms and aspects of a situation until patterns emerge. Later, Glaser and Strauss parted ways on the specifics of how to conduct grounded theory work (Glaser, 1992). Grounded theory is useful in cases in which there are no adequate preexisting theories of a phenomenon. (For overviews, see Corbin & Strauss, 1990; Locke, 1996; Strauss & Corbin, 1994.) However, grounded theorists necessarily bring the frameworks and understandings of theories of social interaction and social organization with them in their analyses of a situation.

CHAPTER ELEVEN

Critical Social
Science and Critical
Social Theory

C ritical social science and critical social theory (we will use these two terms
almost interchangeably) attempt to understand, analyze, criticize, and alter
social, economic, cultural, technological, and psychological structures and phenomena that have features of oppression, domination, exploitation, injustice, and
misery. They do so with a view to changing or eliminating these structures and
phenomena and expanding the scope of freedom, justice, and happiness. The
assumption is that this knowledge will be used in processes of social change by
people to whom understanding their situation is crucial in changing it. The structures and phenomena themselves investigated can be at any level or order of
magnitude from the structure of the global economy, such as an economic system
that produces economic inequality (Habermas, 1975; Sklair, 1995) or environmental destruction (Schnaiberg & Gould, 1994), to the psyche of the individual
person, such as the authoritarian personality (Adorno, Frenkel-Brunswick,
Levinson, & Sanford, 1950) or the impact of sexist child rearing and family
structure on the individual's psyche and behavior (Benjamin, 1988).

■ Orientation to Critical Social Science

No matter how delimited the phenomenon it analyzes, critical social science
always takes into consideration, as much as possible, the complete context in
which that phenomenon occurs. This focus on context is central to critical social
science. For perhaps the most basic thing that sets it apart from other cultures

146

of inquiry is its injunction to think concretely rather than abstractly, and concreteness involves context.

The principle of concrete thinking tells us that we should not look at a phenomenon by removing it, or *abstracting* it (from the Latin word for "withdraw" or "remove"), from its context. To understand it fully—that is, *concretely* (from the Latin words for "growing together")—we need to grasp it in its context. That is, we need to understand how all aspects of the context have grown together, or become concrete, in the individual phenomenon. This is particularly important with regard to knowledge aiming at change. For if the phenomenon is a result of the context, then it will be necessary to change the context to change the phenomenon. If change focuses only on the "abstracted" and hence "abstract" phenomenon, there is the risk that the context will either resist change or restore the phenomenon to its prior state after it has been changed.

The importance of comprehending a phenomenon concretely rather than abstractly derives from the philosopher Hegel. Hegel reversed the commonsense understandings of *concrete* and *abstract*. People usually think of philosophy or theory as using abstract concepts and thinking compared with the concrete concepts and thinking of everyday life. Hegel argued that precisely the reverse is true. In everyday life, we talk about things "out of context." That is, we consider them in isolation from the larger social system and the historical context that give them their specific qualities and meanings. Hegel argued that only the philosopher, who takes these larger contexts into account when considering an individual thing, comprehends it concretely (1977).

Grasping the object concretely has several aspects:

1. *Systems thinking.* For any individual phenomenon, critical social science asks how the larger social system manifests itself in and reproduces itself through the individual phenomenon, while asking what the phenomenon adds to the social system. For example, how does the larger system manifest itself in the authoritarian personality or in how people converse in meetings? Inversely, what does the authoritarian personality or conversation at meetings add to the larger system? Trying to answer such questions helps us see both the phenomenon and the system in richer and more complex ways. By asking such questions, critical social science is a form of systems thinking and systems theory.

2. *Historical specificity.* Critical social science differs from much so-called systems thinking by concretizing its object through the principle of "historical specification" (Korsch, 1938) or "historical specificity" (Calhoun, 1995). Systems are grasped historically. A system persists or evolves in time and at every point of time has a unique configuration. For example, it looks at the authoritarian personality or gender relations or the role of the mass media or how people are socialized in school not in general but in the context of a particular historical period. This is another way in which it is concrete rather than abstract.

3. *Internal contradiction.* According to Hegel, abstract thinking tends to consider individual phenomena not only independently from the system but as simple, internally harmonious unities, when actually they are complex and contradictory things. For Hegel, a thing's unity or identity is not simply given, but rather something achieved in the context of inner antagonisms. In everyday life, a woman or a man, a car or an advertisement, a corporation or a neighborhood is looked at not only as an independent thing, but as a kind of internally consistent thing. Concrete thinking, according to Hegel and many practitioners of critical social science, sees things as beset by internal contradictions that underlie or shape their unity or identity. Becoming a woman or a man may involve the interplay of contradictory or antagonistic forces. An advertisement may contain contradictory messages. A corporation or a neighborhood may be rent by power struggles.

A paradigmatic critical analysis of contradiction in a system is Marx's analysis of capitalism. For example, it is in the interest of the owners of corporations, in order to increase sales and profits, to reduce their labor costs. But if the total income of workers declines through reduction of labor costs, then the effective demand for goods declines, which means lower sales and profits for capitalists. Critical social science draws on the notion of "dialectic" developed by Hegel, Marx, and some of their followers to analyze both small-scale and large-scale phenomena in terms of their "internal contradictions" (Findlay, 1958; Marcuse, 1954). Focusing on contradictions is an important aspect of concrete thinking. Some "systems thinking" abstracts the unity and harmony of a system from their embeddedness in contradictions and antagonisms.

4. *Immanent critique and critique of ideology.* Thinking concretely about human and social affairs involves focusing on the contradiction between the prevailing "official story" (or ideology) and the way things really are. That is why among the key methods of critical theory are immanent critique and the critique of ideology. *Immanent critique* consists of taking a social institution at its word and seeing whether it "keeps its word" or "walks its talk." In other words, if a particular institution or society claims to be free or humane or just, the critical theorist looks to whether these claims are justified and made good. Thus, she criticizes the institution or society not from the outside, according to the researcher's standards, but rather according to its own standards. Some systems thinking does not consider the norms and values of a society as relevant to consideration of that society, abstracting them from their normative or ethical assertion of what "ought" to prevail in a system and redefining them as either biological functions or information components of the social system. Critical theory considers them concretely in their value content, as ideas that "ought" to bear on reality.

This keeping society at its word often involves what critical theorists call a "critique of ideology"—that is, analyzing the ideology or self-justifying ideas that prevail in an institution or society. The intent is to see whether the ideas really describe the reality or rather only serve to justify some particular interest group and its power in and over the institution or society. Weber pointed out that it is distinctive of human beings that they are not content to do things but rather need to believe and assert, to both others and themselves, that what they do is "right" (1968a). In sociological terms, this means that institutions and individuals are under pressure to create ideas, explanations, and belief systems that, among other things, show that they are right and that justify their position, power, and activities—in other words, to create ideology. Often, if not usually, this ideology is at odds with social reality, and this tension provides a basis for the critique of both social reality and ideology. For example, many who promote the worldwide diffusion of information technology assert that it will promote democracy, universal access to information, and the leveling of hierarchy. These are claims that can be examined and compared critically with the social reality.

Grasping the "subject," that is the inquirer or researcher concretely, also has several aspects:

1. *Insider status.* The inquirer approaches social reality not in the impersonal, neutral, and outsider mode with which she might approach the physical world. The inquirer is inside the same social world she studies (even if it is another culture or historical period), for two reasons. First, as hermeneutic philosophers have pointed out, we can only understand and interpret the world of language and meaning because we are inside it as linguistic beings. Second, we can only make sense of the cultural world as one shaped by norms and values because we are shaped by norms and values in our innermost being. So, as a member of the social world, it is appropriate and indeed inevitable for us to incorporate in our perspective a normative, evaluative approach that would be inappropriate for the study of atoms and quanta. "Nothing human is alien to me," Marx's favorite quotation from antiquity, captures well our being inside the social world. For example, without being able to identify with a norm, it would be impossible to critique ideology, which is based on norms and values.

This normativeness is a primary reason that critical theory has been a major critic of positivism, because it rejects the positivist conception of science as value neutral and needing to be protected from evaluative and normative elements. Norms are part of the concrete situation with which the inquirer approaches the social world.

2. *Engagement.* The researcher approaches social reality not as a visitor from Mars or disinterested insider but as an engaged member of society, who as such has a vested interest in social conditions and the solution of social problems. His knowing or cognition is itself a social act, and the knowledge he produces is itself part of the society he is studying. Furthermore, the person's study of society, and indeed of any aspect of the world, always has some social agenda built into it, whether it is for purposes of productivity, healing, social control,

social reform, revolution, status acquisition, membership in a particular knowledge community, and so on. This knowledge is never socially neutral but always plays some role in a specific society or culture. It is thus partisan, whether this partisanship is aware or unaware. Indeed, critical social science in general has argued that such engagement is required for good and significant research, as long as the researcher can at the same time bracket her needs, desires, or biases and be aware of them. For critical theory, it is not the pursuit of needs and interests that is a problem, but rather the pursuit of needs and interests that belong only to a specific social group and cannot be generalized to the whole society (Habermas, 1975). Engagement is part of the concreteness of critical social science, for it makes knowledge serve human beings with concrete social needs, rather than abstract, detached observers.

3. *Cultural specificity.* The researcher is never a generic human being but always a person with a specific social, cultural, class, ethnic, gender, bodily, and sexual background and orientation. Thus knowledge, even the most abstract and universal knowledge, is always knowledge created in a particular society by someone from a particular social class, gender, ethnicity, and so on, and these social envelopes shape the form and content of knowledge. A piece of knowledge is also generically human, but not *only* generically human. It always embodies specific social forces.

4. *Historical specificity.* The researcher is always inside of historical time, and the concreteness of her historical situation and the period in which she thinks and investigates is always a formative part of her research. Her intellectual framework, her ideological orientation, what she perceives as research and researchable questions are all shaped by her roots in history. A knowledge artifact is always the concretion of this historical situation.

In short, critical social science accepts and affirms the researcher as a concrete, engaged, culturally and historically specific insider and requires her to reflect critically on these factors of concreteness and understand their role in her research. It emphasizes that the phenomenon to be studied is systemic, historically specific, internally contradictory, and affected by ideology. This means making concrete both the "object" of knowledge, the phenomenon being studied, and the "subject," we who are studying it.

Critical social science is critical both socially and philosophically. It is critical—and sees good social science research as inherently so—of the society of which it is a part. It is philosophically critical by not accepting a pregiven definition of what knowledge and science are. Instead, it continues the approach that originated in Immanuel Kant's critical philosophy, namely of taking cognizance of the limits and nature of knowledge, the inherent connection between knowledge and freedom, and the active role of knowledge in constructing and construing the objects of knowledge. *Criticism* originally meant discernment and judgment, and Kant expanded it to mean reflection on the scope of knowledge and its limitations (1781/1933). In its current usage in the context of social science and social theory, the phrase "critical theory of society" was introduced by the German social scientist Max Horkheimer (1972). He wanted to reject what he called *traditional theory,* which saw itself as separate from and neutral toward society, as well as uncritical of its own epistemological and social assumptions. According to Horkheimer, this neutral stance unwittingly colluded with social structures of power and domination. To this stance Horkheimer juxtaposed critical theory, which saw itself not only as part of society but as part of changing society.

■ Some Historical Notes on Criticial Social Science

As we noted in Chapter 3, Horkheimer and his associates of the so-called Frankfurt School wanted to rehabilitate the original Marxian conception of an integral relationship between theoretical knowledge of society and the practice of radical social change (Shapiro, 1974). To the critical theorists of society, this meant legitimating and taking seriously as shapers of knowledge the human need and desire for freedom, happiness, and justice. It meant taking the critical, revolutionary social theory of Marx and modifying and expanding it to take account of new social realities and intellectual innovations. To do this, they integrated into Marxism a number of other intellectual currents, including the sociology of Weber, the psychology of Freud, the cultural criticism of Friedrich Nietzsche, and, to some extent, the philosophy of Husserl and Heidegger.

When these thinkers immigrated to the United States in the 1930s, their work began to influence on social science in the English-speaking world. Nevertheless, it remained a small, background current until the social and student movements of the late 1960s and early 1970s. Their critique of advanced industrial society brought about renewed interest in critical theories of society and led to a rediscovery and renewal of the Frankfurt School, especially in the work of Herbert Marcuse (1966b, 1968), Theodor Adorno (1982, 1993; Adorno et al., 1976), and Habermas (1970b, 1971, 1973, 1975).

At the same time, the new feminist movement led to a rebirth of feminist theory. From the 1960s feminists have criticized the social sciences' construction of women. Fraser (1989; Fraser & Bartkly, 1992) has grappled with the heart of the matter in her work on the "subject" in social research as male. Irigary and Whitford (1991) have written of the inability to express women's experience in languages that were developed in patriarchal cultures. The social sciences were founded by mothers, such as the nineteenth-century economist and social critic Harriet Martineau as well as by fathers. Yet the legacies of these mothers have been buried.

Chodorow, a sociologist, has written of the inherently different childhood socialization of women and men, with men having to disidentify with their mothers at an early age (1978). Women never have to in this profound a way, which has been spoken of as the "male wound." Gilligan (1982) described women's moral development in contrast with theories such as Lawrence Kohlberg's, which was developed primarily using male research participants. Belenky et al. (1986) have written of "women's ways of knowing," which they characterize as *connected knowing,* thus implying that men's ways of knowing are disconnected. These insights, however, are based only on women research participants; thus they cannot conclude that men differ, because they have not been studied using the same methods. All of this feminist research is also, explicitly or implicitly, critique: critique of the patriarchal social order and its oppressive and destructive consequences for both women and men.

During this same period, the decolonization of the Third World and antiracism movements in advanced industrial countries engendered postcolonial theory (Fanon, 1966; White, 1990), and the environmental movement and new ecological consciousness have contributed to the development of environmental science and social ecological theory (Miller, 1972; Zimmerman, 1994). Although with different emphases, all of these currents involve a critique of major structures of contemporary society. In combination with some of the thought and work of French poststructuralism, they share with the critical theory of the Frankfurt School central emphasis on the critique of domination in the interest of emancipation.

Calhoun, in his *Critical Social Theory: Culture, History, and the Challenge of Difference* (1995), argues persuasively for an expanded notion of critical theory that includes the original work of the Frankfurt School and its development by Habermas; the "reflexive sociology" of Pierre Bourdieu, with its focus on the reproduction of social and cultural structures of domination and the role of symbolic capital in those processes (Bourdieu, 1977; Bourdieu & Wacquant, 1992); the poststructuralism of Michel Foucault, with its analysis of the interlocking of power and knowledge; the feminist sociology of Dorothy Smith (1987); the critical political philosophy and analysis of Charles Taylor (Taylor, 1979; Taylor et al., 1994); and Donna Haraway's analyses of the relations and boundaries separating and linking gender, race, nature and culture, the human, the animal, and the technical. In this book we consider critical social science as including critical dimensions of feminism, postcolonial thought, poststructuralism, postmodernism, social ecology, cultural studies, legal studies, and science and technology studies. The term is also appropriate because the phrase *critical theory of society* is often associated especially with the work of the Frankfurt School, and many other critical social scientists diverge intellectually in significant ways from this school of thought. It should be noted that the term *critical theory* is also used in literary studies in an entirely different sense.

■ Typical Problems and Concerns

Critical social science is inherently oriented toward practice and social action, following an idea of the "unity of theory and practice" that derives ultimately from two statements of Marx: (1) philosophers have always interpreted the world, whereas the point is to change it; (2) the truth of theory is proven in practice. Many critical theorists see themselves as heirs to the Enlightenment idea that the social sciences are not outside of society looking in on it from a neutral, detached place but rather are part of society's self-improvement process, and therefore inherently are—and should be—partisan and transformative. This does not mean, however, that any particular critical research project needs to be directly part of, connected with, or oriented toward a concrete change project. This is a way that critical theory, despite its practical orientation, is different from action research. For one thing, critical social theory, as a theory of social systems, tends to focus on deep structures of domination that often transcend the individual situation. As a consequence, the changes and actions at which it aims are often systemic ones that might not be easily implemented in a particular setting or project. In addition, because critical theory arises from a tradition that emphasizes human autonomy and consciousness, its approach to change and action is concerned not just with "results," but with results that occur through transformed consciousness and experience. It aims at a consciously transformed life and not merely at objectively measurable improvements.

This focus on both the social whole and the transformation of consciousness can seem to define change at a level that so transcends the immediate situation that change becomes impossible in the absence of a broad, radical social movement. Indeed some critical theorists have been accused of an impractical, idealistic, and romantic utopianism that turns into quietism and the avoidance of social action. Adorno, in particular, has been attacked by social change partisans for engaging in "ivory-tower" sorts of research.

What is most important to critical theory is that its research contribute to a long-term project or goal of human emancipation, even if this goal is unrealized in the present or the immediate future. In Adorno's extreme formulation, it is more important that knowledge aim at "redemption" than whether redemption occurs (Adorno, 1974). In other words, even if human emancipation is unrealizable, the idea of it, the perhaps utopian conception of a better society and a more humane existence, can serve as the basis for critical analysis of the status quo. On the other hand, much of critical social science does inquire into immediate social and political concerns with direct bearing on either social change or education: for example, the causes of the "authoritarian personality," sexist behavior, or manipulative communication. It hopes to influence public policy (Forester, 1993), public opinion, social change movements, or education. It even hopes to influence the way in which individuals live their personal lives: in Shierry Weber Nicholsen's words, "individuation as praxis" (Weber, 1970).

In any case, critical social science has been motivated by many kinds of oppression and injustice that the researcher and, usually, some part of the public, would like to change or eliminate: economic inequality; inequality of information access; environmental destruction; waste of social resources; gender and racial oppression; irrationalistic and fascistic political and religious movements;

social conformity; the impoverishment of experience; the replacement of political by technocratic considerations; the weakening of the public realm; manipulative communication; the mind-numbing effects of advertising and mass culture; subordination of all aspects of social life to the market; addiction to consumerism; and so on. The focus of inquiry becomes to understand and explain the phenomenon in a way that would facilitate changing it. This presupposes that people are fairly rational beings to whom knowledge makes a difference.

■ The Nature of Explanation and the Nature of Knowledge

A critical social science inquiry results in a critique. To be sure, it is a research study that may have many resemblances to any other sort of research study, because critical social science often draws on other cultures of inquiry, overlapping comparative–historical, ethnographic, theoretical, phenomenological, hermeneutic, and quantitative- and behavioral-science inquiry. But, in addition to any of these other things, a work of critical social science is also a critique.

What is a critique? And what makes a critique scientific rather than just an expression of indignation or moral evaluation? What makes it count as knowledge? What is the difference between a critique in this sense and an attack? From what point of view does critical social science conduct its critiques? It is essential to critical theory that it be knowledge, that it be scientific. Otherwise, it would be just opinion and lack the power that comes from the objectivity and validity of knowledge.

Calhoun has argued that in critical theory there are four senses of critique:

1. a critical engagement with the theorist's contemporary social world, recognizing that the existing state of affairs does not exhaust all possibilities, and offering positive implications for future action;
2. a critical account of the historical and cultural conditions (both social and personal) on which the theorist's own intellectual activity depends;
3. a continuous critical reexamination of the constitutive categories and conceptual frameworks of the theorist's understanding, including the historical construction of those frameworks; and
4. a critical confrontation with other works of social explanation that not only establishes their good and bad points but shows the reasons behind their blind spots and misunderstandings and demonstrates the capacity to incorporate their insights on stronger foundations (Calhoun, 1995, p. 35).

A work of critical social science is one that distinguishes between, on the one hand, the human and social potential for freedom, happiness, and justice that exists in a situation and, on the other hand, the structures, processes, and forces that constrain, suppress, limit, or pervert this potential. Marcuse, in his *Eros and Civilization* (1966a), developed for this purpose the concept of "surplus repression," that is, the amount of repression that a society imposes on people over and above that which is necessary for survival. How does one estimate this surplus? How does one know what the potential for freedom, happiness, and justice is, or even that it exists? These are among the deepest questions that can be asked about critical social science. They have been discussed admirably by Brian Fay in his *Critical Social Science: Liberation and Its Limits* (1987), perhaps the most important critique of critical theory, although a sympathetic one. In the present brief introduction, we will limit ourselves to pointing to a few of the sources used by critical social scientists to assess potentials and surplus repression.

1. *Historical and anthropological comparison.* Here the researcher compares what exists in her own society with either another society or a previous period in history. For example, the amount of money spent on advertising or consumer goods is compared with data on such expenditures in other societies to establish what is "socially necessary." Marshall Sahlins took this approach in his "The Original Affluent Society" (1972), comparing the workweek in advanced industrial societies with that in hunter–gatherer societies. Frankfurt School theorists have used eighteenth- and nineteenth-century forms of individualism to critique the fate of the individual in contemporary mass culture (Horkheimer & Adorno, 1975).

2. *Social and cultural movements and experiments.* Here the researcher looks at life in movements and experiments (e.g., utopian communities, voluntary simplicity movement, nontraditional marriages) to establish to what extent prevailing arrangements are necessary. Or she looks at goals and demands advocated by social movements (e.g., a shorter workweek, universal health care, peace) and uses them as part of the critique of contemporary society.

3. *Historical deconstruction.* By looking at the way in which prevailing arrangements came into existence, insight is gained into the social projects behind them and the extent to which they meet general needs or arbitrary political and historical ones.

4. *Different levels of the same society.* Here the researcher uses insights gained at one level of society to critique arrangements at the other level. For example, in *The Pursuit of Loneliness* (Slater, 1976), Philip Slater uses insights gained from family systems and encounter groups about human interdependence to critique the ideology of individualism in American culture.

5. *Suffering.* Just as an individual's suffering is the starting point of a psychotherapeutic process that includes both knowledge and change, so common suffering can be the starting point of a critical theory inquiry. In accordance with

the feminist thesis that "the personal is political," even personal experience can be the basis or stimulus of critique.

6. *The arts.* Influenced ultimately by Freud's model of dream interpretation (1965), which decodes the dream as a disguised wish fulfillment, the critical social scientist decodes artworks as expressions of collective desire, representations of possible fulfillment, and commentary on society. Adorno (1973, 1991c, 1992a) has analyzed individual artists and their work from such a perspective. Marcuse (1966a) has integrated psychoanalytic theory and aesthetic theory to derive from the aesthetic dimension the grounds for a nonrepressive civilization.

7. *Thought experiments and the "objective" analysis of social resources and potentials.* Here the researcher uses data about existing resource distribution, sometimes combined with a kind of input–output analysis, to construct alternative scenarios or models of their use according to different social norms. An example is Len Doyal and Ian Gough's *A Theory of Human Need* (1991), which uses such an "objective" approach to define essential human needs that could be met by the prevailing economic and technological order with appropriate social changes.

8. *Prevailing ideology.* As we pointed out previously in our discussion of immanent critique and the critique of ideology, prevailing ideologies (e.g., democracy, equality, justice) are used to critique factually existing arrangements.

9. *Current need reinterpretations in public discussions.* In contemporary society, social needs are reinterpreted as part of cultural and political discussions. For example, the women's liberation movement has brought into public discussion norms for male and female roles and behavior. The environmental movement has brought into discussion our patterns of consumption and disposal of waste. The issue of assisted suicide has made visible, and subject to discussion, norms and practices about death and dying.

10. *Compassion and identification.* People can have compassion with other suffering beings, identify with them, and speak for them, especially if the sufferers themselves cannot speak, as in the case of nonhuman animals. In the past two decades, taking the perspective of animals and their rights, as well as the perspective of inanimate nature and its rights (Taylor, 1986) has been an important source of critique and of new critical theories of the domination of nature.

These sources of critique are combined with research methods used in other cultures of inquiry. To ensure that the critique is not projection or propaganda, the researcher must take into account countervailing opinions, political beliefs, arguments, evidence, and scholarship regarding the object of her inquiry. Partly because critical social science has borrowed from these other approaches but added a critical perspective, there has been until recently little good methodological literature on how to conduct inquiry in critical social science. Fortunately this situation has been transformed by Raymond Morrow and David Brown's important work, *Critical Theory and Methodology* (1994), which should be studied thoroughly by anyone working in this area. Morrow and Brown identify intensive research designs as the paradigm of critical social science. Intensive research designs consider "small numbers of cases in terms of a great number of individual properties. The primary question becomes that of explicating the operation of causal processes and meaning structures in a single or limited number of cases" (p. 250). "Case study methods coupled with nonstatistical comparative case studies are most compatible with the research problems identified by critical theory and its concern with intensive research designs" (p. 253).

One way to conceptualize this approach practically is for the researcher to choose a case study that is a valuable example of contradictions, tensions, and issues in large-scale social structures and processes and global social, economic, technological, and cultural trends. He would then collect data with a view to analyzing the case in a way that will shed new light on those structures, processes, and trends while making the individual phenomenon understandable in new ways.

Thus, in critical social science even the most microlevel research usually links the particular phenomenon being studied to the macrolevel of the entire society in its contradictory historical dynamics. Critical social science studies the general in order to understand and change the particular and studies the particular in order to understand and change the general.

■ Relationship Between Researcher and Subject Matter

Critical social science requires that the researcher mix moral, political, or social engagement and concern with an attitude of intellectual objectivity and detachment. This form of inquiry presupposes that the researcher consider herself a living and feeling part of her historical and social context and see the knowledge she generates as bearing on and relevant to that context, even if it involves making a considerable detour from the context. Ultimately, for the critical social scientist, the purpose of her inquiry is to change oppressive social conditions and to educate some or all of the public about these conditions and the possibility of changing them. The selection of research problems and material within an individual problem is shaped by these purposes, which constitute a bias. This poses a challenge for the critical social scientist, because the tradition of modern science is built around standards of objectivity designed precisely to eliminate the infiltration of bias into the research process. Because critical social science is animated by values and partisanship—in other words, by bias—the researcher must go to special lengths to be self-critical and, as we have already noted, to ensure that her research is not just a vehicle for projection or ideology. Instead she must strive for objectivity.

In critical theory, the relationship between theory and practice, knowledge and values, is conceived in a dialectical manner. That is, values, concerns, and commitment shape knowledge but are informed and revised by it. The investigator must be open simultaneously to rethinking her commitments in the light of her inquiry and to rethinking her inquiry in the light of her commitments.

Personal Characteristics
of the Researcher

The ideal critical theorist would be one who integrates two tensions or contradictions. The first, already discussed, is the tension between ethical, political, and social concerns and commitment, on the one hand, and the concern for objectivity and truth in knowledge. As we have noted, both foci are necessary for critical theory. Someone who has no reasons for anger at some aspect of society or all of it and no interest in improving or changing it will find critical theory irrelevant or bizarre. But someone who has no interest in contributing to knowledge of society will find critical theory academic and abstruse.

The second tension is that between theory and empirical reality. A critical theorist will want to contribute to an increased, expanded, more complex, and more integrated understanding of human and social affairs. But this understanding is usually won in part through some kind of immersion in the particular realities of human existence, behavior and interaction, social structures and processes. That is why much critical social science research consists of case studies, historical studies, ethnographies, or critical hermeneutic studies of texts, ideologies, advertisements, or other cultural objects such as musical works. So the critical social scientist will integrate theoretical and empirical focus. Most of the major critical social scientists have been both theorists and empirical researchers at the same time.

Examples

In addition to the works already cited, there are many good examples of critical social science inquiry. For studies of mass culture, see Adorno's *Culture Industry* (1991a) and *The Stars Come Down to Earth* (1994) as well as Leo Lowenthal's *Literature, Popular Culture, and Society* (1961). For critical ethnographies, see Michael Burawoy's *Manufacturing Consent* (1979) and Kamala Visweswaran's *Fictions of Feminist Ethnography* (1994). In the area of social and public policy, some important critical studies are John Forester, *Critical Theory and Public Life* (1985) and *Critical Theory, Public Policy, and Planning Practice* (1993); Nancy Fraser, *Justice Interruptus* (1997); Trent Schroyer, *A World That Works* (1997); and Charles Taylor et al., *Multiculturalism* (1994). In the realm of women's and gender studies, a few of the many important critical studies are Nancy Rule Goldberger et al., *Knowledge, Difference, and Power* (1996); Donna Haraway, *Simians, Cyborgs, and Women* (1991); Patricia Hill Collins, *Black Feminist Thought* (1990); David F. Noble, *A World Without Women* (1992); and Carolyn Merchant, *The Death of Nature* (1980). Critical theory has generated an entire branch of aesthetics: see as examples Theodor W. Adorno, *Notes to Literature, Vols. 1 & 2* (1991c, 1992b) and *Quasi Una Fantasia* (1992c); Leo Lowenthal, *Literature and the Image of Man* (1957); Shierry Weber Nicholsen, *Exact Imagination, Late Work* (1997); Albrecht Wellmer, *The Persistence of Modernity* (1991); and Pierre Bourdieu, *Distinction* (1984) and *The Rules of Art* (1995). As examples of the important contemporary area of critical technology studies, see James Boyle, *Shamans, Software, and Spleens* (1996); James Brook and Iain A. Boal, *Resisting the Virtual Life* (1995); Andrew Feenberg, *Critical Theory of Technology* (1991); David J. Hess, *Science and Technology in a Multicultural World* (1995); William Leiss, *Under Technology's Thumb* (1990); Herbert Marcuse, "Some Social Implications of Modern Technology" (1982); Abbe Mowshowitz's "On the Social Relations of Computers" (1985), "Social Dimensions of Office Automation" (1986), and "Virtual Feudalism: A Vision of Political Organization in the Information Age" (1992); Mark Poster's *The Mode of Information* (1990) and *The Second Media Age* (1995); Kirkpatrick Sale, *Rebels Against the Future* (1995); Manuel Castells, *The Informational City* (1989); and Arthur Kroker and Michael A. Weinstein, *Data Trash* (1994).

Conclusion and Magic Formulae

What we have attempted to write is a brief guide through the vast and complicated land of research in the human and social sciences. Our guidebook is not a how-to manual but a way of understanding how the various approaches to social research view the world. The postmodern situation we face in our lifeworlds and as scholars at the turn of the century is unique in that it requires us to return to social philosophy and epistemology. The Tower of Babel of the multiple disciplines, theories, methodologies, cultures of inquiry, and paradigms can only be comprehended and mastered with the senses of a philosopher.

The change in perspective required is equivalent to the change in viewpoint toward the Earth after the first moon landing. One may no longer be aware only of one's own neighborhood, city, or nation. One must comprehend the entire globe to comprehend who we are today. In a similar way, one must comprehend the entire universe of social sciences and humanities discourse (not in every detail, because this is no longer possible for a single human) at the level of philosophical understanding.

Hegel believed that each historical era carried a particular spirit, or "Geist." All that occurs in history is a partial manifestation of this spirit. The uniqueness of modern times, according to Hegel, was that the consciousness of humanity as a whole was beginning to reflect back on itself. In Hegel's time, this self-reflection was seen only in an elite group of social scientists and philosophers. Today, we must all become part of this self-reflection to understand and act meaningfully in relation to the intellectual, social, and environmental chaos surrounding us.

We offer mindful inquiry as a way of navigating in this terrain. In this way, your research will do more than contribute yet another piece of "information" to an information-overloaded world. We see mindful inquiry as a way to keep you (and ourselves) focused and grounded in the process. The Buddhist tradition of mindful awareness, the ability to hold several perspectives respectfully, a belief in the clearing or space underlying insight, and a desire to alleviate suffering are the cornerstones of our approach.

The three other cornerstones of mindful inquiry are critical theory, hermeneutics, and phenomenology. Critical theory brings a rich tradition of insight into ways of raising consciousness of cultural and historical forces of oppression. Phenomenology brings your consciousness and the ways it perceives and apprehends the world into the center of the research process. It offers powerful techniques for apprehending the complexities of the present historical turn. Hermeneutics brings a deep understanding of the intermingling of our symbols of communication and all of our understanding. If, as Heidegger said, "language is the house of Being," then we must work consciously to decipher ourselves and others as texts to reveal our meanings (1971, p. 63).

All knowledge springs from lifeworlds, and it is lifeworlds that must be understood and protected. The ethical obligation of the mindful inquirer is thus to respect lifeworlds and possible future lifeworlds. All mindful inquiry, regardless of the culture of inquiry or method involved, is framed by history and consciousness. It is an interpretive process, and it is implicitly or explicitly interested in cause and meaning. Theory, sequences of events, comparison, experimental logic, and interest in meaning are present and fundamental to all forms of mindful inquiry.

We have addressed this book to scholar–practitioners, to knowledge workers who want to take their knowledge to the kind of explicit, disciplined inquiry that is called research, to students of inquiry and research in both graduate and undergraduate programs. The crisis of understanding characteristics of the postmodern age has affected the major organizations in the world. Their members, managers, leaders are faced with situations that require them to search deeply into the roots of social organization and disorganization to become learned in practice and theory.

In Chapter 5, we presented some tips for becoming scholarly practitioners. The scholarly practitioner must be both a pilot and a ship's captain. She must be able to navigate both the heady air and conflicting winds of the academic heights and the ocean waters as they ebb and flow. As much as mindful inquiry flies in the sky and swims in the deep ocean waters, it comes from the earth and returns there once again. The basis of mindful inquiry is life on earth, and the processes of mindful inquiry fully ground the researcher.

In Chapter 6, we distinguished between cultures of inquiry, research traditions, methods, and techniques. We noted that a mindful inquirer may design a triangulated research borrowing from several traditions, theories, and methods.

We then presented an orientation to the cultures of inquiry, guiding you through the epistemological assumptions of each. We discussed the major questions and concerns and the streams of research typically associated with each. Each culture of inquiry tends to be congruent with certain kinds of relationships to the subjects of study and tends to evoke different styles of engagement of the researcher.

■ Magic Formulae

The process of conducting research and becoming a researcher can seem mysterious, mystifying, intimidating, or overwhelming, and can awaken feelings of insecurity, self-doubt, ignorance, inadequate preparation, and anxiety. As a consequence, people entering it can sometimes feel desperate to find some magical information or formula that will help them do it. In fact, this is probably an important source of the market for books like this one and the dozens of other introductions to research that are available. We do intend to provide you with some "magic formulae." But we would like to assure you that you probably do not actually need them. Inquiry and research and one's ability to conduct them, like many other areas of life, evolve through a simultaneously practical, experiential, intellectual, and psychological process of learning, risk taking, approach and withdrawal, digestion, reflection, and integration. In fact this process is quite a lot like swimming, bicycling, driving a car, or cooking, in that one can start it with just enough preparation to take the plunge and then learn much of the rest while doing it. Of course, intellectual preparation and studying are part of what enables the plunge. At the same time, one will always need to take the plunge without all of the preparation one could wish.

Still, magic formulae sometimes can help focus one's attention and intention and provide what one needs to jump over hurdles and survive confusion. Following, drawn from a number of sources and traditions, especially the component traditions of mindful inquiry, is a mixture of ideas that you can use, as magic formulae or just basic principles, if and when you are confused or disoriented while engaging in inquiry or research. By the way, you may find that some of these formulae contradict one another or reflect opposing viewpoints. In that case, you will have to come up with your own individual resolution of that conflict. That is the way it is with magic formulae.

■ Intend to Learn

Jordan and Margaret Paul (1983) identify two basic intentions that accompany and shape communication in intimate relationships—the intent to learn and the intent to protect. The intent to learn is a genuine openness to exploration and discovery, to go beyond existing boundaries in order to find out something about the other, which may sometimes involve personal discomfort. The intent to protect is an intention to defend one's existing boundaries, feelings, and self-definitions and, in effect, to avoid taking in anything about the other that does not fit in with one's own preexisting feelings, beliefs, values, and ideas. The intent to learn and the intent to protect affect not only what we are open to finding out about others, but what we are open to finding out about ourselves. In intimate relationships, as in other aspects of life, our relationship to others—or to otherness in general—is intertwined with our relationship to ourselves. Being open to another, or to otherness, may involve us in going beyond our own boundaries and self-definitions. By giving up complete control of our own boundaries, we experience novelty, but we may also experience discomfort, anxiety, or confusion. We may have to take seriously ideas and phenomena that make us uncomfortable or that may seem to threaten parts or aspects of our selves.

Many of us often feel that, ideally, we would like to let ourselves be governed by the intent to learn, because communication motivated by the intent to protect is often boring, repetitive, and shallow. In effect, it verges toward pseudo-communication, because the intent to protect usually keeps us from communicating some important aspect of what is really going on with us as well as from taking in information about the other person. Yet, often people do not feel free to exercise the intent to learn, through some combination of fears about the present situation, past experiences that have punished communicative openness, and the existential choice to project one's boundaries and keep a distance from the other person. If we have spent much of our lives, or our communicative experiences, feeling that we needed to protect ourselves from openness to the other, we may not even have an experiential sense of what it is to be open to learn, or we may not believe that we have the capacity to be that way. Furthermore, one can be confused about one's own intent. People often believe that they are communicating with an intent to learn, when in fact they are being affected by an intent to protect and only come to discover their intent indirectly, by its impact on others. Part of this communication model is that others always respond to one's intent, and we may perceive the other as intending to protect when she believes she is intending to learn. Sometimes it is only when the other reflects back to us her perception of our intent that we discover it ourselves. Intent to learn and intent to protect are probably ideal types. In reality, they can be mixed together. A person may have the intent to learn at a certain level, or at a certain time, while still protecting herself at some other level, or at another time. Nevertheless, the pair of concepts is a useful one.

It seems to us that a research project, such as a master's thesis, doctoral dissertation, or professional research project, is also governed at root by one of these two underlying intentions: the intent to learn or the intent to protect. In an ideal situation, a research project would be governed by the intent to learn, to go beyond the boundaries of the already known, understood, and believed in order to discover something currently unknown, something perhaps surprising and even uncomfortable. Yet in reality, even while trying to find out about the world, many people often do so in the mode of intending to protect, of trying simply to confirm their existing beliefs or to reaffirm what they think they already know or to close themselves to new ideas. Part of mindful inquiry is trying to become aware of one's intent to protect and the reasons for it, in order to let one's research be shaped by a more genuine intent to learn.

■ Surrender and Catch

The sociologist Kurt H. Wolff, who comes out of the traditions of phenomenology and continental sociology and philosophy, has developed a principle that he calls "surrender-and-catch" (1995). Surrender-and-catch refers to a process that is cognitive–intellectual on the one hand and existential on the other. In surrender-and-catch, one abandons one's self to something that one is studying—indeed, it can initially be something that one encounters without having thought of studying it. In so surrendering, one catches something of the other (person, thing, artwork, community, natural object, event) to which one surrenders. Through surrendering in this way and catching in this way, one becomes different from what one was at the start. Depending on the context, that to which one surrenders may also become different.

The notion of surrender-and-catch is, in a way, related to the notion of intent to learn. For if one is intending to protect, one cannot really surrender, and therefore cannot catch anything. This points to the peculiar aspect of inquiry, that for one's self to acquire knowledge, one may need to surrender one's self in order to encounter that which leads to knowledge. For if one does not become other than one was, how can one know anything different from what one already knew?

■ Conjecture and Refute

Conjectures and Refutations (Popper, 1965) is the title of an important book on the nature of science and critical thinking by the philosopher Karl Popper, who comes out of the traditions of philosophical analysis of the natural sciences and of the positivist tradition, although he has been a major critic of positivism. This title is also the summary of Popper's influential model of the nature of scientific inquiry. Popper's model turns some fundamental principles of prior epistemology on their head. The prior view is very close both to the conception of the scientific method that many people are exposed to in high school and to positivism. In that view, science consists of using rational thinking and analysis to come up with a hypothesis, which we then corroborate or verify through experimentation and testing. Popper argues that both of these ideas need to be reversed.

We always start processes of inquiry with notions about how something in the world is structured or works. But these notions are conjectures, and it does not matter if they are arrived at in rational, scientific ways or not. What matters is that they can be tested in some way. But we do not test them to verify them or to prove them true because we can never arrive at final truth through scientific inquiry. Even when our conjectures are corroborated, they are eventually replaced by other ideas. We do not try to verify ideas; we try to falsify (or refute) them. If we can refute a conjecture, then we have gained a valuable piece of knowledge. If there is no possible way to refute a conjecture, then we do not gain or learn much from it. Popper's idea of conjectures and refutations is a valuable reminder to us to focus our inquiry not on proving things that we already believe but on disproving them, because it is usually possible to devise some way of convincing ourselves that what we believe is true. The challenge is to convince ourselves that it might be false. Popper's idea is also a reminder that we always start an inquiry into something with some idea about it, some conjecture, and that we should try to choose or tailor conjectures in such a way that they can be refuted. That way we might learn something about reality that does not fit into our ideas about it.

■ To the Things Themselves

"To the things themselves" was a slogan of Husserl and the early phenomenologists. The basic idea is to focus on our actual experience of things rather than on received ideas or mental models or cultural prejudices that we have about them. We believe that most of us, most of the time, have only slight contact with either the things of the world or our own experience. For most of the time we use habitual or cultural categories to describe both our inner and outer experience. To take the sort of example beloved of phenomenologists, we look at a coin. If someone were to ask us to describe what shape we see, we are most likely to say that we see a circle. But we are likely to be looking at the coin from an angle in which what we see is not a circle but an ellipse. Nevertheless, we describe what we perceive as a circle. We have substituted an idea for our own perception. Our substitution of ideas and conventions for perception and experience occurs constantly, even more so in the realm of our experience of other people and society than in our visual perceptions. It can even occur in our relation to our own experience. Adorno described certain people as "not being able to tell a lie without believing it themselves" (Adorno, 1974, p. 110). A similar idea is expressed in the title of the recent book *Hello, He Lied* (Obst, 1996). The phenomenological goal of going "to the things themselves" is an attempt to break with convention and preconceived ideas to arrive at genuine knowledge of the world, of society, and of ourselves. We can do so by focusing rigorously on what we and others actually experience instead of adopting conventions and preconceived ideas.

■ Let Everything Human Be Spoken to You

The hermeneutic philosophers Heidegger and Gadamer have placed great emphasis on the way in which our understanding and knowledge is mediated by and through language. Not only the realm of cultural and social experience but our own sense of ourselves is something to which we have access through language. And the concepts and terms through which we describe and order the natural world are linguistic. Our construction of reality, our attribution of Being to things, our knowledge that they "are," our knowledge of Being, occur in and through language. Understanding, interpretation, meaning, and language are intertwined. For the inquirer in the human and social sciences, this means that openness to human phenomena and our ability to understand them are intimately connected with our ability to interpret. Our inability or unwillingness to interpret may be an expression of an intent to protect. That is why being an inquirer involves our development as interpreting beings. And our openness to what is human requires us to be attuned to the languages and symbolisms in which human existence and human meaning express themselves and speak to us. That is why Gadamer writes that "we should let everything human be spoken to us" (1976).

■ Regard All Things as They Present Themselves
From the Standpoint of Redemption

The tradition of critical theory asks us to be aware of the ways in which our selves, our lives, our relationships, our society, and the things of the world are distorted and deformed by economic, social, political, cultural, and psychological oppression, domination, exploitation, violence, and repression. An important implication of this approach is the idea that, because of oppression and domination, we do not encounter people and things as they truly are. For people and things are not what they could be if it were not for oppression and domination. We have all experienced this in one form or another. If someone is trying to sell you something, neither you nor the other person can experience each other as a full human being. You experience the other as someone with a vested interest, and he experiences you as someone to get something out of or "close on," as some salespeople say. In a relationship of power with a "superior," it is hard to reveal yourself fully as yourself. There is always the danger that if you do, you will be punished, abused, fired, put down, demoted, or humiliated for some aspect of yourself. If a natural environment is turned into either a tourist trap or a source of minerals to be exploited, it is hard for it to be what it otherwise was, and hard for us to experience it in its natural beauty. Adorno enjoined us to "regard all things as they present themselves from the standpoint of redemption" (1974, p. 247). By *redemption* he means whatever historical, social, or political process would eliminate the domination and exploitation that keeps things from being in accord with their potential and thereby would "free" people and things to be what they truly are. The inquirer is reminded to see things in terms of their potential and of their undeformed, undistorted nature. The standpoint of redemption is something that one can adopt deliberately in inquiry, in order to see this nature.

■ Cultivate a Boundless Heart
Toward All Beings

A profound and amazing aspect of Buddhist doctrine is the way it links nonattachment and love. In the Western tradition, love is often associated with intense involvement and with loss of awareness. Much of the romantic tradition describes love as a state in which one loses one's consciousness. Presumably, one does so to give up one's self to the other. You abandon your self by submerging it in the other person. The problem with this notion is that, if there is no self, then there is no one left to be aware of the other. Thus the selflessness of love can turn into selfishness, as one abandons not only one's self as self but the other as other. The other can become a mere means for one's self. But because one's self has by this time abandoned itself to unconsciousness, the other has become a means, not for one's conscious self, but for one's unconscious self.

Buddhism, too, preaches the ultimate unity of all beings and the illusion of duality—of the distinction between self and other, even of the existence of self at all. But this unity is attained through increased mindfulness rather than mindlessness. It can be said that the Buddhist notion of Nirvana is a kind of mindlessness; but it is one that is attained through mindfulness and through compassion for and love of all beings. The Buddha said, "Just as a mother would protect her only child even at the risk of her own life, even so let one cultivate a boundless heart towards all beings" (Rahula, 1974, p. 97). With regard to inquiry, this can be taken to imply that love and compassion are the underlying attitude that we should take toward all beings: that our knowledge should be generated from within such an attitude. It is particularly noteworthy that this advocacy of love occurs in a passage devoted to the attainment of calm. It is followed almost immediately by the statement "whether one stands, walks, sits or lies down, as long as one is awake, one should maintain this mindfulness" (Rahula, 1974, p. 98).

■ Look Diligently at Your Own Mind

The ancient Greek philosopher Heraclitus is known for his profound and sometimes obscure pronouncements. Among them is his statement, "I have looked

168   MINDFUL INQUIRY

diligently at my own mind" (1979). This is the first historical record of the act
of self-consciousness. Because of this and our belief in inquiry as an extension
of philosophy, and of our emphasis on mindfulness in inquiry, we want Heraclitus's record of self-consciousness to have the last word. We hope that in all your
inquiry and research, you will be aware of your own mind and that, especially
at moments of confusion, doubt, disappointment, or despair, you look diligently
at your own mind.

In summary, here are the magic formulae that we encourage you to remember and to recite whenever you find it useful:

- Intend to learn
- Surrender and catch
- Conjecture and refute
- To the things themselves
- Let everything human be spoken to you
- Regard all things as they present themselves from the standpoint of redemption
- Cultivate a boundless heart toward all beings
- Look diligently at your own mind

Glossary

Being-in-the-world A concept of twentieth-century philosopher Martin Heidegger that focuses attention on the actual nature of human existence as bounded by the physical environment at a particular time and place with a physical body that has a biography and history and a being who exists in a linguistically infused world.

Cognition The active process of knowing by which knowledge is produced. Cognitive science seeks to explain all thought, knowledge, and understanding in terms of brain functioning and its evolution.

Community of inquirers–investigators–researchers–scientists–scholars Each research tradition is carried on by researchers or scholars who operate in a shared network that includes a shared language.

Critical theory A body of thought developed by a group of scholars associated with the University of Frankfurt in the 1930s. Critical theorists, such as Max Horkheimer, Theodor Adorno, Herbert Marcuse, and Leo Lowenthal, blended the thinking of Marx and Freud into cogent and incisive analyses of culture. They contended that cultural forms, such as music, law, art, and the mass media, exercise a force on culture just as economic forms and psychological forms influence culture. Critical theory is dedicated to human and world emancipation from humanly created forms of oppression, such as fascism.

Culture of inquiry A way of knowing, with a shared set of assumptions, language, and understandings about appropriate ways of conducting research.

Epistemology The study of valid knowledge, its status, and its conditions. In the modern period, with Descartes and, especially, with Kant, epistemology has concentrated especially on the way in which features of the knowing human mind shape, structure, and set conditions for anything that we can know. The underlying idea of modern epistemology is that, because all knowledge is produced by the human mind, and because the mind is a more or less subjective thing, we need to understand how the mind can arrive at more or less objective knowledge of the world outside it. We need to investigate various features of the mind itself in order to grasp its knowledge capacities. Epistemology is not psychology. That is, it does not study how human minds actually operate in the world to produce what is considered knowledge. Rather, it studies how the human mind can arrive at valid knowledge of reality. A psychologist might observe people to find out how they come to form the idea that there is a sun and a moon and that these objects move in certain paths. An epistemologist is concerned with how we could ascertain that these ideas are valid. Indeed, an epistemologist would evaluate what would make the psychologist's claims about this valid.

Feminism   A worldview that holds that women and men should be treated in all respects as social equals. Some forms of feminism seek to portray women as superior to men and to make claims for female supremacy. Feminist critiques of all forms of knowing are being conducted.

Hermeneutic circle   The relationship between an interpreter and her or his interpretation of the text as she or he moves toward greater understanding.

Hermeneutic spiral   A concept used to correct the image of the hermeneutic process as a closed circle. The hermeneutic spiral moves forward in time in a continual process toward deeper and richer understanding.

Hermeneutics   Hermeneutics is the interpretation of texts. Developed from the tradition of biblical scholarship, hermeneutic strategies were later employed in the analysis of all textual materials by scholars in the humanities and social sciences. In the later half of the twentieth century, texts other than verbal, such as clothing, geography, architecture, conversations, and group interactions, have come to be viewed as kinds of texts and treated hermeneutically.

Human science   A broader term than social science because it emphasizes the connection between the social sciences and the humanities. A human science is a discipline that seeks to use systematic scientific means to study human beings and their forms of social organization. It includes the disciplines of history, literature, and social philosophy as they interface with the social sciences.

The term *human science* parallels the German terms *Geisteswissenschaft* and *Kulturwissenschaft,* meaning "sciences of spirit" and "sciences of culture." Dilthey, a German historian of the late nineteenth and early twentieth centuries, distinguished them from the natural sciences or *Naturwissenschaft* because of the way in which human beings not only observe other humans but understand the meaning of their actions from the inside.

Ideal type   A model of a type of action, person, or social situation. It highlights some characteristics of the phenomenon in order to explore the nature and effects of the phenomenon as it relates to other phenomena. For example, Max Weber developed an ideal type of the "Protestant ethic" and an ideal type of the "spirit of capitalism" and showed how the one fostered the other in the history of the west.

Inquiry   A sustained investigation involving careful reflection, the purpose of which is to disclose truth. Truth may be reached when one has made a sincere, self-critical, and socially verifiable attempt to understand or explain a phenomenon. Truth is always partial and temporary, as fuller disclosures may lead to deeper understanding.

Lifeworld   The lived experiences of human beings and other living creatures as formed into more or less coherent grounds for their existence. This consists of the whole system of interactions with others and objects in an environment that is fused with meaning and language (for human actors) and that sustains the life of all creatures from birth through death. It is the fundamental ground of all experience for human beings.

Metaculture of inquiry   A culture of inquiry that carries power that transcends all other cultures of inquiry. (We contend that phenomenology, hermeneutics, and critical theory are metacultures of inquiry.)

Methodology   The study of ways of gaining knowledge. It involves a reflective analysis of the kinds of knowledge desired and the nature of knowledge claims that can be made according to the procedures followed.

Mindful inquiry   Mindful inquiry combines the Buddhist concept of mindfulness with phenomenology, critical theory, and hermeneutics in a process that puts the inquirer in the center.

Mindfulness   A concept from Buddhism that stresses focus, intention, and awareness of whatever is present in a situation or experience. It requires the acceptance of complete responsibility for the effects of all one's actions, thoughts, and experiences. Mindfulness itself is antithetical to cruelty and bears a natural affinity to compassion.

Modern   The historical period called *modern* is marked by the shift from a traditional, agriculturally based society to an industrial–urban society. It is characterized by a detached, scientific attitude toward the world and an attempt to view everything with the light of reason and logic.

Ontology   The knowledge of being of all and anything that is, and of its features, properties, or qualities. In its nontechnical sense, *ontology* means fundamental conceptions or assumptions about reality and about how it is structured. For example, one could say that people who believe the world consists only of observable behavior have a different ontology from those who believe it also consists of intentions. In a similar way, people who believe that only individuals exist have a different ontology from people who believe that there are features of groups or systems that cannot be reduced to the individuals that are part of them. All of the sciences study aspects of being or of what is. For example, physics studies material being, biology studies living beings or being, anthropology and psychology study human being, and so on.

In the Western philosophical tradition, especially since Aristotle, *ontology* has meant primarily the study of being *as* being—that is, the features, properties, and qualities that things have just by being and that are common to all beings as such. An example would be the idea that, regardless of any particular qualities that differentiate physical, living, and human beings, all beings have properties, or essences, and all have quantitative and qualitative features. Furthermore, there are different types, or regions, of being. For example, numbers have being. Frogs have being. Fantasies have being. And, just because they are, there are certain things that are common to all of them. But because they are in different ways, both their similarities and differences are subject matter for ontology.

In the twentieth century, Martin Heidegger has criticized the Western ontological tradition for studying being as though it were just another, more general particular being. Heidegger argued that being is very different from beings and that humans have a special relationship to the being of beings that enables them to understand beings. According to Heidegger, being is neither an object nor a concept, but rather something that we relate to through our existence in a way that makes beings accessible or available to us. He points out that the question of why there is being rather than nothing points to a very different sort of answer than the question of why there is any particular being.

Phenomenology Phenomenology is the study of experiences of consciousness. Edmund Husserl, a key founder of phenomenology, used the phrase "back to the things themselves" to describe the objective of phenomenology. Things to human beings are experienced by and through consciousness. This fundamental reality had been ignored in the twentieth century in the rush to develop social sciences to parallel the natural sciences.

Postcolonial A concept from anthropology that viewed the anthropological tradition as having been linked with the colonization of much of the world by Western European and American powers. Postcolonial thought sets itself in opposition to this framework and emphasizes the voices and powers of those who are native to a culture.

Postmodern A trend in intellectual circles of the late twentieth century used to characterize forms of art, architecture, scholarship, literature, social science, and social organization itself. The postmodern tends to be characterized by an eclecticism of styles, combining forms from different eras and geographic locations, which at prior times would have been thought to be incompatible. There is an irreverence for past achievements, which postmodernists wish to "deconstruct," destroy, or ignore. Grand theories, enlightenment ideals, and fundamental motives are viewed with suspicion by postmodern thinkers. The human identity or self is seen as a fictional construct, and indeed fact and fiction are indistinguishable.

Reification   The use of a concept or abstraction as if it were an objective, physical reality. For example, one may say that the concepts *husband* and *wife* are reified terms that carry meanings that distort the lived experience of persons who act as husbands and wives.

Research   Literally, *research* means to "search again" or "look again." In the traditional academy of the late nineteenth century and through the twentieth century, *research* has meant a scientific approach modeled after the methods of the natural sciences. However, research actually includes methods such as logical analysis, semiotics, historical methods, hermeneutics, and phenomenology.

Research tradition   A body of research on a particular topic or with a particular perspective. For example, within the field of sociology, there is a research tradition on complex organizations. In the same way, psychoanalytically inspired researchers carry on a research tradition. Research traditions typically are brought forward in a journal or several related journals, in monograph series, and in conferences.

Social science   A general term for those disciplines that have adopted the scientific model for understanding human beings and their forms of social organization. The social sciences include sociology, psychology, political science, anthropology, economics, and social geography.

Typification   A mental construct of attributes about a person or thing. It is a concept from social phenomenology, which stresses that we only know others and objects based on judgments from prior knowledge.

Undistorted/uncoercive communication   Jürgen Habermas, a well-known theorist of the late twentieth century, working in the tradition of critical theory, developed a concept of undistorted communication. Communication is usually distorted by the power relationships and hidden agendas of members of groups and organizations. Habermas developed guidelines for communication that were designed to alleviate some of these distortions so that truthful discourse could occur. These norms are (a) understandability (speakers should share enough norms and ways of speaking and writing that they can accurately interpret each other's meaning); (b) truth (speakers should have cogent and recognized means of relating their assertions about the nature of the world to the actual world); (c) truthfulness (speakers should be sincere and have self-critical abilities to detect ideological distortions coming from their own experiences and strategies); and (d) rightness (speakers should follow valid moral norms). In undistorted communication, all items may be placed on the agenda, and all assumptions must be available for discussion and critique.

Research
Competencies

This listing of research competencies was developed by the five consulting faculty of the Fielding Institute, each of whom has vast experience in serving as a methods advisor on dissertation committees. This list is a proposed integration of the research competency lists drawn up by Fielding faculty research committees and consulting faculty.

I. Intersection of Research and Scholarship

    A. Ability to critique existing research, including

        1. the logic of the arguments presented

        2. the methods used

        3. the interpretations made of the data

    B. Ability to make and present an argument, including

        1. looking at all sides of the issue

        2. bringing in past research in support of and against the argument

        3. framing the argument in terms of theory, schools of thought, and cultures of inquiry

        4. using language correctly and according to standards of relevant professional associations

    C. Ability to develop research questions that

        1. are framed in such a way as to add to existing thought and understanding in theory, literature, and schools of thought

        2. are attached to a larger frame of reference

        3. can be invalidated by data (for quantitative)

        4. orient the researcher to finding that preconceived ideas are wrong or incomplete (for qualitative)

        5. are well matched with one or more identified cultures of inquiry

        6. will result in new knowledge

    D. Ability to understand and implement research according to ethical standards, including

     1. understanding the researcher's accountability
     2. not inflicting harm to research participants
     3. providing for support where unintentional harm is done
     4. evaluating the appropriate use of methods for questions related to ethno–racial, gender, age, disability and lifestyle issues

II. A theoretical and practical understanding of quantitative research methods, including

   A. Research design

     1. that is appropriate to the research question being addressed
     2. that allows for invalidation of hypotheses
     3. that includes appropriate consideration of confounding variables
     4. that controls appropriately for sources of internal and external invalidity

   B. Sampling

     1. that considers representativeness and the effects of sampling bias
     2. that avoids sampling bias
     3. that considers sample sizes that are appropriate to the question and the effects the researcher wants to detect

   C. Data collection techniques

     1. that maximize validity and reliability
     2. that maximize participation and minimize attrition

III. An understanding of the logic of and interpretation of the most common statistical techniques used in the social science literature, including

   A. Basic statistics

     1. Univariate descriptors
     2. t-tests
     3. chi-squares

   B. The logic of inference and statistical significance

   C. Statistics involving more than one independent variable

     1. ANOVA and the partitioning of variance
     2. Multiple regression

   D. Interpretation of statistical results

   E. Presentation of statistical results

IV. An understanding of the place of more specialized techniques in the scholarly literature, and the types of questions they address, including

   A. Discrimination of groups

     1. Discriminant function analysis

        2. Nonparametric tree methods

        3. Logistic regression

   B. Analysis of multiple dependent variables and mediating variables

        1. MANOVA

        2. Causal modeling

   C. Measurement of underlying, unobserved constructs

        1. Factor analysis

        2. Scaling

   D. Analysis of categorical data

        1. Loglinear

   E. Classification of cases

        1. Cluster analysis

   F. Nonparametrics

V. A theoretical and practical knowledge of basic qualitative methods of research, including the ability to

   A. choose a culture of inquiry appropriate to the research question

   B. match a method to the research question

   C. design a qualitative study that allows initial assumptions to be invalidated

   D. address the effects of sampling methods on results

   E. address issues of trustworthiness, authenticity, and transferability

   F. interpret qualitative data to bring out the underlying structure of meaning

   G. collect qualitative data at a level that supports scholarly interpretation

   H. present interpretations and the data on which they are based

VI. Familiarity with the common approaches to qualitative research, their appropriate use, their similarities and their differences, including

   A. Grounded theory

   B. Phenomenology

   C. Narrative analysis

   D. Hermeneutics

   E. Ethnography

   F. Ethnomethodology

   G. Action research

Key Ideas
of Positivism

We present here a brief statement of interrelated ideas, each of which has been part of some conception of positivism. Looking at the separate ideas in this way can help make sense of what positivism is and is not. Over the past 30 years, positivism has come under withering criticism as a social and political ideology, as a general theory of knowledge, and as a valid basis for the human sciences. As a consequence, after every positivist notion, we have provided a counter-idea or counterposition that has some weight in philosophy or in the social and human sciences. This is not meant to imply that the positivist idea is automatically wrong and the counterposition is automatically right. We want mainly to indicate that these are complex and controversial issues.

1. Knowledge consists primarily of turning "facts," derived from observation, into sciences organized according to theories formulated as general laws.

There are no pure facts: All facts are theory laden and exist within prior conceptual or theoretical frameworks or paradigms. Through their activities and the active processes of knowing, human beings shape the "facts" that surround them. Although there is an external reality, it is constructed (Berger & Luckmann, 1967) and relative to conceptual frameworks.

2. Distinct from religious or philosophical speculation, these fact-oriented, or "positive," sciences are the only legitimate form of knowledge. Metaphysics is meaningless, obsolete, or both. Only that which can be verified empirically is meaningful. Propositions containing unverifiable statements are meaningless. Metaphysical or ethical statements are meaningless in this sense.

All forms of knowledge rest on some prior doctrine about knowledge that goes beyond what can be derived from empirical knowledge and thus rest on some kind of metaphysics. Metaphysical doctrines of various kinds continue within philosophy, despite the importance of the positive sciences. The philosopher Karl Popper has stressed that it is impossible to verify scientific hypotheses and theories. At best one can hope to falsify them (Popper, 1965).

3. There is a single scientific method, that of the natural sciences, primarily physics and astronomy. For Comte, the official founder of positivism, astronomy was the model science (Comte, 1963). For twentieth-century logical positivists, physics is the model science. It is valid everywhere, at all times, and in all domains of knowledge, and only the results of applying that method can count as true knowledge. Disciplines or areas that do not yet operate according to this single scientific method are still in a prescientific stage of development. This belief is sometimes also called *scientism.*

In the nineteenth and early twentieth centuries, scholars in the human and social sciences started to develop methods for studying human beings objectively to parallel the efforts of natural scientists in studying nature objectively. However, because human beings act in the world and express themselves in terms of meanings, subjective experience, and symbols, much inquiry in the human sciences consisted of, and still consists of, understanding and interpreting human beings' subjective experience and action as expressed in language and other forms of symbolic communication. Thus, starting in the nineteenth century, historians interpreted documents, inscriptions, artifacts, and artworks in order to create accurate pictures of societies at different times in their history. Anthropologists and ethnographers traveled to different parts of the world, living among native peoples in order to describe and analyze their cultures. Psychologists and psychiatrists interacted with their patients to develop detailed case histories and analyses of different forms of problematic human behavior and experience. Sociologists observed the lives of people in their own societies undergoing industrialization and urbanization in order to understand the social structures and tendencies of modern societies. Thus, the original research methods in the human sciences consisted of capturing and understanding human communication and subjective experience.

Around the turn of the century, German and French social scientists and philosophers developed the idea that the human sciences are based on distinctive methods that involve the use of understanding and interpretation. That is, in the human sciences the observer or scholar studies the phenomenon by virtue of being similar to the phenomena themselves. The researcher and the researched interact through shared culture and communicative ability. It is by virtue of being able to share communication and subjective experience that the investigator can come to understand the data. The natural scientist, on the other hand, does not resemble the data he or she studies and does not communicate with them or understand them. Much current research in the human sciences continues in this tradition of understanding

*and interpretation as sociologists, anthropologists, historians, political sci-
entists, and many psychologists continue to study human beings as they
reveal themselves in actions and expressions occurring in, or shaped by,
meanings and symbols.*

*In the twentieth century, the human sciences have also been affected
strongly by a current of thought that stresses similarity between the human
sciences and the natural sciences. This way of thinking has sought to transfer to the study of human beings the experimental methods and search for
mathematically formulated laws that originated much earlier in the natural
sciences. Quantitative and experimental methods are sometimes very useful
in isolating patterns and relationships among different aspects of human
and social phenomena. However, they are not the only "scientific" approach.*

4. Only hypotheses that can be formulated as potential general laws involving relationships among measurable variables and verified through experiment
and sensory observation can count as knowledge. These laws are what constitute
explanation.

*Much of the work of the human and social sciences rests on understanding
unique human situations and does not involve measurement or experiment.
This understanding draws on the way we understand unique situations in
everyday life (Habermas, 1971). All human behavior, action, and experience is shaped by, and occurs within systems of language, meaning, and
symbolism that cannot just be described and explained but must be understood and interpreted. This means that the researcher must be to some extent
"inside" of, or sharing, the language or symbol system of those who are
being studied. Otherwise the researcher has no access to the meanings involved (Habermas, 1971, 1984).*

5. The ability to generate confirmable predictions is the test of the validity
of a hypothesis and the sign of its holding up as a general law.

*Prediction is irrelevant to much of the work of the human sciences. The
human sciences are concerned with fully comprehending the unique features of an event, situation, or organization, and even their general conclusions rarely make predictions possible. Furthermore, because human beings have freedom and the possibility of action, they can change the course
of events, so predictions cannot play the same role in human affairs that
they can in nonhuman affairs.*

6. In the human realm, only observable and measurable behavior is legitimate data for science. The realm of subjective or internal experience and meaning is irrelevant to science unless it manifests itself in measurable, observable

behavior that follows law-like regularities. This doctrine is also referred to as *behaviorism.*

> *As we pointed out, much of twentieth-century social science is based on the understanding of subjective meaning. Max Weber claimed that the basis of social science is the understanding of the meaning of social action. Although the status of the understanding and interpretation of meaning is controversial, many social scientists accept it as foundational to their science. This involves intentionality—a concern with the "interior" (cognitive, emotional) meaning of action (to the actors involved) rather than merely with the observed behavior by itself (Weber, 1949)*

7. To count as knowledge, these general laws have to be formulated mathematically and follow from one another according to logical deduction.

> *Even in the natural sciences, the organization of knowledge as a system of mathematically formulated laws interconnected by deduction has only limited applicability. In the social and human sciences, it has even more limited applicability. The fact that the social sciences are generally not organized in this way is not because they are still in an undeveloped state but because the model is not appropriate.*

8. Values have no relevance to science except as expressions of irrational human emotions and preferences. Behavior originating in values can be studied scientifically, but values themselves have no application to knowledge. To the contrary, the entire realm of values, the "ought," and the normative need to be rigorously excluded from science. There is no way to be rational about ethical or political values or norms, for these are, strictly speaking, nonrational or irrational. Thus, there is no such thing as practical reason—rationality that applies to action or practice—except for the instrumental rationality that can be used to evaluate whether particular means are appropriate to the realization of ultimately irrational goals or values.

> *Major philosophical traditions and positions argue that values can have a cognitive basis and that there is such a thing as practical reason or practical rationality. For a critical exposition of the influential Kantian conception of practical reason, see Wolff (1973). For some recent discussions of the notion of practical rationality, especially with regard to Habermas's conception of "communicative ethics," see Benhabib and Dallmayr (1990).*

9. The only things that we can know exist for sure are individual, isolated occasions of observation of the external world ("atomism"), because everything else is really only inferred from them. In some versions of positivism, this led to the notion that there really are no "wholes" or "systems." In scientific expla-

nation, "holistic" or "system" properties were to be "reduced" to properties of the system's elements or component parts. Other versions, however, as in some forms of systems theory, emphasize the priority of the system over the part or the individual. In the human and social sphere, this form of systems theory usually severs the system from any sort of moral or normative regulation or action (Dallmayr, 1987). It can also be argued that phenomenological, subjectivistic, or interpretive approaches to reality are positivistic when they take the "facts" of consciousness or meaning as ultimate, irreducible givens.

Critics of the atomistic version of positivism have stressed the importance of "holism," "systemness," and "systematicity" (Rescher, 1979), rather than merely the individuals that comprise them. Although there are positivistic ways of conceptualizing systematicity, the notion of system properties that go beyond the facts can serve as a critical, rather than positivistic, notion (Harris, 1987; Marcuse, 1954).

10. Because all genuine knowledge consists of either scientifically formulated statements and theories that obey the preceding rules or the logical analysis of such statements and theories, strictly speaking there is no need to justify or ground knowledge epistemologically or philosophically. Because philosophical statements do not obey these rules, they are not really scientific. Indeed, most of them are, strictly speaking, meaningless, and philosophical problems are pseudo-problems. Philosophy and epistemology are really relics of the prescientific age, and are valid and useful only to the extent that they clarify and advocate scientific knowledge. Therefore, positivism does not need to justify itself.

"Empiricism cannot be justified empirically or scientism by means of scientific method" (Dallmayr, 1987, p. 248). Habermas pointed to the denial of the need for or possibility of epistemological reflection as the most basic positivistic notion. These critics of positivism point out that positivism undermines itself by having to ground itself in a "meta-language" that itself does not obey the rules of positivism.

11. Knowledge is essentially the product of a "knower" and conceived from the perspective of an individual observer and knower of reality. Although knowledge is formulated in language and communicated, essentially shared knowledge is the knowledge of a collection of such individual, solitary knowers.

Much of the recent philosophy and sociology of science and of knowledge shows that knowledge arises in and is created by communities, and many of its characteristics follow from the role of these communities, and not just from interaction between an individual "knower" and an individual known. See, for example, Toulmin (1972).

12. The fundamental relationship of the knower to reality is essentially a passive or neutral one, consisting primarily of observing facts or sensory data and then building up knowledge from these observed facts. True, experimentation is an active process. But ultimately knowledge is derived from observation, and these observations are "given" to the observer.

Contemporary thought has argued for both the inevitability and legitimacy of the knower's active role in both perception and conceptualization as well as the knower's engagement with the known. In the human and social sciences, in particular, involvement with the subjects of one's study may be necessary and appropriate. It has come to be recognized that detachment, or neutrality, is itself a form of engagement with or relation to these subjects, which may make certain phenomena visible but render others invisible. Furthermore, our knowledge is connected with our embodiment. Recent philosophy is concerned with the way in which the human bodily relation to the world mediates, frames, and shapes our knowledge of it (Merleau-Ponty, 1981). And practice, or action, may be combined with knowledge.

13. The observer's or knower's context does not enter into knowledge, because context exists just as another source of intruding subjective and irrational elements into the research or knowledge process. Making knowledge valid and scientific requires excluding contexts or situations in the same way that values and preferences need to be excluded. Thus, knowledge is fundamentally impersonal, and the person of the knower, scientist, or researcher has no bearing on and does not enter into the research, except as a negative factor.

The importance of context in the generation of knowledge, especially in the social sciences, is a primary thrust of important currents in the theory of knowledge over the past three decades. It is central to hermeneutics, which sees all interpretation as occurring within the horizon of a historical and cultural context (Gadamer, 1975); critical theory, which sees all knowledge as shaped by its historical, class, gender, and ethnic context (Collins, 1990; Harding, 1996; Horkheimer, 1972); and constructionism and constructivism of different varieties (Berger & Luckmann, 1967; Hess, 1995).

14. Knowledge serves as a means of control, and this orientation toward control is built into knowledge itself. This can be seen in the way that knowledge is validated or established through experimentation and prediction. The experimental method is based on control, because an experiment is precisely a situation in which one can produce a particular result through controlling the factors of the situation. And prediction is a way of controlling the future (e.g., the results of an experiment) or of enabling control of the future (e.g., if we can predict when the sun will set, we know when to turn on the lights). So there is a built-in "instrumental" or "technical" approach to knowledge, and positivism tends to

assume an instrumental orientation of knowledge and of knowledge processes (Habermas, 1971). This instrumental orientation may seem to contradict the idea of the knower relating to reality in a neutral or passive manner, but it is in fact connected with it. For it is precisely by adopting a neutral stance, by being outside of a context with reality, that the observer can then control it. Part of the scientific critique of magical, prescientific thinking is that magic presumes the ability to control or influence reality, which ends up being more wish fulfillment than real control. Science, to the contrary, can achieve real control precisely by adopting a neutral or passive relationship.

> *Since the seventeenth century, the idea that scientific knowledge is a means to increase humans' power over, or domination of, nature has been a key element in the modern European worldview (Leiss, 1994). The ability to dominate nature has been taken—and still is taken by many—to be an obvious, unquestioned value. But it is currently being called into question from a number of points of view, both ethical (Taylor, 1986) and scientific (Schroyer, 1983). In the human sciences in particular, the interpretive stream of thought has argued that although the domination of nature may be appropriate for the explanatory knowledge of the natural sciences, it is inappropriate for understanding the point of view and lifeworld of human beings and societies, which are of equal human status to the interpreter and need to be considered as subjects, not objects.*

15. Just as there is no such thing as context, strictly speaking there is no such thing as history, because history is context or situation—and action within that context or situation—that changes over time. Because scientific knowledge consists of general laws that are true universally and at all times and that are verified through repetition or recurrence—because the ability to make verifiable predictions implies a future that is fundamentally like the past—the existence of history is either denied or deemphasized. The world is a totality of facts without context, history, or system. For positivism, history is fundamentally the transition from the prescientific age and mentality to the scientific. That is, the only real history is the history of positivism itself. In the same way that the knower's person cannot and should not enter into research, the knower's social or historical situation, including social, gender, or ethnic background or context, cannot and should not enter into the research.

> *Recent work in the human and social sciences has become much more historicist than in the previous generation. Historicism is concerned with comprehending the unique by seeing it in a multidimensional, historical situation. This applies to both the researcher and the object of inquiry. Although the researcher may invoke or be interested in discovering laws that transcend the situation, the uniqueness is part of the essence of what the researcher is trying to understand or explain.*

16. Progress in knowledge—and, by implication, in civilization—results automatically from applying and extending this positive approach to knowledge. Removing the obstacles to science will bring about social improvement as scientific knowledge is applied piecemeal to different provinces of social life through a process of social engineering. The social order of the status quo is alright as it is and requires no fundamental or structural change, except to the extent that it is an obstacle to the spread of positivism and the positive sciences themselves. Nevertheless, positivism will contribute to an entire new level of civilization, by helping eradicate religious, philosophical, or metaphysical beliefs and ways of thinking that impede the development of science and its positive impact on human life and society. Thus, for example, Comte, the founder of positivism, saw positivism as contributing to a new "religion of humanity." For him, positivism and its slogan, "order and progress," were solutions to the social and political conflicts that emerged in modern society during the French Revolution (Comte, 1963). Comte considered it essential to educate working-class people in positivist philosophy in order to help create a new, positivistic social order (1963).

> *Progress in knowledge can contribute to barbarism and reinforce the power of the status quo unless it is allied with the transformation of fundamental social, structural, and political structures (Horkheimer & Adorno, 1975). The way science and technology have been put at the service of the destruction of human beings, nature, and culture—from concentration camps to nuclear waste to environmental pollution to instruments of torture and surveillance—shows that science by itself does not lead to human progress and that technology does not lead to affluence.*

17. Positivism rejects "negative" thinking, that is, thinking that either invokes principles that have not been verified experimentally or that applies to the current social order principles, norms, standards, or values that go beyond it or that are more than generalizations of behavior or statements of subjective preference. According to positivists, we must be limited to the facts; everything else is speculation or emotion. Social critique and "negative" or "critical thinking" are seen as expressions of confused thinking, resentment, ideology, or totalitarian hopes and visions.

> *Positivism is a fundamentally conservative political ideology. Herbert Marcuse emphasized positivism's reaction against the critical and radical power of "negative thinking" as manifested especially in Hegelian philosophy (Marcuse, 1954). Social critique is a legitimate and indeed primary goal of the human and social sciences. These sciences should explicitly and deliberately criticize the ideologies prevalent in the surrounding society, including the worship of decontextualized "facts" and the alleged value neutrality of social science. In the critique of ideology, researchers are concerned with*

unmasking individual and social illusions that are part of the social fabric and that sustain social and political domination and oppression. Almost every social arrangement, whether an entire society, an organization, a town, or a social group, has some set of ideas that justify or rationalize or legitimate it. Because almost all such ideas are based on something that cannot be justified on a rational basis; that incorporates fantasies, distortions, projections, or illusions; and that is used for purposes of social control or to maintain power, research that shows the illusory quality of the ideas may function, intentionally or unintentionally, to undermine the illusions, the power structure, or the social cohesion of that arrangement. Research may not be neutral in relation to what it studies; instead it may alter it or disrupt it (Fay, 1987).

Introductory
Reading List

E ach of the topic areas of this book is a rather large one, with a voluminous literature. Although we have referred to a number of works in the body of the text, they are not always the best ones for getting started in an area. Following is a short list of books that can serve as introductions to the different areas we have covered.

Historical Context of the Present

Harvey, David. (1989). *The condition of postmodernity: An enquiry into the origins of cultural change.* Cambridge, MA: Basil Blackwell.

Hobsbawm, Eric. (1994). *The age of extremes: A history of the world, 1914–1991.* New York: Random House.

Reich, Robert. (1991). *The work of nations: Preparing ourselves for 21st-century capitalism.* New York: Random House.

Stavrianos, Leften Stavros. (1995). *A global history: From prehistory to the present* (6th ed.). Englewood Cliffs, NJ: Prentice Hall.

Postmodernism

Best, Steven, & Douglas M. Kellner. (1991). *Postmodern theory: Critical interrogations.* New York: Guilford Press.

Docherty, Thomas. (Ed.). (1993). *Postmodernism: A reader.* New York: Columbia University Press.

Jencks, Charles. (1989). *What is post-modernism?* (3rd ed., enlarged). New York: St. Martin's Press.

Lyon, David. (1994). *Postmodernity.* Minneapolis: University of Minnesota Press.

General Philosophy

Appleby, Joyce, Elizabeth Covington, David Hoyt, Michael Latham, & Allison Sneider (Eds.). (1996). *Knowledge and postmodernism in historical perspective.* New York and London: Routledge.

Cornford, Francis Macdonald. (1993). *Before and after Socrates.* Cambridge: Cambridge University Press.

Nagel, Thomas. (1986). *The view from nowhere.* New York: Oxford University Press.

Wolff, Robert Paul. (1995). *About philosophy* (6th ed.). Englewood Cliffs, NJ: Prentice Hall.

Philosophy of Science

Fisher, Alec. (1988). *The logic of real arguments.* Cambridge: Cambridge University Press.

Hempel, Carl G. (1966). *Philosophy of natural science.* Englewood Cliffs, NJ: Prentice Hall.

Kuhn, Thomas S. (1970). *The structure of scientific revolutions* (2nd ed., enlarged). Chicago: University of Chicago Press.

Popper, Karl. (1965). *Conjectures and refutations: The growth of scientific knowledge.* New York: Harper and Row.

Quine, W. V., & J. S. Ullian. (1978). *The web of belief* (2nd ed.). New York: Random House.

Ziman, John. (1978). *Reliable knowledge: An exploration of the grounds for belief in science.* Cambridge: Cambridge University Press.

Philosophy of the Social Sciences

Bohman, James. (1991). *New philosophy of social science: Problems of indeterminacy.* Cambridge, MA: MIT Press.

Dallmayr, Fred, & Thomas A. McCarthy (Eds.). (1977). *Understanding and social inquiry.* Notre Dame, IN: University of Notre Dame Press.

Manicas, Peter T. (1987). *A philosophy and history of the social sciences.* Oxford: Basil Blackwell.

Rosenberg, Alexander. (1995). *Philosophy of social science.* Boulder, CO: Westview Press.

Skinner, Quentin (Ed.). (1985). *The return of grand theory in the human sciences.* Cambridge: Cambridge University Press.

Toulmin, Stephen, & June Goodfield. (1965). *The discovery of time.* New York: Harper and Row.

Multicultural and Gender Perspectives on Science and Knowledge

Belenky, Mary Field, Blythe McVicker Clinchy, Nancy Rule Goldberger, & Jill Mattuck Tarule. (1986). *Women's ways of knowing.* New York: Basic Books.

Goldberger, Nancy Rule, Jill Mattuck Tarule, Blythe McVicker Clinchy, & Mary Field Belenky. (1996). *Knowledge, difference, and power: Essays inspired by women's ways of knowing.* New York: Basic Books.

Hess, David J. (1995). *Science and technology in a multicultural world: The cultural politics of facts and artifacts.* New York: Columbia University Press.

San Juan, E., Jr. (1992). *Racial formations/critical transformations.* Atlantic Highlands: Humanities Press.

White, Robert. (1990). *White mythologies: Writing history and the west.* London: Routledge.

Mindful Inquiry

Buddhism

Conze, Edward. (1959). *Buddhism: Its essence and development.* New York: Harper and Row.

Nhat Hanh, Thich. (1974). *Zen keys.* (Albert Low and Jean Low, Trans.). Garden City, NY: Doubleday Anchor.

Rahula, Walpola. (1974). *What the Buddha taught* (2nd ed., enlarged). New York: Grove Press.

Phenomenology

Ihde, Don. (1986). *Experimental phenomenology: An introduction.* Albany: State University of New York Press.

Psathas, George (Ed.). (1989). *Phenomenology and sociology: Theory and research.* Washington, DC: Center for Advanced Research in Phenomenology and University Press of America.

Wagner, Helmut R. (1983). *Phenomenology of consciousness and sociology of the life-world: An introductory study.* Edmonton: University of Alberta Press.

Young, Iris Marion. (1990). "Throwing like a girl: A phenomenology of feminine body comportment, motility, and spatiality." In *Throwing like a girl and other essays in feminist philosophy and social theory.* Bloomington: Indiana University Press.

Hermeneutics

Howard, Roy J. (1982). *Three faces of hermeneutics: An introduction to current theories of understanding.* Berkeley: University of California Press.

Palmer, Richard E. (1969). *Hermeneutics: Interpretation theory in Schleiermacher, Dilthey, Heidegger, and Gadamer.* Evanston, IL: Northwestern University Press.

Ricoeur, Paul. (1977). "The model of the text: Meaningful action considered as a text." In Fred Dallmayr & Thomas A. McCarthy (Eds.), *Understanding and social inquiry* (John B. Thompson, Trans.). Notre Dame, IN: University of Notre Dame Press.

Ricoeur, Paul. (1981). *Hermeneutics and human sciences: Essays on language, action, and interpretation* (John B. Thompson, Ed.; John B. Thompson, Trans.). Cambridge: Cambridge University Press.

Critical Social Science and Critical Theory

Benhabib, Seyla, Judith Butler, Drucilla Cornell, & Nancy Fraser. (1995). *Feminist contentions: A philosophical exchange.* New York: Routledge.

Braaten, Jane. (1991). *Habermas's critical theory of society.* Albany: State University of New York Press.

Calhoun, Craig. (1995). *Critical social theory: Culture, history, and the challenge of difference.* Oxford: Blackwell.

Collins, Patricia Hill. (1990). *Black feminist thought: Knowledge, consciousness, and the politics of empowerment.* Boston: Unwin Hyman.

Fay, Brian. (1987). *Critical social science: Liberation and its limits.* Ithaca, NY: Cornell University Press.

Harding, Sandra (Ed.). (1987). *Feminism and methodology: Social science issues.* Bloomington: Indiana University Press.

Held, David. (1980). *Introduction to critical theory: Horkheimer to Habermas.* Berkeley: University of California Press.

Morrow, Raymond A., & David A. Brown. (1994). *Critical theory and methodology: Interpretive structuralism as a research program.* Thousand Oaks, CA: Sage.

Smith, Dorothy. (1987). *The everyday world as problematic: A feminist sociology.* Boston: Northeastern Press.

Young, Iris Marion. (1990). "Humanism, gynocentrism, and feminist politics." In *Throwing like a girl and other essays in feminist philosophy and social theory.* Bloomington: Indiana University Press.

Sociological Theory

Collins, Randall. (1994). *Four sociological traditions.* New York: Oxford University Press.

Collins, Randall (Ed.). (1994). *Four sociological traditions: Selected readings.* New York: Oxford University Press.

Coser, Lewis A. (1977). *Masters of sociological thought: Ideas in historical and social context.* New York: Harcourt Brace Jovanovich.

Ritzer, George. (1992). *Contemporary sociological theory* (3rd ed.). New York: McGraw-Hill.

General Introductions to Research

Golden, M. Patricia (Ed.). (1976). *The research experience*. Itasca, IL: F. E. Peacock.

Robson, Colin. (1993). *Real world research: A resource for social scientists and practitioner-researchers*. Oxford: Blackwell.

Quantitative and Behavioral Science

Bausell, R. Barker. (1986). *A practical guide to conducting empirical research*. New York: Harper and Row.

Kerlinger, Fred N. (1979). *Behavioral research: A conceptual approach*. New York: Holt, Rinehart, and Winston.

Meek, Ronald L. (1971). *Figuring out society*. London: William Collins Sons.

Qualitative Research in General

Berger, Peter, & Thomas Luckmann. (1967). *The social construction of reality*. New York: Doubleday Anchor.

Creswell, John W. (1998). *Qualitative inquiry and research design: Choosing among five traditions*. Thousand Oaks, CA: Sage.

Denzin, Norman K., & Yvonna S. Lincoln. (1994). *Handbook of qualitative research*. Thousand Oaks, CA: Sage.

Lofland, John, & Lyn H. Lofland. (1995). *Analyzing social settings: A guide to qualitative observation and analysis* (3rd ed.) Belmont, CA: Wadsworth.

Schatzman, Leonard, & Anselm Strauss. (1973). *Field research: Strategies for a natural sociology*. Englewood Cliffs, NJ: Prentice Hall.

Silverman, David. (1993). *Interpreting qualitative data*. London: Sage.

Strauss, Anselm, & Juliet Corbin. (1990). *Basics of qualitative research: Grounded theory procedures and techniques*. Newbury Park, CA: Sage.

Ethnography

Agar, Michael H. (1986). *The professional stranger: An informal introduction to ethnography* (2nd ed.) San Diego, CA: Academic Press.

Marcus, George E., & Michael M. J. Fischer. (1986). *Anthropology as cultural critique: An experimental moment in the human sciences*. Chicago: University of Chicago Press.

Spradley, James P., & David W. McCurdy (Eds.). 1997. *Conformity and conflict: Readings in cultural anthropology*. New York: Longman.

Action Research

Park, Peter. (1992). "The discovery of participatory research as a new scientific paradigm: Personal and intellectual accounts." *The American Sociologist, 23,* 2–42.

Park, Peter (Ed.). (1993). *Voices of change: Participatory research in the United States and Canada.* Westport, CT: Bergin and Garvey.

Whyte, William Foote (Ed.). (1991). *Participatory action research.* Newbury Park, CA: Sage.

Evaluation Research

Patton, Michael Quinn. (1997). *Utilization-focused evaluation: The new century text.* Thousand Oaks, CA: Sage.

Rossi, Peter H., & Howard E. Freeman. (1993). *Evaluation: A systematic approach* (5th ed.). Newbury Park, CA: Sage.

Comparative–Historical Inquiry

Bloch, Marc. (1953). *The historian's craft.* (Peter Putnam, Trans.). New York: Vintage.

Fischer, David Hackett. (1970). *Historians' fallacies: Toward a logic of historical thought.* New York: Harper and Row.

Theoretical Inquiry

Stinchcombe, Arthur L. (1968). *Constructing social theories.* Chicago: University of Chicago Press.

Critical Thinking and Argumentation

Fisher, Alec. (1988). *The logic of real arguments.* Cambridge: Cambridge University Press.

Jones, Morgan, D. (1995). *The Thinker's Toolkit: Fourteen skills for making smarter decisions in business and in life.* New York: Random House.

Quine, W. V., & J. S. Ullian. (1978). *The web of belief,* (2nd ed.). New York: Random House.

References

Aanstoos, Christopher M. (1987). "A comparative survey of human science psychologies." *Methods, 12,* 1–36.

Adorno, Theodor W. (1973). *Philosophy of modern music* (Anna G. Mitchell and Wesley V. Blomster, Trans.). New York: Continuum.

Adorno, Theodor W. (1974). *Minima moralia: Reflections from damaged life* (E. F. N. Jephcott, Trans.). London: NLB.

Adorno, Theodor W. (1982). *Negative dialectics* (2nd ed.) (E. B. Ashton, Trans.). New York: Continuum.

Adorno, Theodor W. (1991a). *Culture industry: Selected essays on mass culture* (Stephen Crook, Ed.; J. M. Bernstein, Trans.). London: Routledge.

Adorno, Theodor W. (1991b). *In search of Wagner* (Rodney Livingstone, Trans.). London: Routledge.

Adorno, Theodor W. (1991c). *Notes to literature: Volume one* (Lawrence D. Kritzman and Richard Wolin, Eds.; Shierry W. Nicholsen, Trans.). New York: Columbia University Press.

Adorno, Theodor W. (1992a). *Mahler: A musical physiognomy* (Edmund Jephcott, Trans.). Chicago: University of Chicago Press.

Adorno, Theodor W. (1992b). *Notes to literature: Volume two* (Shierry W. Nicholsen, Trans.). New York: Columbia University Press.

Adorno, Theodor W. (1992c). *Quasi una fantasia: Essays on music & culture* (Rodney Livingstone, Trans.). New York: W. W. Norton.

Adorno, Theodor W. (1993). *Hegel: Three studies* (Shierry W. Nicholsen, Trans.). Cambridge, MA: MIT Press.

Adorno, Theodor W. (1994). *The stars come down to earth and other essays on the irrational in culture* (Stephen Crook, Ed.). London: Routledge.

Adorno, Theodor W., Hans Albert, Ralf Dahrendorf, Jürgen Habermas, Harald Pilot, & Karl R. Popper. (1976). *The positivist dispute in German sociology* (Glyn Adey and David Frisby, Trans.). London: Heinemann. (Original work published 1969)

Adorno, Theodor W., Else Frenkel-Brunswick, Daniel J. Levinson, & R. Nevitt Sanford. (1950). *The authoritarian personality.* New York: Harper and Brothers.

Alexander, Christopher, Sara Ishikawa, Murray Silverstein, Max Jacobson, Ingrid Fiksdahl-King, & Shlomo Angel. (1977). *A pattern language: Towns, building, construction.* New York: Oxford University Press.

American Psychiatric Association. (1994). *Diagnostic and statistical manual of mental disorders* (4th ed.). Washington, DC: Author.

Anderson, Adrienne. (1998). *Report on sociological practicum.* Unpublished manuscript, The Fielding Institute, Santa Barbara.

Apel, Karl-Otto. (1984). *Understanding and explanation: A transcendental-pragmatic perspective* (Georgia Warnke, Trans.). Cambridge, MA: MIT Press.

Appadurai, Arjun. (1996). *Modernity at large: Cultural dimensions of globalization.* Minneapolis: University of Minnesota Press.

Auerbach, Erich. (1953). *Mimesis: The representation of reality in western literature* (Willard R. Trask, Trans.). Princeton, NJ: Princeton University Press.

Ayer, Alfred Jules. (1952). *Language, truth, and logic.* New York: Dover.

Ayer, Alfred Jules. (1957). "The Vienna circle." In A. J. Ayer et al. (Eds.), *The revolution in philosophy.* London: Macmillan.

Barber, Benjamin R. (1995). *Jihad vs. McWorld.* New York: Random House.

Baron, Larry, & Murray A. Straus. (1989). *Four theories of rape in American society.* New Haven, CT: Yale University Press.

Barrell, James J., Christopher M. Aanstoos, Anne C. Richards, & Mike Arons. (1987). "Human science research methods." *Journal of Humanistic Psychology, 27,* 424–457.

Bart, Pauline B., & Peter Kimball. (1992). "Four theories of rape in American society: A state-level analysis." *The Annals of the American Academy of Political and Social Science, 521,* 213–215.

Barthes, Roland. (1968). *Elements of semiology.* New York: Hill and Wang.

Barthes, Roland. (1972). *Mythologies* (Annette Lavers, Trans.) New York: Hill and Wang. (Original work published 1957)

Barthes, Roland. (1990). *The fashion system* (Matthew Ward and Richard Howard, Trans.). Berkeley: University of California Press.

Bechert, Heinz, & Richard Francis Gombrich. (1984). *The world of Buddhism: Buddhist monks and nuns in society and culture.* London: Thames and Hudson.

Belenky, Mary Field, Blythe McVicker Clinchy, Nancy Rule Goldberger, & Jill Mattuck Tarule. (1986). *Women's ways of knowing.* New York: Basic Books.

Bendix, Reinhard. (1962). *Max Weber: An intellectual portrait.* Garden City, NJ: Doubleday.

Benhabib, Seyla, Judith Butler, Drucilla Cornell, & Nancy Fraser. (1995). *Feminist contentions: A philosophical exchange.* New York: Routledge.

Benhabib, Seyla, & Fred Dallmayr. (1990). *The communicative ethics controversy.* Cambridge: Cambridge University Press.

Beniger, James R. (1986). *The control revolution: Technological and economic origins of the information society.* Cambridge, MA: Harvard University Press.

Benjamin, Jessica. (1988). *The bonds of love: Psychoanalysis, feminism, and the problem of domination.* New York: Pantheon Books.

Bentz, Valerie Malhotra. (1989). "Simmel and power in a dyadic relationship: Illustrations from a dance work." Paper presented at the annual meeting of the American Sociological Association.

Bentz, Valerie Malhotra. (1993). "Creating images in dance: Works of Hanstein and Ziaks." In Valerie Malhotra Bentz & Philip E. F. Mayes (Eds.), *Women's power and roles as portrayed in visual images of women in the arts and mass media.* Lewiston, PA: Edwin Mellen Press.

Bentz, Valerie Malhotra. (1995). "Husserl, Schutz, Paul and Me: Reflections on writing phenomenology." *Human Studies, 18,* 41–62.

Bentz, Valerie Malhotra, & Wade Kenny. (1997). ""Body-as-World": Kenneth Burke's answer to the postmodernist charges against sociology." *Sociological Theory, 15,* 81–96.

Berger, Peter, & Thomas Luckmann. (1967). *The social construction of reality.* New York: Doubleday Anchor.

Berger, Peter L., & Hansfried Kellner. (1970). "Marriage and the construction of reality." In Hans Peter Dreitzel (Ed.). *Recent sociology #2,* New York: Macmillan.

Bernstein, Richard J. (1978). *The restructuring of social and political theory*. Philadelphia: University of Pennsylvania Press.

Best, Steven, & Douglas M. Kellner. (1991). *Postmodern theory: Critical interrogations*. New York: Guilford Press.

Binswanger, Ludwig. (1967). *Being-in-the-world* (Jacob Needleman, Ed. and Trans.). New York: Harper and Row.

Blalock, Hubert M. (1964). *Causal inferences in nonexperimental research*. Chapel Hill: University of North Carolina Press.

Bloom, Harold. (1992). *The American religion: The emergence of the post-Christian nation*. New York: Simon and Schuster.

Bolter, J. David. (1984). *Turing's man: Western culture in the computer age*. Chapel Hill: University of North Carolina Press.

Bourdieu, Pierre. (1977). *Outline of a theory of practice* (Richard Nice, Trans.). Cambridge: Cambridge University Press.

Bourdieu, Pierre. (1984). *Distinction: A social critique of the judgement of taste*. (Richard Nice, Trans.). Cambridge: Harvard University Press.

Bourdieu, Pierre. (1995). *The rules of art: Genesis and structure of the literary field* (Susan Emanuel, Trans.). Stanford, CA: Stanford University Press.

Bourdieu, Pierre, & Loïc J. D. Wacquant. (1992). *An invitation to reflexive sociology*. Chicago: University of Chicago Press.

Boyle, James. (1996). *Shamans, software, and spleens: Law and the construction of the information society*. Cambridge, MA: Harvard University Press.

Braudel, Fernand. (1972). *The Mediterranean and the Mediterranean world in the age of Phillip II, Vol. 1* (Sian Reynolds, Trans.). New York: Harper and Row.

Braudel, Fernand. (1973). *Capitalism and material life 1400-1800*. (M. Kochan, Trans.). New York: Harper and Row.

Braudel, Fernand. (1980). *On history* (Sarah Matthews, Trans.). Chicago: University of Chicago Press.

Brook, James, & Iain A. Boal (Eds.). (1995). *Resisting the virtual life: The culture and politics of information*. San Francisco: City Lights Books.

Brown, Richard Harvey. (1987). *Society as text: Essays on rhetoric, reason, and reality*. Chicago: University of Chicago Press.

Brown, Richard Harvey. (1992). *Writing the social text: Poetics and politics in social science discourse*. New York: A. de Gruyter.

Buddha. (1974). "Setting in Motion the Wheel of Truth." In Walpola Rahula (Ed.), *What the Buddha taught*. New York: Grove Press.

Burawoy, Michael. (1979). *Manufacturing consent: Changes in the labor process under monopoly capitalism*. Chicago: University of Chicago Press.

Butler, Christopher. (1994). *Early modernism: Literature, music, and painting in Europe 1900–1916*. Oxford: Clarendon Press.

Calhoun, Craig. (1995). *Critical social theory: Culture, history, and the challenge of difference*. Oxford: Blackwell.

Campbell, Joseph. (1968). *The masks of God: Creative mythology*. New York: Viking Penguin.

Casey, Edward S. (1987). *Remembering: A phenomenological study*. Bloomington: Indiana University Press.

Casey, Edward S. (1993). *Getting back into place: Toward a renewed understanding of the place-world*. Bloomington: Indiana University Press.

Castaneda, Carlos. (1968). *The teachings of Don Juan: A Yaqui way of knowledge*. Berkeley: University of California Press.

Castells, Manuel. (1989). *The informational city: Information technology, economic restructuring, and the urban-regional process*. Oxford: Basil Blackwell.

Catton, William R., Jr., & Riley E. Dunlap. (1980). "A new ecological paradigm for post-exuberant sociology." *American Behavioral Scientist, 24,* 15–47.

Chafetz, Janet Saltzman. (1995). "Four theories of rape in American society: A state-level analysis." *Social Forces, 73,* 1631–1632.

Chattopadhyaya, D. P., Lester Embree, & Jitendranath Mohanty (Eds.). (1992). *Phenomenology and Indian philosophy.* Albany: State University of New York Press.

Chaudhuri, Jewel Ray. (1996). *Research: A way of knowing.* Unpublished paper, The Fielding Institute, Santa Barbara, California.

Chirot, Daniel. (1986). *Social change in the modern era.* San Diego, CA: Harcourt, Brace, Jovanovich.

Chodorow, Nancy. (1978). *The reproduction of mothering: Psychoanalysis and the sociology of gender.* Berkeley: University of California Press.

Cicourel, Aaron V. (1977). *The social organization of juvenile justice.* Philadelphia: Taylor and Francis.

Clancy, Ann Leone. (1996). *Toward a holistic concept of time: Exploring the link between internal and external temporal experiences.* Doctoral dissertation, Human and Organization Development, The Fielding Institute, Santa Barbara, CA.

Clark, Stuart. (1985). "The *Annales* historians." In Quentin Skinner, *The return of grand theory in the human sciences.* Cambridge: Cambridge University Press.

Clayman, Steven E., & Don H. Zimmerman. (1987). *"I'm sorry but we're out of time": Coordinating closings in televised news interviews.* American Sociological Association.

Clifton, Thomas J. (1983). *Music as heard: A study in applied phenomenology.* New Haven, CT: Yale University Press.

Coch, L., & J. R. P. French. (1948). Overcoming resistance to change. *Human Relations, 1,* 512–532.

Collier, John. (1945). "United States Indian Administration as a laboratory of ethnic relations." *Social Research, 12,* 275–286.

Collins, Patricia Hill. (1990). *Black feminist thought: Knowledge, consciousness, and the politics of empowerment.* Boston: Unwin Hyman.

Collins, Randall. (1986). *Max Weber: A skeleton key.* Beverly Hills, CA: Sage.

Collins, Randall. (1994). *Four sociological traditions.* New York: Oxford University Press.

Collins, Richard, James Curran, Nicholas Garnham, Paddy Scannell, Philip Schlesinger, & Colin Sparks (Eds.). (1986). *Media, culture, and society: A critical reader.* London: Sage.

Comte, Auguste. (1963). *Discours sur l'Esprit Positif suivi de cinq documents annexes* (Paul Arbousse-Bastide, Ed.). Paris: Union Générale d'éditions. (Original publication 1844)

Comte, Auguste. (1974). *The positive philosophy* (Abraham S. Blumberg, Trans.). New York: AMS Press.

Corbin, Juliet, & Anselm Strauss. (1990). "Grounded theory research: Procedures, canons, and evaluative criteria." *Qualitative Sociology, 13,* 3–21.

Coser, Lewis A. (1971). *Masters of sociological thought: Ideas in historical and social context.* New York: Harcourt Brace Jovanovich.

Dallmayr, Fred R. (1987). "System, state, and polis: Luhmann." In *Critical encounters: Between philosophy and politics.* Notre Dame: University of Notre Dame Press.

Davis, Murray S. (1983). *Smut: Erotic reality/obscene ideology.* Chicago: University of Chicago Press.

Deleuze, Gilles, & Félix Guattari. (1983). *Anti-Oedipus: Capitalism and schizophrenia* (Mark Seem Robert & Helen Lane, Trans.). Minneapolis: University of Minnesota Press.

Denzin, Norman K. (1989). *The research act: A theoretical introduction to sociological methods* (3rd ed.). Englewood Cliffs, NJ: Prentice Hall.

Derrida, Jacques. (1976). *Of grammatology* (Gayatri Chakravorty Spivak, Trans.). Baltimore: Johns Hopkins University Press.

Dickens, A. G. (1966). *Reformation and society in sixteenth-century Europe.* New York: Harcourt, Brace and World.

Dobb, Maurice. (1947). *Studies in the development of capitalism.* New York: International Publishers.

Docherty, Thomas (Ed.). (1993). *Postmodernism: A reader.* New York: Columbia University Press.

Doyal, Len, & Ian Gough. (1991). *A theory of human need.* New York: Guilford Press.

Dreyfus, Hubert. (1992). *What computers still can't do: A critique of artificial reason* (2nd ed.). Cambridge, MA: MIT Press.

Duncan, Hugh Dalziel. (1964). *Communication and social order.* New York: Oxford University Press.

Dupré, Louis. (1993). *Passage to modernity: An essay in the hermeneutics of nature and culture.* New Haven, CT: Yale University Press.

Durand, Gilbert. (1969). *Les structures anthropologiques de l'imaginaire: Introduction à l'archétypologie générale* (3rd ed.). Paris: Bordas.

Durkheim, Emile. (1947). *Division of labor in society* (George Simpson, Trans.). Glencoe, IL: Free Press.

Elias, Norbert. (1994). *The civilizing process: The history of manners and state formation and civilization* (Edmund Jephcott, Trans.). Oxford: Blackwell.

Ellis, Lee. (1995). "Four theories of rape in American society: A state-level analysis." *Women and Health, 22,* 75–78.

Erikson, Erik H. (1958). *Young man Luther: A study in psychoanalysis and history.* New York: Norton.

Fanon, Frantz. (1966). *The wretched of the earth* (Constance Farrington, Trans.). New York: Grove Press.

Fay, Brian. (1987). *Critical social science: Liberation and its limits.* Ithaca, NY: Cornell University Press.

Feenberg, Andrew. (1991). *Critical theory of technology.* New York: Oxford University Press.

Findlay, John Niemeyer. (1958). *Hegel: A reexamination.* London: George Allen and Unwin.

Fischer, David Hackett. (1970). *Historians' fallacies: Toward a logic of historical thought.* New York: Harper and Row.

Fischer, William F. (Ed.). (1988). *Theories of anxiety* (2nd ed.). Washington, DC: Center for Advanced Research in Phenomenology and University Press of America.

Fiske, John. (1994). "Audiencing: Cultural practice and cultural studies." In Norman K. Denzin & Yvonna S. Lincoln (Eds.), *Handbook of qualitative research.* Thousand Oaks, CA: Sage.

Foglia, Wanda D. (1990). "Four theories of rape in American society: A state-level analysis." *Qualitative Sociology, 13,* 281–284.

Forester, John (Ed.). (1985). *Critical theory and public life.* Cambridge, MA: MIT Press.

Forester, John. (1993). *Critical theory, public policy, and planning practice.* Albany: State University of New York Press.

Foucault, Michel. (1975). *The birth of the clinic: An archaeology of medical perception* (A. M. Sheridan Smith, Trans.). New York: Vintage Books.

Foucault, Michel. (1980). *Power/knowledge: Selected interviews and other writings, 1972–77.* (Colin Gordon, Ed.; Colin Gordon, Leo Marshall, John Mepham, and Kate Soper, Trans.). New York: Pantheon Books.

Frank, Manfred. (1988). *L'ultime raison du sujet.* (Veronique Zanettie, Trans.). Arles, France: Actes Sud.

Fraser, Nancy. (1989). *Unruly practices: Power, discourse, and gender in contemporary social theory.* Minneapolis: University of Minnesota Press.

Fraser, Nancy. (1997). *Justice interruptus: Critical reflections on the "postsocialist" condition.* New York: Routledge.

Fraser, Nancy, & Sandra Lee Bartky. (1992). *Revaluing French feminism: Critical essays on difference, agency, and culture.* Bloomington: Indiana University Press.

Freud, Sigmund. (1965). *The interpretation of dreams* (8th rev. ed.; James Strachey, Trans.). New York: Avon.

Gadamer, Hans-Georg. (1975). *Truth and method* (Garrett Barden and John Cumming, Trans.). New York: Seabury Press.

Gadamer, Hans-Georg. (1976). *Philosophical hermeneutics* (David. E. Linge, Trans.). Berkeley: University of California Press.

Garfinkel, Harold. (1967). *Studies in ethnomethodology.* Englewood Cliffs, NJ: Prentice Hall.

Giddens, Anthony (Ed.). (1974). *Positivism and sociology.* London: Heinemann.

Giddens, Anthony. (1984). *The constitution of society.* Berkeley: University of California Press.

Giddens, Anthony. (1986). "Action, subjectivity, and the constitution of meaning." *Social Research, 53,* 529–545.

Gilligan, Carol. (1982). *In a different voice: Psychological theory and women's development.* Cambridge, MA: Harvard University Press.

Gillispie, Charles Coulston. (1960). *The edge of objectivity: An essay in the history of scientific ideas.* Princeton, NJ: Princeton University Press.

Giorgi, Amedeo, William F. Fischer, & Rolf Von Eckartsberg (Eds.). (1971). *Duquesne studies in phenomenological psychology.* Pittsburgh, PA: Duquesne University Press and Humanities Press.

Glaser, Barney, G. (1992). *Emergence vs. forcing: Basics of grounded theory analysis.* Mill Valley, CA: Sociology Press.

Glaser, Barney G., & Anselm L. Strauss. (1967). *The discovery of grounded theory: Strategies for qualitative research.* New York: Aldine.

Glass, James M. (1993). *Shattered selves: Multiple personality in a postmodern world.* Ithaca, NY: Cornell University Press.

Goffman, Erving. (1961). *Asylums: Essays on the social situation of mental patients & other inmates.* New York: Aldine de Gruyter.

Goldberger, Nancy Rule, Jill Mattuck Tarule, Blythe McVicker Clinchy, & Mary Field Belenky. (1996). *Knowledge, difference, and power: Essays inspired by women's ways of knowing.* New York: Basic Books.

Golden, M. Patricia (Ed.). (1976). *The research experience.* Itasca, IL: F. E. Peacock.

Gottdiener, Mark. (1995). *Postmodern semiotics: Material culture and the forms of postmodern life.* Oxford: Blackwell.

Grossberg, Lawrence, Cary Nelson, & Paula A. Treichler. (1992). *Cultural studies.* New York: Routledge.

Haag, Karl Heinz. (1985). *Der Fortschritt in der Philosophie.* Frankfurt am Main: Suhrkamp Verlag.

Habermas, Jürgen. (1970a). "Science and technology as 'Ideology.' " In *Toward a Rational Society: Student Protest, Science, & Politics* (Jeremy J. Shapiro, Trans.). Boston: Beacon Press.

Habermas, Jürgen. (1970b). *Toward a rational society: Student protest, science, and politics.* (Jeremy J. Shapiro, Trans.). Boston: Beacon Press.

Habermas, Jürgen. (1970c). "Toward a theory of communicative competence." In Hans Peter Dreitzel (Ed.), *Recent sociology, Vol. #2.* New York: Macmillan.

Habermas, Jürgen. (1971). *Knowledge and human interests* (Jeremy J. Shapiro, Trans.). Boston: Beacon Press.

Habermas, Jürgen. (1973). *Theory and practice* (John Viertel, Trans.). Boston: Beacon Press.

Habermas, Jürgen. (1975). *Legitimation crisis* (Thomas McCarthy, Trans.). Boston: Beacon Press.

Habermas, Jürgen. (1984). *The theory of communicative action, vol. 1: Reason and the rationalization of society* (Thomas McCarthy, Trans.). Boston: Beacon Press.

Habermas, Jürgen. (1988). *The theory of communicative action, vol. 2: Lifeworld and system: A critique of functionalist reason* (Thomas McCarthy, Trans.). Boston: Beacon Press.

Habermas, Jürgen. (1990). *Moral consciousness and communicative action* (Shierry W. Nicholsen, Trans.). Cambridge, MA: MIT Press.

Habermas, Jürgen. (1996). *Between facts and norms: Contributions to a discourse theory of law and democracy* (William Rehg, Trans.). Cambridge, MA: MIT Press.

Hale, John. (1994). *The civilization of Europe in the Renaissance.* New York: Atheneum.

Hamabata, Matthews. (1986). "Ethnographic boundaries: Culture, class and sexuality in Tokyo." *Qualitative Sociology, 9,* 354–371.

Hamabata, Matthews. (1991). *The crested kimono.* Ithaca, NY: Cornell University Press.

Hannerz, Ulf. (1992). *Cultural complexity: Studies in the social organization of meaning.* New York: Columbia University Press.

Haraway, Donna. (1991). *Simians, cyborgs, and women.* New York: Routledge.

Harding, Sandra. (1996). "Ways of knowing and the 'epistemological crisis' of the west." In Nancy Rule Goldberger, Jill Mattuck Tarule, Blythe McVicker Clinchy, & Mary Field Belenky (Eds.), *Knowledge, difference, and power: Essays inspired by women's ways of knowing.* New York: Basic Books.

Harris, Errol E. (1987). *Formal, transcendental, and dialectical thinking: Logic and reality.* Albany: State University of New York Press.

Harvey, David. (1989). *The condition of postmodernity: An enquiry into the origins of cultural change.* Cambridge, MA: Basil Blackwell.

Hazard, Paul. (1963). *European thought in the eighteenth century: From Montesquieu to Lessing* (J. Lewis May, Trans.). Cleveland, OH: World.

Heap, James L. (1982). "Practical reasoning in depression: A practice." *Human Studies, 5,* 345–356.

Heelan, Patrick A. (1983). *Space-perception and the philosophy of science.* Berkeley: University of California Press.

Hegel, Georg Wilhelm Friedrich. (1977). "Who thinks abstractly?" In Walter Kaufmann (Ed. and Trans.), *Hegel: Texts and commentary.* Notre Dame: University of Notre Dame Press.

Heidegger, Martin. (1971). The nature of language. In *On the way to language* (Peter Hertz, Trans.). San Francisco: Harper and Row.

Heidegger, Martin. (1993). "The origin of the work of art." In David Farrell Krell (Ed.), *Basic writings from Being and Time (1927) to The Task of Thinking (1964)* (David Farrell Krell, Joan Stambaugh, John Sallis, Frank A. Capuzzi, and J. Glenn Gray, Trans.). San Francisco: HarperCollins.

Heilbroner, Robert L. (1961). *The future as history: The historic currents of our time and the direction in which they are taking America.* New York: Grove Press.

Heim, Michael. (1993). *The metaphysics of virtual reality.* New York: Oxford University Press.

Heraclitus. (1979). "Fragments." In Guy Davenport (Ed. and Trans.), *Herakleitos and Diogenes.* Bolinas, CA: Grey Fox Press.

Heritage, John. (1984). *Garfinkel and ethnomethodology.* Cambridge, MA: Polity Press.

Hess, David J. (1995). *Science and technology in a multicultural world: The cultural politics of facts and artifacts.* New York: Columbia University Press.

Hobsbawm, Eric. (1962). *The age of revolution: 1789–1848.* New York: New American Library.

Horkheimer, Max. (1972). *Critical theory* (Matthew O'Connell, Trans.). New York: Herder and Herder.

Horkheimer, Max, & Theodor W. Adorno. (1975). *Dialectic of enlightenment* (John Cumming, Trans.). New York: Continuum.

Husserl, Edmund. (1962). *Ideas: General introduction to pure phenomenology* (W. R. Gibson Boyce, Trans.). New York: Collier Books.

Husserl, Edmund. (1970). *The crisis of European sciences and transcendental phenomenology: An introduction to phenomenological philosophy* (David Carr, Trans). Evanston, IL: Northwestern University Press.

Husserl, Edmund. (1977). *Cartesian meditations: An introduction to phenomenology* (Dorion Cairns, Trans). The Hague: Martinus Nijhoff.

Ihde, Don. (1990). *Technology and the lifeworld: From garden to earth.* Bloomington: Indiana University Press.

Irigaray, Luce, & Margaret Whitford. (1991). *The Irigaray reader.* Cambridge, MA: Basil Blackwell.

Iyer, Pico. (1988). *Video night in Kathmandu and other reports from the not-so-far-East.* New York: Vintage Books.

Jencks, Charles. (1989). *What is post-modernism?* (3rd rev. ed.). New York: St. Martin's Press.

Jung, Carl Gustav. (1960). *The structure and dynamics of the psyche* (R. F. C. Hull, Trans.). New York: Pantheon Books.

Jung, Hwa Yol. (1979). *The crisis of political understanding: A phenomenological perspective in the conduct of political inquiry.* Pittsburgh, PA: Duquesne University Press.

Kabat-Zinn, Jon. (1994). *Wherever you go, there you are: Mindfulness meditation in everyday life.* New York: Hyperion.

Kant, Immanuel. (1933). *Critique of pure reason* (Norman Kemp Smith, Trans.). London: Macmillan.

Kegan, Robert. (1994). *In over our heads: The mental demands of modern life.* Cambridge, MA: Harvard University Press.

Kennedy, Paul M. (1987). *The rise and fall of the great powers: Economic change and military conflict from 1500 to 2000.* New York: Random House.

Kockelmans, Joseph J. (Ed.). (1987). *Phenomenological psychology: The Dutch school.* Dordrecht: Martinus Nijhoff.

Kondo, Dorinne K. (1985). "Gender, self and work in Japan: Some issues in the study of self and other." *Culture, Medicine and Psychiatry, 9,* 3, 19–328.

Kondo, Dorinne K. (1990). *Crafting selves: Power, gender, and discourses of identity in a Japanese workplace.* Chicago: University of Chicago Press.

Korsch, Karl. (1938). *Karl Marx.* New York: John Wiley.

Kroker, Arthur, & Michael A. Weinstein. (1994). *Data trash: The theory of the virtual class.* New York: St. Martin's Press.

Kuhn, Thomas S. (1970). *The structure of scientific revolutions* (2nd enlarged ed.). Chicago: University of Chicago Press.

LaFree, Gary. (1990). "Four theories of rape in American society: A state-level analysis." *Social Forces, 69,* 326–328.

Laing, Ronald D. (1965). *The divided self.* Harmondsworth: Penguin Books.

Landes, David S. (1969). *The unbound Prometheus: Technological change and industrial development in Western Europe from 1750 to the present.* Cambridge: Cambridge University Press.

Landgrebe, Ludwig. (1968). "Die Phänomenologie der Leiblichkeit und das Problem der Materie." In *Phänomenologie und Geschichte.* Gütersloh: Gütersloher Verlagshaus Gerd Mohn.

Latour, Bruno. (1993). *We have never been modern* (Catherine Porter, Trans.). Cambridge, MA: Harvard University Press.

Leiss, William. (1990). *Under technology's thumb.* Montreal: McGill-Queen's University Press.

Leiss, William. (1994). *The domination of nature.* Montreal: McGill-Queen's University Press.

Lemert, Charles (Ed.). (1993). *Social theory: The multicultural and classic readings.* Boulder, CO: Westview Press.

Lerner, Melvin J. (1980). *The belief in a just world: A fundamental delusion.* New York: Plenum Press.

Levesque-Lopman, Louise. (1988). *Claiming reality: Phenomenology and women's experience.* Totowa, NJ: Rowman and Littlefield.

Levin, David Michael. (1989). *The listening self: Personal growth, social change, and the closure of metaphysics.* London: Routledge.

Levy, Pierre. (1987). *La Machine Univers: Creation, Cognition, et Culture Informatique.* Paris: Éditions La Découverte.

Lewin, Kurt. (1946). "Action research and minority problems." *Journal of Social Issues,* 34–36.

Lewin, Kurt. (1952). "Group decision and social change." In Theodore Newcomb & E. L. Hartley (Eds.), *Readings in social psychology.* New York: Henry Holt.

Locke, Karen. (1996). "Rewriting the discovery of grounded theory after 25 years?" *Journal of Management Inquiry, 5,* 239–245.

Lowenthal, Leo. (1957). *Literature and the image of man.* Boston: Beacon Press.

Lowenthal, Leo. (1961). *Literature, popular culture, and society.* Palo Alto, CA: Pacific Books.

Lyon, David. (1994). *Postmodernity.* Minneapolis: University of Minnesota Press.

Lyotard, Jean-François. (1984). *The postmodern condition: A report on knowledge* (Geoff Bennington and Brian Massumi, Trans.). Minneapolis: University of Minnesota Press.

Mann, Thomas. (1986). *A guide to library research methods.* New York: Oxford University Press.

Mannheim, Karl. (1985). *Ideology and utopia: An introduction to the sociology of knowledge.* San Diego, CA: Harcourt Brace Jovanovich.

Marcus, George E., & Michael M. J. Fischer. (1986). *Anthropology as cultural critique: An experimental moment in the human sciences.* Chicago: University of Chicago Press.

Marcuse, Herbert. (1954). *Reason and revolution: Hegel and the rise of social theory* (2nd ed.). Boston: Beacon Press.

Marcuse, Herbert. (1966a). *Eros and civilization: A philosophical inquiry into Freud* (2nd ed.). Boston: Beacon Press.

Marcuse, Herbert. (1966b). *One-dimensional man.* Boston: Beacon Press.

Marcuse, Herbert. (1968). *Negations: Essays in critical theory* (Jeremy J. Shapiro, Trans.). Boston: Beacon Press.

Marcuse, Herbert. (1982). "Some social implications of modern technology." In Andrew Arato & Eike Gebhardt, *The essential Frankfurt school reader.* New York: Continuum.

Marx, Karl. (1960). Theses on Feuerbach. In Loyd D. Easton & Kurt H. Guddat (Eds. and Trans.), *Writings of the young Marx on philosophy and society.* Garden City, NJ: Doubleday Anchor.

May, Rollo, Ernest Angel, & Henri F. Ellenberger (Eds.). (1958). *Existence: A new dimension in psychiatry and psychology.* New York: Simon and Schuster.

McKibben, Bill. (1992). *The age of missing information.* New York: Random House.

McLane, Janice. "Thinking as victim/acting as violator: The mind of the abuser." Paper presented at the Annual Conference of the Society for Phenomenology and the Human Sciences.

McLuhan, Marshall. (1967). *The mechanical bride: Folklore of industrial man.* Boston: Beacon Press.

Mead, George Herbert. (1934). *Mind, self, and society: From the standpoint of a social behaviorist* (Charles W. Morris, (Ed.). Chicago: University of Chicago.

Mead, Margaret. (1973). *Coming of age in Samoa: A psychological study of primitive youth for Western civilization.* New York: Morrow.

Mensch, James. (1996). *Knowing and being: A postmodern reversal.* University Park: Pennsylvania State University Press.

Merchant, Carolyn. (1980). *The death of nature: Women, ecology, and the scientific revolution.* San Francisco: Harper and Row.

Merleau-Ponty, Maurice. (1964). *L'Oeil et l'Esprit.* Paris: Gallimard.

Merleau-Ponty, Maurice. (1981). *Phenomenology of perception* (Colin Smith, Trans.). London: Routledge.

Michael, Mary Lou. (1996). *Salt and light: The lived experience of evangelical Protestant women influencing public education.* Doctoral dissertation, Human and Organization Development, The Fielding Institute, Santa Barbara, CA.

Milgram, Stanley. (1974). *Obedience to authority: An experimental view.* New York: Harper and Row.

Miller, G. Tyler, Jr. (1972). *Replenish the Earth: A primer in human ecology.* Belmont, CA: Wadsworth.

Miller, Michael B. (1981). *The Bon Marché: Bourgeois culture and the department store, 1869–1920*. Princeton, NJ: Princeton University Press.

Miller, Richard W. (1987). *Fact and method: Explanation, confirmation, and reality in the natural and social sciences*. Princeton, NJ: Princeton University Press.

Mills, C. Wright. (1959). *The sociological imagination*. New York: Grove Press.

Moore, Barrington, Jr. (1966). *Social origins of dictatorship and democracy: Lord and peasant in the making of the modern world*. Boston: Beacon Press.

Morris, Charles W. (1973). *Paths of life: Preface to a world religion*. Chicago: University of Chicago Press.

Morrow, Raymond A., & David A. Brown. (1994). *Critical theory and methodology: Interpretive structuralism as a research program*. Thousand Oaks, CA: Sage.

Mosley, Erma Dianne. (1991). *The history and social context of an African American family cemetery and its influence on social organization and mental health*. Doctoral dissertation, Texas Woman's University.

Moustakas, Clark E. (1961). *Loneliness*. Englewood Cliffs, NJ: Prentice-Hall.

Mowshowitz, Abbe. (1985). "On the social relations of computers." *Human Systems Management, 5*, 99–110.

Mowshowitz, Abbe. (1986). "Social dimensions of office automation." In M. Yovits (Ed.), *Advances in computers*. New York: Academic Press.

Mowshowitz, Abbe. (1992). "Virtual feudalism: A vision of political organization in the Information Age." *Informatization and the Public Sector, 2*, 213–251.

Mowshowitz, Abbe. (1994). "Information as a commodity: Assessment of market value." In M. Yorits (Ed.), *Advances in computers*. New York: Academic Press.

Moynihan, Mary Beth. (1996). "Walking the mystical path with practical feet." Paper presented at the Annual Conference of the Society for Phenomenology and the Human Sciences.

Müller-Vollmer, Kurt (Ed.). (1988). *The hermeneutics reader: Texts of the German tradition from the enlightenment to the present* (Kurt Müller-Vollmer, Trans.). New York: Continuum.

Myers, Isabel Briggs, Mary H. McCaulley, & Robert Most. (1985). *Manual, a guide to the development and use of the Myers-Briggs type indicator*. Palo Alto, CA: Consulting Psychologists Press.

Nhat Hanh, Thich. (1974). *Zen keys* (Albert Low and Jean Low, Trans.). Garden City, NJ: Doubleday Anchor.

Nicholsen, Shierry Weber. (1997). *Exact imagination, late work: On Adorno's aesthetics*. Cambridge, MA: MIT Press.

Nietzsche, Friedrich. (1967). *On the genealogy of morals* (Walter Kaufmann and R. J. Hollingdale, Trans.). New York: Random House.

Noble, David F. (1992). *A world without women: The Christian clerical culture of Western science*. New York: Knopf.

Obst, Lynda R. (1996). *"Hello, he lied": And other truths from the Hollywood trenches*. Boston: Little, Brown.

Olafson, Frederick. A. (1979). *The dialectic of action: A philosophical interpretation of history and the humanities*. Chicago: University of Chicago.

Packer, Martin J. (1985). "Hermeneutic inquiry in the study of human conduct." *American Psychologist, 40*, 1081–1093.

Park, Peter (Ed.). (1993). *Voices of change: Participatory research in the United States and Canada*. Westport, CT: Bergin and Garvey.

Parsons, Talcott. (1949). *The structure of social action* (2nd ed.). Glencoe, IL: Free Press.

Pasmore, William, & Frank Friedlander. (1982). "An action-research program for increasing employee involvement in problem solving." *Administrative Science Quarterly, 27*, 343–362.

Paul, Jordan, & Margaret Paul. (1983). *Do I have to give up me to be loved by you?* Minneapolis, MN: Compcare.

Pearce, W. Barnett, & Stephen W. Littlejohn. (1997). *Moral conflict: When social worlds collide.* Thousand Oaks, CA: Sage.

Phillips, David P., & Daniel G. Smith. (1990). "Postponement of death until symbolically meaningful occasions." *The Journal of the American Medical Association, 263,* 1947–1952.

Polanyi, Michael. (1966). *The tacit dimension.* Garden City, NJ: Doubleday.

Polkinghorne, Donald. E. (1983). *Methodology for the human sciences: Systems of inquiry.* Albany: State University of New York Press.

Polkinghorne, Donald E. (1988). *Narrative knowing and the human sciences.* Albany: State University of New York Press.

Popper, Karl. (1965). *Conjectures and refutations: The growth of scientific knowledge.* New York: Harper and Row.

Poster, Mark. (1990). *The mode of information: Poststructuralism and social context.* Chicago: University of Chicago Press.

Poster, Mark. (1995). *The second media age.* Cambridge, MA: Polity Press.

Prior, Michael. (1997). *Surviving transition at ABC Limited: A study of heuristic research and action research interventions to effect employee anxiety reduction in changing times.* Doctoral dissertation, Human and Organization Development, The Fielding Institute, Santa Barbara, CA.

Psathas, George. (1995). *Conversation analysis: The study of talk-in-interaction.* Thousand Oaks, CA: Sage.

Rahula, Walpola. (1974). *What the Buddha taught* (2nd enlarged ed.). New York: Grove Press.

Reason, Peter (Ed.). (1988). *Human inquiry in action: Developments in new paradigm research.* London: Sage.

Reason, Peter, & John Rowan (Eds.). (1981). *Human inquiry: A sourcebook of new paradigm research.* New York: John Wiley.

Reich, Robert. (1991). *The work of nations: Preparing ourselves for 21st-century capitalism.* New York: Random House.

Rescher, Nicholas. (1979). *Cognitive systematization: A systems-theoretic approach to a coherentist theory of knowledge.* Totowa, NJ: Rowman and Littlefield.

Ricoeur, Paul. (1981). *Hermeneutics and human sciences: Essays on language, action, and interpretation* (John B. Thompson, Ed. and Trans.). Cambridge: Cambridge University Press.

Ritzer, George. (1992). *Contemporary sociological theory* (3rd ed.). New York: McGraw-Hill.

Robson, Colin. (1993). *Real world research: A resource for social scientists and practitioner-researchers.* Oxford: Blackwell Publishers.

Ropers, Richard H. (1988). *The invisible homeless.* New York: Insight Books.

Rosenthal, Robert. (1976). *Experimenter effects in behavioral research.* New York: Irvington.

Rossi, Peter H. (1989). *Down and out in America.* Chicago: University of Chicago Press.

Russell, Bertrand. (1956). "Logical positivism." In Robert Charles Marsh (Ed.), *Logic and knowledge: Essays 1901–1950.* London: Allen and Unwin.

Sahlins, Marshall. (1972). "The original affluent society." In *Stone age economics.* New York: Aldine de Gruyter.

Said, Edward W. (1978). *Orientalism.* New York: Pantheon Books.

Sale, Kirkpatrick. (1995). *Rebels against the future: The Luddites and their war on the industrial revolution—Lessons for the computer age.* Reading, MA: Addison-Wesley.

Sartre, Jean Paul. (1976). *Anti-semite and Jew* (George Joseph Becker, Trans.) New York: Schocken Books.

Schnaiberg, Allan, & Kenneth Alan Gould. (1994). *Environment and society: The enduring conflict.* New York: St. Martin's Press.

Schor, Juliet B. (1992). *The overworked American: The unexpected decline of leisure.* New York: Basic Books.

Schroyer, Trent. (1983). "Critique of the instrumental interest in nature." *Social Research, 50,* 158–184.

Schroyer, Trent (Ed.). (1997). *A world that works: Building blocks for a just and sustainable society.* New York: Bootstrap Press.

Schutz, Alfred. (1970). *On phenomenology and social relations: Selected writings* (Helmut Wagner, Ed.). Chicago: University of Chicago Press.

Schutz, Alfred. (1973a). *Collected papers of Alfred Schutz* (Maurice Natanson, Ed.). The Hague: Martinus Nijhoff.

Schutz, Alfred. (1976a). *Collected papers of Alfred Schutz, Vol. 2* (Arvid Brodersen, Ed.). The Hague: Martinus Nijhoff.

Schutz, Alfred. (1976b). "Making music together." In *Collected papers of Alfred Schutz, Vol. 2* (Arvid Brodersen, Ed.). The Hague: Martinus Nijhoff.

Schutz, Alfred. (1976c). "The stranger." In *Collected papers of Alfred Schutz, Vol. 2* (Arvid Brodersen, Ed.). The Hague: Martinus Nijhoff.

Sculco, Lois. (1997). *The empowerment of African American college women through storytelling.* Doctoral dissertation, Human and Organization Development, The Fielding Institute, Santa Barbara, CA.

Seamon, David (Ed.) (1993). *Dwelling, seeing, and designing: Toward a phenomenological ecology.* Albany: SUNY Press.

Seamon, David, & Robert Mugerauer. (1989). *Dwelling, place and environment: Towards a phenomenology of person and world.* New York: Columbia University Press.

Shapiro, Jeremy J. (1974, October 4). "The critical theory of Frankfurt." *Times Literary Supplement, 3,* 787.

Shapiro, Jeremy J. (1970). "One-dimensionality: The universal semiotic of technological experience." In Paul Breines (Ed.), *Critical interruptions.* New York: Herder and Herder.

Shenk, David. (1997). *Data smog: Surviving the information glut.* San Francisco: HarperCollins.

Shklar, Judith N. (1986). "Squaring the hermeneutic circle." *Social Research, 53,* 449–473.

Simmel, Georg. (1950). *The sociology of Georg Simmel* (Kurt H. Wolff, Ed. and Trans.). Glencoe, IL: Free Press.

Simon, W. M. (1963). *European positivism in the 19th century: An essay in intellectual history.* Ithaca, NY: Cornell University Press.

Sklair, Leslie. (1995). *Sociology of the global system* (2nd ed.). Baltimore: Johns Hopkins University Press.

Slater, Philip. (1976). *The pursuit of loneliness: American culture at the breaking point* (Rev. ed.). Boston: Beacon Press.

Smith, Dorothy. (1987). *The everyday world as problematic: A feminist sociology.* Boston: Northeastern Press.

Snyder, Paula J. (1993). "Four theories of rape in American society: A state level analysis." *Deviant Behavior, 14,* 377–379.

Sorokin, Pitirim Aleksandrovich. (1937). *Social and cultural dynamics.* New York: American Book.

Spender, Stephen. (1963). *The struggle of the modern.* Berkeley: University of California Press.

Stein, Murray. (1983). *In midlife: A Jungian perspective.* Dallas, TX: Spring.

Stinchcombe, Arthur L. (1968). *Constructing social theories.* Chicago: University of Chicago Press.

Strauss, Anselm, & Juliet Corbin. (1994). "Grounded theory methodology: An overview." In Norman K. Denzin & Yvonna S. Lincoln (Eds.), *Handbook of qualitative research.* Thousand Oaks, CA: Sage.

Strauss, Anselm, & Barney G. Glaser. (1977). *Anguish: The case history of a dying trajectory.* Van Nuys, CA: Sociology Press.

Strauss, Leo. (1959). *What is political philosophy? and other studies.* Glencoe, IL: Free Press.

Sudnow, David. (1967). *Passing on: The social organization of dying.* Englewood Cliffs, NJ: Prentice Hall.

Sudnow, David. (1978). *Ways of the hand: The organization of improvised conduct.* London: Routledge and Kegan Paul.

Suransky, Valerie Polakow. (1982). *The erosion of childhood.* Chicago: University of Chicago Press.

Sweezy, Paul Marlor. (1962). *The present as history: Essays and reviews on capitalism and socialism.* New York: Monthly Review Press.

Talarico, Susette M. (1991). "Four theories of rape in American society: A state-level analysis." *Crime, Law and Social Change, 15,* 155–157.

Taylor, Charles. (1979). *Hegel and modern society.* Cambridge: Cambridge University Press.

Taylor, Charles, K. Anthony Appiah, Jürgen Habermas, Steven C. Rockefeller, Michael Walzer, & Susan Wolf. (1994). *Multiculturalism: Examining the politics of recognition* (Amy Gutmann, Ed.). Princeton, NJ: Princeton University Press.

Taylor, Paul W. (1986). *Respect for nature: A theory of environmental ethics.* Princeton, NJ: Princeton University Press.

Toulmin, Stephen. (1972). *Human understanding: The collective use and evolution of concepts.* Princeton, NJ: Princeton University Press.

Turnbull, Colin M. (1972). *The mountain people.* New York: Simon and Schuster.

Turner, Jonathan. (1991). *The structure of sociological theory* (5th ed.). Belmont, CA: Wadsworth.

Turner, Jonathan. (1992). "The promise of positivism." In Steven Seidman & David G. Wagner (Eds.), *Postmodernism and social theory: The debate over general theory.* Oxford: Blackwell.

Van Manen, Max. (1990). *Researching lived experience: Human science for an action sensitive pedagogy.* Albany: State University of New York Press.

Veroff, Susie. (1996). *Using art to create knowledge or create issuma from art: A multi-media participatory education project with post-secondary Inuit students in Montreal.* Doctoral dissertation, Human and Organization Development, The Fielding Institute, Santa Barbara, CA.

Visweswaran, Kamala. (1994). *Fictions of feminist ethnography.* Minneapolis: University of Minnesota Press.

Wagner, Helmut R. (1983a). *Alfred Schutz: An intellectual biography.* Chicago: University of Chicago Press.

Wagner, Helmut R. (1983b). *Phenomenology of consciousness and sociology of the life-world: An introductory study.* Edmonton: University of Alberta Press.

Wallerstein, Immanuel. (1976). *The modern world-system: Capitalist agriculture and the origins of the European world-economy in the sixteenth century.* New York: Academic Press.

Warr, Mark. (1990). "Four theories of rape in American society: A state-level analysis." *American Journal of Sociology, 96,* 511–513.

Weber, Max. (1949). *The methodology of the social sciences* (Edward A. Shils and Henry A. Finch, Trans.). New York: Free Press.

Weber, Max. (1961). *General economic history* (Frank H. Knight, Trans.). New York: Collier Books.

Weber, Max. (1967a). *Ancient Judaism* (Hans Gerth and Don Martindale, Ed. and Trans.). New York: Free Press.

Weber, Max. (1967b). *The religion of India: The sociology of Hinduism and Buddhism* (Hans Gerth, Don Martindale, Ed. and Trans.). New York: Free Press.

Weber, Max. (1968a). *Economy and society: An outline of interpretive sociology* (Günther Roth and Claus Wittich, Ed.; Ephraim Fischoff, Hans Gerth, A. M. Henderson, Ferdinand Kolegar, C. Wright Mills, Talcott Parsons, Max Rheinstein, Guenther Roth, Edward Shils, & Claus Wittich, Trans.). New York: Bedminster Press.

Weber, Max. (1968b). *The religion of China: Confucianism and Taoism* (Hans Gerth, Ed. and Trans.). New York: Free Press.

Weber, Max. (1992). *The Protestant ethic and the spirit of capitalism.* London: Routledge.

Weber, Shierry M. (1970). "Individuation as praxis." In Paul Breines (Ed.), *Critical interruptions.* New York: Herder and Herder.

Weinstein, Michael A. (1985). *Finite perfection: Reflections on virtue.* Amherst: University of Massachusetts Press.

Weinstein, Michael A. (1995). *Culture/flesh.* Lanham, MD: Rowman and Littlefield.

Wellmer, Albrecht. (1991). *The persistence of modernity: Essays on aesthetics, ethics, and postmodernism* (David Midgley, Trans.). Cambridge, MA: MIT Press.

Weppner, Robert S. (1977). *Street ethnography: Selected studies of crime and drug use in natural settings*. Beverly Hills, CA: Sage.

Whalen, Jack, & Don H. Zimmerman. (1990a). *Categorizing and describing "emergencies" in 9-1-1 communications*. Paper presented at the annual meeting of the American Sociological Association.

Whalen, Marilyn R., & Don H. Zimmerman. (1990b). "Describing trouble: Practical epistemology in citizen calls to the police." *Language in Society, 19,* 465–492.

White, Lynn, Jr. (1962). *Medieval technology and social change*. London: Oxford University Press.

White, Robert. (1990). *White mythologies: Writing history and the West*. London: Routledge.

Whyte, William Foote (Ed.). (1991). *Participatory action research*. Newbury Park, CA: Sage.

Williamson, Judith. (1978). *Decoding advertisements: Ideology and meaning in advertising*. London: Marion Boyars.

Wilson, William Julius. (1987). *The truly disadvantaged: The inner city, the underclass, and public policy*. Chicago: University of Chicago Press.

Winograd, Terry, & Fernando Flores. (1986). *Understanding computers and cognition: A new foundation for design*. Norwood: Ablex.

Wolfe, Minna Sheryl. (1984). *Construction of social reality in a lesbian group: Gender and role in culture, structure, and person*. Doctoral dissertation, Texas Woman's University.

Wolff, Kurt H. (1995). *Transformation in the writing: A case of surrender-and-catch*. Dordrecht: Kluwer Academic.

Wolff, Robert Paul. (1973). *The autonomy of reason: A commentary on Kant's Groundwork of the Metaphysic of Morals*. New York: Harper and Row.

Young, Iris Marion. (1990). "Throwing like a girl: A phenomenology of feminine body comportment, motility, and spatiality." In *Throwing like a girl and other essays in feminist philosophy and social theory*. Bloomington: Indiana University Press.

Zagzebski, Linda Trinkaus. (1996). *Virtues of the mind: An inquiry into the nature of virtue and the ethical foundations of knowledge*. Cambridge: Cambridge University Press.

Zimmer, Heinrich Robert. (1993). *The king and the corpse: Tales of the soul's conquest of evil* (Joseph Campbell, Ed.). Princeton, NJ: Princeton University Press.

Zimmerman, Michael E. (1994). *Contesting earth's future: Radical ecology and postmodernity*. Berkeley: University of California Press.

Zuboff, Shoshana. (1984). *In the age of the smart machine: The future of work and power*. New York: Basic Books.

Index

About the Authors

Valerie Malhotra Bentz, PhD, is Associate Dean and Professor on the Graduate Faculty in the Human and Organization Development Program at the Fielding Institute, Santa Barbara. She has taught and published in the areas of sociological theory, social psychology, phenomenology, symbolic interaction, dramatism and hermeneutics, and is a classical musician. She is editor of *Phenomenology and the Human Sciences*. Currently she is writing a book about her emotional and intellectual relationships with George Herbert Mead, Martin Heidegger, and other philosophers. She is the author of *Becoming Mature: Childhood Ghosts and Spirits in Adult Life* (1989) and *Visual Images of Women in the Arts and Mass Media*. A practicing psychotherapist for 20 years, she consults internationally and offers workshops on deep learning, a way of knowing that integrates philosophical, bodily, and emotional understanding. She is a licensed body therapist in Santa Barbara, and she is Associate Editor of *Sociological Practice: A Journal of Clinical and Applied Sociology*.

Jeremy J. Shapiro is Professor of Human and Organization Development and Senior Consultant for Academic Information Projects at the Fielding Institute, New York. With a background in sociology, philosophy, information systems, and the history of ideas, he is active as a scholar and translator in the area of critical social theory, with publications and interests focusing on the cultural and social impact of information technology, the integration of social and personal change, the politics of communication theory, and aesthetic experience. He serves on the editorial board of *Theory and Society*. As an educator, he has specialized in the teaching of research, critical thinking, and information literacy. He has also worked as an information systems professional for 15 years; been active nationally in efforts to use networked information resources and computer networks in higher education; published and presented on information literacy, the virtual university, and the social consequences of the Internet; served as institutional representative to EDUCOM and the Coalition for Networked Information; and been involved in efforts to bring computer technology to community, grassroots, and nonprofit organizations. He has also taught peer counseling. He graduated from Harvard College, studied with Max Horkheimer, Theodor Adorno, Herbert Marcuse, and Jürgen Habermas at the University of Frankfurt am Main, and obtained his doctorate from Brandeis University under Kurt Wolff and Maurice Stein. His passions are classical music and travel. He lives in New York City with his wife Pamela Walsh and his cat Deeda.